FILL *these* ROOMS

A Story of God's Faithfulness

Dotty Hash

CP
cadence press

FILL *these* ROOMS

A Story of God's Faithfulness

Printed by Back to the Bible Printing

Cover design and formatting: Intrinsic Designs
First Printing, 1998
Printed in the United States of America

Some segments are adapted from *Prisoner of Hope* by Jesse Miller
2930 S. DeFrame Way, Lakewood, CO 80228.

LIBRARY OF CONGRESS CATALOGING-IN-PUBLICATION DATA
Hash, Dorothy, M.
Fill These Rooms : A Story of God's Faithfulness / Dorothy Hash.
p. cm.
ISBN 0-9664572-0-X
1.Missions—Autobiography. I. Title

To order additional copies of *Fill These Rooms*, use order form in back or send $13.00* per copy or $20.00 per audio tape set, plus $3.00 for shipping to:

Cadence Press
Tom and Dotty Hash
13803 W. Amherst Way
Lakewood, CO 80228
(303) 989-5659
E-mail: INTERNET:75147,3564@compuserve.com

*Colorado residents add 4.3% sales tax
*Quantity discounts available
*Price may be subject to change

Endorsements

I am excited with *Fill These Rooms.* Certainly because I know the players personally, but mostly because young people today are in desperate need of role models, heroes, and exposure to real life mentors. God, of course, is keeping the books, but the story of OCSC's Tom and Dotty Hash and C.P. Tarkington is for me one of the great heroic missionary stories. I want all young people to be exposed to these things, the recent history of the church and the power of God expressed through people who offered their all and God multiplied it a hundred fold.

—*Jay Kesler*
President, Taylor University

In a world desperately in need of mentors, here's the story of God working through two very real people to achieve his purposes but, more significantly, to reveal his heart to theirs. The message of a mentor to those following along is "God is worthy of trust. It can be done. He is enough!" *Fill These Rooms* makes that message clear.

—*Larry Crabb*
Psychologist, Author, and Speaker

A readable, down-to-earth modern-day missionary biography—a personal narrative of common daily experiences by missionaries who effectively shared the Gospel and their lives with the American military community.

—*Jesse and Nettie Miller*
Founders, OCSC/Cadence
Author, *Prisoner of Hope*

We in the military think we understand the concept of "service," but OCSC's Tom and Dotty Hash have truly serve—both their fellow man and their God. For 23 years they "filled" the hearts of service members in remote locations with a genuine sense of home and a contagious love of the Lord.

—*Captain Curt Kemp*
U.S. Navy

Many other things did Tom and Dotty Hash which are not written in this book. But these are written that others who read may rejoice and give glory to God who is faithful and does all things well.

This may be the "crowning jewel" of all their ministries over the years, as missionaries and others are blessed by their effort to write it down.

—*David L. Meschke*
General Director of OCSC/Cadence 1978-1995

What an exciting walk through the history of two lives God chose to use to impact so many with the kindness and saving grace He offers! My own faith was deepened as I read story after story of God's provision for the Hash family!

—*Stephanie Nelson*
Senior Editor, *Women of the Harvest*

Fill These Rooms vividly captures the heart of Cadence to open our homes and lives to military people. Tom and Dotty embody this heart and share it powerfully with you in this stirring account.

—*David Schroeder*
General Director, Cadence International

Foreword

When you are asked to say a word about a book containing subjects you know and love, it is easy to give a ringing endorsement because of the emotional attachments. However, to me *Fill These Rooms* is far more than that. Though I have known Tom and Dotty Hash for many years and have seen their extraordinary ministry firsthand, I can enthusiastically recommend this book because it has such wide appeal and is so beautifully written.

Fill These Rooms is really about God's faithfulness to a family. The eternal truths of God's love and plans for us are woven throughout and beautifully illustrated by personal accounts that make these truths come alive.

As Dotty shares of her reluctance to become a missionary and how God gave her a special commitment to this ministry, many of us can identify with the struggle of total commitment. The highs and lows, the sunshine and the darkness, the triumphs and the defeats, are all bared in such a way they give hope and encouragement to the reader.

This faithfulness of God is also about the men and women who make up the United States military. The book gives some very special insight into what it is like to be thousands of miles from home and subject to temptations that one would rarely face at home. The hospitality houses are cities of refuge where those in the military can receive sound Bible teaching in an atmosphere of love and fellowship. I remember Tom telling me one time if they could reach the Christian serviceman or woman within the first thirty days of their assignment overseas, the success of keeping them away from immorality or other activities that were displeasing to the Lord was high.

Fill These Rooms also deals with the personal challenge of the ministry. It is not easy to have guests for dinner every night, especially when you have no idea how many are going to show up. I came to a fresh appreciation for the flexibility of those who serve Cadence International as a visitor to the center when resources were scarce and they didn't want to waste food and yet had to have casseroles ready to pop in the oven if more than expected showed up.

I also think of the relationship Biola University and many other Christian colleges have with this ministry as we have benefitted from the faithfulness of those who staff the hospitality houses. Young men and women would find the Savior and many of them would commit their lives to serve the Lord in ministry and so would enroll in our schools.

God's faithfulness is also reflected in the Hashes' story as I believe one of the greatest ways of inspiring young people for ministry is reading about the lives of others whom God has used in a very special way. *Fill These Rooms* excels in this department as you actually feel part of the Hash family as they face the challenges of living in countries that are not as stable nor have the comforts that we have in the United States.

The reader is included in many delightful family stories as we walk through the serious illnesses that the children faced as well as having to share their father and mother with so many others.

As you read these pages ask God to speak to you about his love for the world and how he can use you, just an ordinary person as were the Hashes, to touch the lives of thousands of people for his honor and glory.

—*Clyde Cook*
La Mirada
March 1998

This Book is Dedicated to

Jesse and Nettie Miller, Tom's spiritual parents and founders of OCSC/Cadence who, in their faithfulness to God's call, blazed the trail and taught us how to *fill these rooms.*

The men and women of the U.S. Armed Forces who *filled our rooms* and responded to our ministry.

Our faithful donors and Prayer warriors who often gave sacrificially so we could have *rooms to fill.*

Our children, Lori, David, and Danny, who also *filled our rooms* and grew up to honor the Lord.

OCSC/Cadence missionaries, past, present, and future, who, with open hearts and open homes, trust God to *fill their rooms.*

And to our Lord Jesus, who bought us with the price of his blood, and has gone ahead to prepare many *rooms for us to fill* eternally.

CONTENTS

Acknowledgements

Thanks, Ron Dice, for the day you plunked a computer on my desk in the OCSC personnel department and said, "Dotty, by tonight I want you to have one letter ready to mail." That was the beginning of my computer literacy, without which this story probably wouldn't have been written.

Thanks, Carey and Janie Matthews, for the money to buy the computer for this project. It is my daily companion.

Thanks, Dave Meschke, Marijane West, Anne Koch, Ron Dice, and Bill Needham for your help in editing the manuscript.

Thanks, Philip Steers, for assuring the accuracy of the Panama years; Ken Brooks, for the Philippine years; and Dave Meschke, for the military segments.

Thanks, Nettie Miller, Stephanie Nelson, Brad Ellgen, and Dan Hash for reading the manuscript and offering your comments and encouragement.

Thanks, Duncan Sprague at Intrinsic Designs, for formatting the book and designing the cover. You made it look great!

Thanks, anonymous benefactors, who gave and loaned us the money to have the book printed.

And thanks, Tom, my ever-patient husband, life companion, and best friend who with eternal optimism led our family from "room" to "room," investing your life in people and in us. Your day-by-day reassurance encouraged me to persevere.

INTRODUCTION

Why Write this Book?

F*ill These Rooms* ends in 1978 when Tom and I stepped aside from direct ministry to the military to assume the role of Director of Asia Ministries for OCSC.

At the end of one of our trips to visit our missionaries in Asia, we stopped for a day or two in Yokosuka, Japan, before returning to the U.S. While there, I had an opportunity to do one of my favorite things—read a missionary biography. After closing the book I tried to go to sleep. Until 2 a.m. I wrestled with the Lord over an overwhelming urge I had experienced the year before and which returned in those morning hours: to write the story of our years in servicemen's center/hospitality house ministry.

That night, May 21, 1981, I surrendered to the Lord. In the next three months in my regular Bible reading, he confirmed that commissioning to write with these verses:

I Peter 2:9 "That you may proclaim the excellencies of him who has called you."

I John 2:20 "But you have an anointing from the Holy One."

II Cor. 4:7 "But we have this treasure in earthen vessels that the surpassing greatness of the power may be of God and not from ourselves."

II Cor. 12:9 "My grace is sufficient for thee, for my strength is made perfect in weakness."

What I didn't know was that it would be sixteen years before I could fulfill that commission.

In 1982 I was asked to assume the role of Personnel Secretary in our home office while still assisting Tom in his leadership role. For the next ten years I corresponded with hundreds of potential missionaries, taking them through the application process, appointment as missionaries, and preparation to leave for the field. I also learned how to use the computer, developed new methods for keeping track of missionaries, and compiled a 300-page handbook for the mission.

In 1994 Tom and I stepped aside from our leadership roles to become the mission historians. For two years I sifted through boxes and boxes of archives, recording significant data that would someday become historical books.

In February 1997 I once again felt compelled to write our story. Now, more than a year later, the task is complete.

Hopefully, this account of God's faithfulness will be of encouragement to you in your journey of faith and that you also will be challenged to invite God to fill your rooms.

PREFACE

Fill These Rooms is our story, Tom's and mine. But it's also an account of God's faithfulness.

It was God who called us from very ordinary beginnings to experience his salvation through his Son, Jesus Christ; it was he who promised to fulfill the work he had begun in our hearts (Philippians 1:6) and to feed us with the finest of the wheat and honey out of the rock (Psalm 81:16).

It was God who gave us our deep love for military men and women; who gave us prayer warriors and financial donors to sustain us through the years; and who endowed us with health and energy to serve those who filled our rooms.

No matter who they were or where they came from, these third-culture people (expatriates) were away from home, lonely, and searching for something significant in which to invest their lives. They were longing for love and we were privileged to be there with rooms to fill.

The style of open-home ministry portrayed in this book represents how we did it in the early years of OCSC. Some methods have changed with the times, but the message remains the same.

I have used the King James version of the Bible for scriptural quotations because that was the translation we used in the early years.

Through the early part of this account, I refer almost exclusively to "the guys" in our ministry. I have not left the women out—there simply weren't many military women deployed overseas then. We did have a significant ministry to those who were there—nurses, Department of Defense teachers, and other civilian workers—who also came regularly to fill our rooms.

Our lifetime maxim has been to invest our lives in people, for only people and the Word of God last for eternity.

Part I

The Early Years — Tom's Story

Chapter 1

A BOY LOOKING FOR A HOME

Tom's earliest recollections are of a wooden casket in a roughhewn one room log cabin in the hills of Kentucky. That blustery February in 1934 when his sister Deloras was being born, a blizzard prevented the doctor from coming until an uncle, armed with a rifle, persuaded him of the urgency. But by then it was too late. Tom's mother, Oma Ethel DeSpain Hash, had died, leaving Howard Taylor Hash a widower with four small children. Harold (later to use his middle name "Tom") was the oldest, just turned five; Helen was three; and Lonnie two. Miraculously, Deloras survived so a childless aunt, Ida Heaverin, took her as her own.

Those Great Depression years were difficult for everyone, and the Kentucky Hashes were no exception. When Howard married again, his wife, Lou, also had four small children. Sustaining such a large family soon proved too difficult, so little Helen went to live with another aunt.

When Harold was six, Grandmother (Hash) Elmore journeyed from Kansas to Kentucky to take him, suffering from rickets and malnutrition, to live on the farm with her.

Adjustment from a rural southern culture to that of the Kansas plains was difficult. Sitting in the big chair at the barbershop getting his first haircut, Harold winced as the men of the town tried to get him to talk, laughing uproariously at his Kentucky drawl. Confused, he determined never to speak in public again.

The first day of school was not much better. His shyness was so acute that the teacher of the one-room school allowed him to sit with his Uncle Garland, a mighty eighth-grader. She took the attendance, calling each child by name. "Harold," she sang out. Silence.

"Harold?" Again no answer. Finally, "Harold Hash?"

"Oh, heah mayam!"

"Why didn't you answer the first time?" she questioned.

"But, mayam, mah name haint Harold. It's Hurl!" Ripples of laughter spread through the room, doubling his resolve to keep silent forever among those foreigners.

But inhaling the clean farm air, taking care of animals, and helping his grandpa cultivate the dusty earth restored his health and soon provided him the confidence necessary to converse in Kansan.

The dust bowl years eventually took their toll, and Grandma and Harold moved to Peoria, Illinois, to live with Uncle Bernie, a widower with two daughters. This was Harold's first encounter with "sisters," an awesome experience for an eleven-year-old boy. Later, with World War II in full swing, he was able to get a job at a drive-in for $2.00 a night—his first spending money.

During this time, he occasionally attended a small church. One morning when the invitation was given, he felt compelled to go forward. Kneeling at the altar weeping for his sins, he wanted desperately to be "saved" like the preacher had said. But when the service ended, the pastor congratulated him, pumping his hand and patting his back. He would have gladly received Christ that morning if someone had just shown him the way. He left the church with an empty heart.

The following year was spent back in rural Kentucky with his father. By now, two more children had been added to the family—Ruby Doris and Harlan. Though welcomed into the home, Harold just didn't feel he belonged, but he learned much about his heritage that year. A favorite story in the family was about the moonshining activities of one of his uncles. When the revenuers caught up with him, they said, "Now you go on home and take care of your family. We'll meet you on the road on Monday morning to go to jail." The thought of skipping out never entered his mind. Tom and his siblings' favorite game was not "cops and robbers" but "rev'nooers and moonshiners." Of course, the moonshiners were the "good guys!"

The next year Tom moved to Louisville to live with Aunt Ida who was rearing his youngest sister, Deloras. In spite of all his moving, he had managed to pass all grades and was now a sophomore in high school. Feeling the necessity to provide for himself, for the next three years he worked full time at a print shop during the day and attended high school in the evening. Frequently the teacher took pity on the weary young man, allowing him to sleep through class. It's no wonder that when he walked down the aisle to receive his diploma in 1948, his education was sorely deficient. At nineteen, with no future goals, he enlisted in the U.S. Air Force.

After basic training at Lackland Air Force Base in Texas and at tech school to become a clerk typist, he received orders to West Germany to participate in the Berlin Air Lift. When he returned to the States, he was sent to tech school in Denver, Colorado to learn accounting. Then with the Korean Conflict just beginning, he received orders to the Far East.

Tom in 1949 before becoming a Christian

He soon found himself on board a troop ship crossing the Pacific ocean—not exactly a pleasure cruise! The ship was old, having been hurriedly taken out of moth balls for the trip. As men flocked on board, hefting their duffle bags down the ladders, each one scrambled for a space to call his own. Only then did they learn that each bunk had to be shared by three men sleeping in eight-hour shifts.

Tom made his way to the very back of the ship where, to his amazement, he found a tiny unclaimed area. Smug over his good fortune, he settled in. But when they got underway, he discovered his bunk was directly under the fan-tail just over the propeller. The constant noise was bad enough, but when the seas were rough, the screw pitched clear out of the water, causing a bone-jarring vibration. But he did have the bunk to himself!

Another problem was the water. Fresh water could be used only for drinking, requiring the men to shower and do their laundry in salt water. Before long the stench was unbearable.

With little to occupy their time, the men played cards, told stories, and speculated about where they were going. On the twenty-first day at sea, the public address system cracked, "Now hear this! We will soon be landing in the Philippines. The following men report to the quarter deck with full gear in one hour." Among the names called were Tom Hash and C. P. Tarkington.

Assembled on the deck in the blazing tropical sun, the troops stood at attention. Again names were called. "You men will board those buses and proceed to Clark Field," a sergeant commanded. As the group shuffled down the gangplank, Tom and Tark stared at each other—they were two of eighteen remaining. "Do you think they know about us stealing that food from the galley? Maybe someone squealed on us for getting fresh water," they whispered.

Their questions were interrupted by the sergeant calling their names. They snapped to attention. "You men will be assigned to the U.S. Military Port here in Manila. Just head that way," he barked, indicating a building beside the pier.

Chapter 2

PRISONER OF HOPE

(Some incidents in this chapter are adapted from Prisoner of Hope by Jesse L. Miller)

Within a few hours they had reported in, settled in their barracks, and toured the entire base—two square city blocks. They learned that because of an uprising of the local Communist movement (Huks), they were restricted to the base for the weekend.

By Sunday morning boredom was so acute that they willingly accepted an invitation to attend services at the base chapel. After the traditional songs and liturgy, the speaker was introduced, a missionary named Jesse Miller. Unimpressed, they watched him approach the pulpit. He was of average height, skinny, a little stoop-shouldered, with ordinary features—almost homely, and his voice quavered as he spoke.

"Let's pray, men." Bowing his head, he spoke softly and reverently, "Dear Father, I pray that these men won't see me this morning...."

Tom and Tark looked at each other. "Oh, boy, we've got some kind of a nut here! Of course we can see him—he's right there!"

Jesse continued, "Just let them see your son, the Lord Jesus Christ. In his precious name I pray, Amen."

"Men," Jesse began, "I wouldn't be here this morning if it were not for the grace of our Lord Jesus Christ. Just eight years ago I was a young soldier like you. When the Japanese bombed the Philippines, we retreated to the Bataan Peninsula, just over there." He gestured toward the bay and the land in the distance. "By then we were exhausted, rations were reduced, and most of us were sick. My body began to swell; ulcers appeared on my flesh. I had seen sores like that on the Filipinos and hated them for it. Now I realized it wasn't their fault—they didn't have enough to eat.

"One evening it was my turn to teach the Bible class to these men who were filled with hatred and who had seen more than their share of death, disease, and starvation. I opened my Bible and read, 'And, as Moses lifted up the serpent in the wilderness, even so must the Son of man be lifted up.' (John 3:14). 'Look unto me, and be saved, all the ends of the earth: for I am God....' (Isaiah 45:22) There were nine there who didn't know that Jesus had died on the cross for them. All of them received him as their Savior that night. The next day Bataan fell into Japanese hands and all of us stepped out on the infamous 'Bataan Death March.' All nine of those men died. I am the only one who survived.

"Memories of the next six days still haunt me. Stumbling along in the blazing tropical sun, my body screamed from thirst and starvation. Malarial fever burned within me, acute dysentery sapped my strength. The Japanese guards were incredibly cruel, waiting sadistically to club or bayonet to death anyone falling behind. They cursed and taunted us with food and water, then threw it away. Filipino nationals who tried to help us were driven off or killed. At night, when the scraggly column stopped, we fell exhausted to the ground, mosquitoes swarming over our bodies. Sixty thousand American and Filipino soldiers began that death march. Six days and seventy miles later, ten thousand had died.

"When we reached San Fernando, numb with shock, we were herded into a barbed wire compound. There many died of malaria, dengue fever, dysentery, beri-beri, and scurvy. I suffered from all of them.

"Then we were herded into boxcars like cattle, without room to move. The only ventilation came from small slits in the roof. Many were overcome by the stifling heat, foul air, and stench. When they died, their bodies remained upright until the three-hour ride was over. We tried to step over them as we stumbled out. We were marched another seven miles to the prison camp to become prisoners of war.

"The Japanese had an ingenious way of preventing escapes. We were placed into squads of ten men. Each morning when roll call was taken, if anyone was missing, the others in the squad were executed immediately. One morning a man from our squad was gone.

"The roll call began. 'First squad: all present. Second squad: all present. Third squad...' our nerves grew more tense. Why did this have to happen? Could he really have escaped? 'Oh God, be merciful. Put a little love in those Japs' hearts if that's possible.'

"'Fourth squad: all present.' As the bango (roll call) came closer, our hearts beat frantically. We knew the penalty—we had seen it before. But now it was happening to us. Fifth, sixth, seventh, eighth squad: all present. Ninth squad: one man absent!

"Immediately we were rushed to headquarters. Nip guards ran out of the building, pumping ammunition into the chambers of their rifles. 'Get over there!' a guard howled in Japanese. 'God, have mercy!' one man pleaded.

"But deep within there was a peace that only God could give, for death was not a threat to me. I had placed my trust in Jesus Christ in 1937 and I knew I would go immediately to be with him. As I stared at the guards and the rifles, I prayed, 'Thank you, Lord, for being my Savior. It looks like I'm coming to be with you.'

"Ready, aim...

"I couldn't have felt any closer to Jesus than I did at that moment. Then he spoke softly from within me, Will you reveal me to others who don't know the peace that you have? How about these other eight men, the Filipinos outside the fence staring in, or the Japanese guard aiming his rifle at you? Will you tell them of me?

"Yes, Lord, I will—even if it means going to the uttermost parts of the earth for you.

"I knew immediately there would be no execution. As badly as those guards wanted to pull the triggers, they couldn't. Seconds dragged into minutes. One by one we looked up. The soldiers awaited the command. Then the order was given for them to shoulder their rifles. They marched off. 'You men be ready to die tomorrow at sunrise!' the captain snarled. Our legs turned to jelly. We slid to the ground in relief. Tomorrow came and went. There was no massacre.

"Many times in the next three-and-a-half years I wondered about my promise to the Lord. Would I ever live to fulfill it? In the prison camp I shared my faith in Christ with many men, most of whom are no longer alive. As our bodies deteriorated and hopes grew dim, the only source of strength we had was the Bible verses I had memorized just before the war.

"A missionary couple, Cyril and Anna Brooks, living here in Manila had invited us to their home on Saturday nights. There we studied the Bible and committed verses to memory. During those months my faith grew stronger—God was preparing me for what was to come.

"As the tables of war turned against the Japanese, they shipped prisoners to Japan to labor in the mines. One day my name was on the roster. But I was so ill from disease that a friend, Bernard Humphrey, erased my name, putting his own there. He was placed in the hold of a ship for the voyage. Not knowing prisoners were on board, the American planes bombed and sank the ship. Once again I should have died, but God had a plan for me. Later it was learned that Bernard's cousin was in that bomber.

"Later I did go to Japan, ending up in a prison camp near Fukuoka. There we were forced to work in the coal mines from before dawn until after dark, never seeing the light of day. I was in the mine when the atom bomb was dropped on Nagasaki on August 9, 1945. When Japan surrendered, I was liberated and returned home.

"I didn't forget my promise to the Lord. As soon as I was well enough, I enrolled at the Bible Institute of Los Angeles (BIOLA) to study the Bible and prepare for missionary service. Now I am back. God graciously preserved my life over and over again so that I could be here this morning to tell you of his love."

Then Jesse Miller gently shared how God loved them so much he had sent his son Jesus to the cross to die for their sins. If they accepted his payment, they would be forgiven and receive the gift of eternal life.

Tom and Tark sat spellbound. They had never heard anyone speak like that before. Amazed, they realized they had caught a glimpse of Jesus. They hadn't seen Jesse Miller, but the Christ he loved so dearly.

Filing out of the little chapel, Jesse approached them smiling. "Would you men like to come to a Bible study on Wednesday night?" In the awesomeness of the moment, they agreed.

But by Wednesday night both men had lost interest. When they saw Jesse approaching the barracks, Tom quickly grabbed a towel and headed for the shower in the Quonset hut next door. He stood under the tepid water for an interminable time and then peeked out the door. Jesse was sitting patiently on Tom's bunk beside the clothes he had left behind. Wrapping his towel around him, Tom stood waiting in the cool evening air. Before long goose bumps stood up on his flesh as he shivered with cold. He finally surrendered, walking sheepishly into the barracks. Dressing quickly, they headed for the Bible study.

Jesse and Nettie Miller in Manila in 1951

Jesse faithfully taught the handful of men each week for several months. Often he would ask them to memorize a Scripture verse and then have them quote it the following week. It was Tom's turn to quote John 1:12: "But as many as received him, to them gave he power to become the sons of God, even to them that believe on his name."

"Tom, do you believe that's true—that you can receive Christ as your Savior?" Jesse asked. Then he asked the men to bow their heads, challenging them to commit their lives to

Christ and to raise their hands when they had done so. Tom's was the first hand in the air.

Tark wanted very much to open his heart to Christ, but he knew what a sinner he was. How could God accept him? Then peeking between his fingers, he saw Tom's hand. Well, if that rascal can be saved, so can I! he reasoned, lifting his hand high. Both men point to that night in November 1950 as their spiritual birthday. Tom also celebrated his twenty-first birthday that month.

Chapter 3

A CHANGED LIFE

Tom's conversion wasn't a particularly emotional experience, but in the next few days it became obvious he had changed. Walking to work one morning, he stubbed his toe. The usual stream of profanity gushed out as he stood there cursing the curb. Instantly conviction swept over him. *Oh, Lord,* he pleaded, *please wash out my mouth so I never swear again.* The prayer was answered immediately.

One night after Bible study he stopped at the club for a drink. He didn't enjoy liquor but had recently started drinking to be one of the guys. He struck up a conversation with one of the men when suddenly the man stopped short. "What is that?" he snapped, pointing to Tom's Bible lying on the table.

"It's my Bible. Why?"

"That thing doesn't belong in here!" he blurted. Tom was hurt. He was just learning to love the person of that book. If the Bible wasn't welcome at the club, then he wouldn't go there either.

Before long the Holy Spirit began to deal with him about smoking. But this deeply rooted habit wasn't easily conquered. About that time Jesse was planning a trip to visit some missionaries in a tribal area. "I'd like to take you along," he told Tom and Tark, "but with you still smoking I just can't. It would be a hindrance to the work."

Okay, Lord, Tom rationalized, *I'll quit the cigarettes!* He started smoking cigars. One day while reading the Bible, he came across II Corinthians 6:17: "Wherefore, come out from among them, and be ye separate, saith the Lord, and touch not the unclean thing..." In his mind's eye he could see the dark ring the cigars left around his mouth. *All right, Lord, I'll give up the cigars!*

The pipe was next. But there was no peace in his heart about that either. One dark night, under deep conviction, vowing he would never smoke again, he stood beside a field and threw his pipe and lighter as far as he could into the tall weeds. The next morning when Tark went to work, there was Tom in the throes of a nicotine fit, crawling on his hands and knees in the foliage desperately searching. He never did find them.

But Jesse helped him through the ordeal. "Tom, we don't separate ourselves *from* these things. We separate ourselves *to* Christ. When we are separated to him, the trash falls away. We leave it behind and are drawn to Christ. It's not a negative concept, but a positive one." Tom didn't smoke again, and gradually the cravings subsided.

However years later after becoming a missionary, he frequently dreamed he was preaching fervently, only to duck down behind the pulpit, take a puff on a cigarette, and raise up to resume his message. This distressed him greatly because the desire to smoke had been gone for years, so he asked the Lord to stop the dream. Eventually it went away.

As Tom and Tark witnessed to the men in their barracks, Chuck Hall came to the Lord, and these three men along with

Bill Pleins and Johnny Blackwell became the nucleus of Jesse and Nettie Miller's early ministry to the GIs. The men spent all their off-duty hours in the Millers' 20' x 20' Quonset on the campus of Far Eastern Bible Institute and Seminary (FEBIAS), where the Millers were serving.

They began the GI Gospel Hour, a Saturday night evangelistic outreach. Because Tom and Tark ran the base movie theater, they received permission to have the meetings there. The men invited their friends, led the meetings, and asked different missionaries to speak. Many came to the Lord as a result. Tom and Tark and the other new believers grew in their faith as they reached out to others.

Chuck Hall tells his story like this:

> Tark lived across the aisle from me in the barracks and frequently tried to witness to me. More than once I told him to "bug off" but he didn't stop. He always recited John 1:12 to me. (He told me later he had memorized many verses of Scripture intending to give me a new one but always ended up saying John 1:12.) We also played together on the Port All Stars Basketball Team. Tark was the only really good player and the only Christian. One night we played Adamson University over in Manila and were badly beaten. Only seven of us were sober enough to play. Tark was the only one who hadn't been drinking.
>
> Riding back to base in the old deuce-and-a half truck, the other guys were cussing, blaming the other team. I turned to them to say, *Shut up, it's our own fault!* when I saw Tark sitting on the tailgate of the truck with his head on his knees. *The guy's praying again!* I thought. It was the first time I saw the contrast between believers and nonbelievers: believers knew how to pray, unbelievers didn't. I was an unbeliever. So I turned around, faced the

front of the truck, and said to the Lord, *Whatever he has, I want.*

Walking to the barracks when we got to base, I sidled up to Tark and said, "Tark, I think I believe, but don't tell anyone until I see if it works." I was dead serious. Tark told Nettie Miller what I had said. Later, in a testimony meeting at the GI Gospel Hour, Nettie was sitting beside me. She leaned over and said, "Chuck, I hear you believed." I was struck with fear and irritation but nevertheless was convicted. I didn't say anything. Then she showed me Romans 10:9 and 10 from the Bible: "That if thou shalt confess with thy mouth the Lord Jesus, and shalt believe in thine heart that God hath raised him from the dead, thou shalt be saved. For with the heart man believeth unto righteousness, and with the mouth confession is made unto salvation." I knew I believed in my heart, but I sure didn't want to confess with my mouth. I didn't say anything but just sat there for awhile. When a lull came in the testimony time, I came under conviction. Then another lull came, and I jumped up and said, "I'm saved!" and sat down. That was my first testimony.

Sometime later in another GI Gospel Hour they were having another testimony meeting. It was customary for the guys to read their Bibles every day and then during the meetings share what a passage meant to them. I didn't know the difference between Genesis and Revelation but had found a passage in the book of Malachi. I bravely stood to my feet and said, "I've been reading in the book of Malahchee...." They roared with laughter. Embarrassed, I sat down. But I've learned since then. Just like olives are hard to get out of a bottle until you turn it upside down and stick a knife in it until the first one comes out and all of them follow, so it has been with me. The Lord helped me give many, many testimonies after that, and I even became a teacher. I'm thankful to the Lord for his grace in my life.

The little group soon filled the Millers' home as Jesse taught them the Word of God. By Christmas of 1951 not only was the house too small, but those young GIs—some not yet believers, the others new in their faith—were a disturbance to the structured life of the Filipino Bible school students on the campus. (This story is recorded in Jesse Miller's book, *Prisoner of Hope.*)

Jesse and the men began looking for a suitable home for the budding ministry. The Millers were serving under Far Eastern Gospel Crusade (FEGC) but were released from their teaching responsibilities at Far Eastern Bible Institute and Seminary (FEBIAS) with the blessing of their mission's leadership to work full time with the GIs. They knew their meager missionary salary of $200 a month was inadequate to pay for a place large enough for all of them, so the young servicemen enthusiastically promised to pay the rent if a place could be found. When a home was found for $125 a month, they moved in, trusting the Lord to provide. On February 2, 1952, the Manila Christian Servicemen's Home became a reality.

During Tom's early days as a Christian, he made a commitment to study God's Word. Early each morning he found a quiet, secluded spot where he could be alone—where the men in the barracks wouldn't harass him. It was during those times he learned that the Bible was a unique book—it was alive—it was God's word. He determined to read it the rest of his life.

Another significant event occurred when Jesse Miller took the new believers to the South China Sea where they were led into the water for believers' baptism—a testimony before their friends that they had been buried in Christ and now had newness of life. Tom had no idea that day how many times he would have the privilege of baptizing others in those very same waters in years to come.

Many of the men attended a church for Chinese Christians led by missionary Ed Spahr. Tom became a faithful member of the choir. One morning as the offering plate was passed, he opened his wallet—there was a ten-dollar bill in military scrip and some pesos. Removing what he thought was a peso, he placed it into the plate. But then he glanced down the row. *There's scrip in the plate. I wonder who else in the choir has scrip?"* Panicking, he reopened his wallet—the ten-dollar bill was gone. It was the most money he had ever given.

Tom and Tark were responsible for collecting the rent money for the home. One month a new shipment of stereo equipment had arrived in the PX and when they went around to all the guys for their contributions, no one had any money. Remembering their commitment, Tark said to Tom, "I'll give fifty if you'll give fifty." Since they each received only $70 a month in pay, it was an awesome figure. Jesse had taught the men, "...Freely ye have received, freely give." (Matthew 10:8.) God's Word was bearing fruit in their lives.

In those post-war days, the Filipinos joyfully received anything from the Americans including gospel tracts, reading them eagerly. The men organized themselves into an outreach group called the "GI Gospel Gang." Because the servicemen were authorized to check out military vehicles for recreational purposes for a minimal cost, sometimes they did that and drove through downtown Manila handing out tracts to the bustling crowds. Those "gospel bombs" were rolled in colorful cellophane with a return card enclosed. One question on the card asked, "Where did you receive this gospel tract?" One enterprising Filipino wrote, "I don't know where it came from. It just came flying through my living room window and landed on the floor." Another said, "I was riding in a local bus, and it flew through the bus window onto my lap."

From left: Tom, Chuck Hall, Bill Pleins and Tark on a "Gospel Bomb" run

Not all of the tract ministry was effective. Tom recalls the group passing tracts in the local Chinese cemetery during the Easter weekend. He became separated from the others and was on the back side of a very large, elaborate tomb. As he handed the tract to a Chinese gentleman, the man turned with anger in his eyes, took the tract, laid it on Tom's nose and ripped it in two. Frightened, Tom hurried back to the group.

Another time he found himself surrounded by several "billy boys," homosexual Filipino men dressed in women's clothes. One of them approached Tom, propositioning him. When Tom resisted, he snarled, "I can kill you, you know!" Undaunted by the knife in the assailant's hand, courageous beyond his own strength, Tom replied, "No, you can't harm me. I belong to the Lord Jesus Christ!"

Visually shaken, the man replied, "Tell me about Jesus!"

"No!" Tom retorted. "Not when you're dressed like that. Go home, change your clothes, dress like a man, and I'll meet you here tomorrow and tell you about Jesus."

To Tom's amazement, the man did just that. The next day Tom led him to Christ, his first "convert."

On one of the Gospel Gang outings, one of the missionaries mentioned he needed to move a refrigerator. Since the men had the military truck, they thought nothing of using it to help. Shortly after returning to the base, they were met by the military police. "You are charged with using a military vehicle in unauthorized activity," they announced, "and we hear you are part of a gang." After a brief investigation by the authorities, the airmen were reprimanded and let off without punishment, but they were more careful after that.

G.I. Gospel Gang
From left: Bill Fordham, Tom, Tark, Chuck Hall, Bill Pleins

The tract ministry had a definite follow-up system through the Bible School of the Air led by Cyril (Dad) and Anna (Mom) Brooks, missionaries with Christian Missions in Many Lands (CMML). The servicemen met at the missionary compound weekly to help check and mail out lessons in response to the cards sent in. The men loved Mrs. Brooks' homemade cinnamon rolls—their reward for a job well done.

One night Bill Fordham had CQ (charge of quarters) on the base, so Mom Brooks asked Tark to take four of her rolls to him. En route back to the base, unable to resist the sweet aroma, Tark ate two of them. When they arrived at Bill's desk, Tark gave him the two remaining rolls. As Bill opened the napkin, Tark said, "After I went to all the trouble to bring these to you, aren't you going to share one with me?" Reluctantly he handed one to Tark.

Eventually the tract ministry led to the formation of an English Bible study for Filipinos who had received Christ through reading them. Jesse began teaching the group and later turned it over to the young GIs, always available when they needed help.

Jesse frequently took the men on trips to visit missionaries. Sometimes they took leave from the military to journey to remote mission stations. Many men, including Tom and Tark, sensed the Lord compelling them to give their lives to him as missionaries during those trips.

Some months before Tom, Tark, and Chuck were due to return to the U.S. for discharge, they were given the opportunity to test for Officers' Candidate School (OCS). If they passed, they would all make the military their career. When the test results were returned, Tark had missed by one point, Chuck by two, whereas Tom had passed by one point. They were disappointed, but because the Lord had been speaking to

Tom's heart about going to Bible school and entering missionary service, he eventually turned down the OCS appointment. By thus declaring his disinterest in pursuing the military as a career, he assumed promotion to staff sergeant was out of the question. But he was called before the promotion board. "If promoted, will you make the military your career?" they asked.

"No, sir, it is my plan to go to Bible school to prepare for missionary service," Tom replied. To his amazement promotion to staff sergeant was granted. He felt this was God's way of honoring his decision. Also, he had promised the Lord he would give the difference in pay to the Christian Servicemen's Home, a commitment he fulfilled.

Sensing God's call to be a missionary, Tom began praying for the Lord's guidance to the right school. Several missionaries tried to recruit him for their schools, but Tom finally concluded he would look at all the missionaries, find the ones he wanted to emulate, and consider their schools. Two of the men he chose were Ken Engle and Ben Haglund—both graduates of Moody Bible Institute. His decision was made.

At the end of the Korean Conflict, many of the men whose return to the U.S. had been delayed by the "Truman year" received orders home. When Tom's turn came, he was disappointed that none of the other Christians were sailing on the troop ship with him. The first morning at sea, when roll call was taken, the sergeants were put in charge of work details—kitchen duties, cleanup, military police, etc. Each was given fifteen to twenty men to fulfill the detail. Finally, Tom was standing all alone—the last sergeant. One lone sailor was assigned to his detail. Having been handed the work assignment, he and the sailor went hunting for their particular project. They found it—a small storage room containing only the admiral's staff car. Their duty was to clean the floor each day, a fifteen minute process. "Gee, Sarge, I'm sure glad to be on your work detail," the young sailor remarked. They were free to do as they pleased the rest of the day.

Tom found a secluded spot underneath a life boat. To encourage his walk with the Lord on the long voyage home, he had taken a number of Christian books to read. One of the books was William R. Newell's, *The Book of the Revelation* (1935 Moody Press). To this day the end times remain a strong love in Tom's teaching. Sometimes in the evening when he was lonely for Christian fellowship, he would look up at the stars shining over the ocean and feel God saying, *Tom, you are sitting in my living room. I am turning on the lights just for you.* This confirmation of God's presence was of great encouragement for years to come.

Chapter 4

A NEW MISSION

After his discharge from the Air Force in July 1952, Tom entered Moody Bible Institute to prepare for missionary service. There were many veterans in that class, utilizing the GI Bill to pay their expenses. Tom received $110 a month. He spent $70 for school, $30 for living expenses and offerings, and $10 for tithe.

In his third year unexpected expenses prevented him from giving his tithe. For three more months he borrowed God's money for other things. Convinced this was wrong, he determined to repay the Lord in full. As soon as his pay arrived, he put the forty dollars into an envelope, addressed it to a missionary, rushed to the mailbox, and dropped it in. *What will I live on all month?* he wondered fearfully. He walked back through the mail room, glancing at his box, which he had just checked. There he saw an envelope with just his name on it. Opening it, he found four crisp ten-dollar bills. He learned a vital lesson that day that never needed to be repeated.

Tom was surprised how young and immature most of the students seemed. It was also his first time to meet young, single Christian women. He had been taught by the missionaries to be careful to marry only a Christian. Now here was a whole school full of potentials. Before long he met one who, like himself, was planning to be a missionary to China. After a period of time they became engaged.

In 1953 the Millers returned to the U.S. for a year of furlough. A reunion of the men who had been in the Manila home was planned for the next summer. Since Tom was centrally located, he requested permission from the China Inland Mission to have the meetings at their guest house in North Chicago.

Of concern to the Millers was how to continue the work in Manila. Their mission, Far Eastern Gospel Crusade (FEGC), was incorporated to work with Filipino nationals. Their leadership was uncertain if they should officially embrace this new ministry to Americans. Phil Armstrong, General Director of FEGC, came to the meetings, as well as Cyril (Dad) Brooks. These men gave valuable counsel to the group. At that time there was no other mission organization working exclusively with American military personnel overseas.

During those meetings requests from other military areas were presented: Okinawa, Japan, Alaska, and Germany. Christians in those areas had heard about the effective ministry in Manila and wanted a similar work established. Dick Patty, director of the Oxnard Servicemen's Center in California, had become concerned about the needs of the sailors at Subic Bay in the Philippines, so he came also.

From those meetings in June of 1954 came the formation of Overseas Christian Servicemen's Centers (OCSC). Jesse Miller, Dick Patty, Tom Hash, Bob Stout, and C.P.(Tark) Tarkington, elected as the steering committee, were later to become the Mission Council. Tom's fiancé attended those meetings with him. After the organization was confirmed, they walked into the back yard. "Tom, you have changed your calling and I am not interested in this work with servicemen. Here is your ring," she said. He was devastated. Already the cost was proving to be dear.

After the foundation meetings, Tom drove to Tennessee to fulfill his commitment to work at Cedine Bible Camp, a ministry to underprivileged black children. On the way, he visited his relatives in Kentucky. The hilly, curving country road was slick from a recent downpour. Coming down the hill in "bald holler" he lost control and the car went into a spin. "God, help me!" he cried as the car careened out of control. Then it abruptly came to rest at the edge of a steep embankment. Still gripping tightly to the steering wheel, Tom looked out the drivers' side window into the deep ravine. He slumped over the steering wheel while the reality of what had happened sunk in. "God, you just handed me my life on a silver platter," he murmured. "I don't know why you spared my life, but thank you. I give it back to you now. It's yours to do whatever you want."

When he returned for his final year at Moody that fall he dated a young lady several times. When he chose not to ask her to a special school function, her roommate met with him. "How can you break her heart like that?" she rebuked him. Not wanting to hurt anyone, Tom determined to not date casually anymore, but to place his relationship with women into God's hands.

"From now on I'll wait on you to bring someone into my life, Lord," he prayed.

In December the OCSC Mission Council met in Denver at the invitation of Sid Hendry, the director of a local servicemen's center. Jesse, Dick, Tom, Tark, and Chuck Hall attended this meeting. At this time the mission's constitution and by laws were drawn up. When Dick returned to California, he enlisted the services of a Christian lawyer friend who formally drew up the incorporation papers under the laws of California. Financial records were established and kept by Mrs. Bruce Swor of Oxnard. Jesse Miller was elected as chairman and Tom as home secretary of the mission, since Jesse, Dick and Tark all planned to return to the Philippines.

In June of 1955 Tom graduated from Moody and Tark from Taylor University. Tark with his wife Alma and little Timmy set out to raise financial support to return to the Philippines to take over the Manila home. Tom agreed to assist them in their deputation. Using Tom's 1950 Ford station wagon, they went to any church or group of people who would listen to their burden for the military, trusting God to meet their needs and provide future support for the Tarkingtons. Trials were abundant, especially with the car. It needed constant repair. One time they drove from Detroit to Louisville without a reverse gear!

A friend of Tark's invited them to the Berean Fundamental Church in North Platte, Nebraska. The warm welcome they received from Pastor Ivan Olsen was surprising. A true visionary, he had been the instrument God used to start small evangelical churches throughout the rural and small town areas of the surrounding states. He not only invited Tark and Tom into his pulpit to present the work among the military but also encouraged other Berean pastors to do likewise. This was remarkable! From a human standpoint, who would be interested in helping a couple of young men in their twenties who had begun their own mission? It was risky at best! But God burdened those godly pastors for the fledgling mission, encouraging their congregations to support it with prayer and funds. Slowly Tark and Alma's promised support began to grow.

Part II

The Early Years — Dotty's Story

Chapter 5

SEARCHING

Joe and Esther Keeler and two-year old Lawrence had just moved into the two room log cabin. The big barrel set on legs in the living room glowed red as logs were piled in, lit, and coaxed to a glow to fight off the bitter cold outside in the north woods of Wisconsin in 1932. The morning of January 15th, Esther said, "Joe, I think you had better go for the doctor." Cranking his car, it shuddered in response and he drove as quickly as possible on the snow-covered dirt roads to the next town. Before long the doctor was attending to the birth of little Dorothy May.

My first memories of those next five years are happy ones. My dog, the little wood rifle Daddy had carved for me, and the tall pines were my playmates and play yard. Munching on wintergreen berries from the forest floor as the sun streaked through the trees and hearing the crunch of pine needles beneath my feet are still some of my fondest memories. I do remember waking up some wintry mornings to see snow on the blankets on my bed where it had blown in through the plaster chinking during the night. And there was the time when Daddy rushed in, warning us all to get away from the door for a huge bear was foraging outside. During those deep Depression years, my father hunted in the winter and fished in the summer to provide for us. Occasionally a logging job was found. But I was unaware we were poor—the occasional treat of lard spread on homemade bread sprinkled with brown sugar seemed like the finest delicacy to me.

Log cabin in the north woods of Wisconsin where Dotty was born

My mother had grown up in the parsonage as a Methodist minister's daughter, so attending church was normal for her. But it wasn't until she was playing the piano for a local "revival" that she acknowledged Jesus as her Savior. After moving into the log cabin, occasionally she would persuade Daddy to drive us to the Lutheran church, the only one nearby. I began first grade at age five in a two-room school, walking a mile each way. By the middle of the year I could read quite well.

With the promise of a bricklaying job, my father moved the family to Milwaukee that Christmas. A fine, three-story school and a Methodist church were right in our south side neighborhood. They became the center of my life. We lived in a two-story "flat." Mrs. Haun, the lady upstairs, also attended our church. She began a "Good News Club" in her home, sponsored by a newly organized group called Child Evangelism Fellowship.

The offer of prizes for learning memory verses appealed to my highly competitive nature. As award after award was added to my collection, the Word of God hidden away in my heart began to bear fruit. One day the teacher, Mrs. Baker, told the story of the death of Jesus. I listened and watched as the pictures were put on the flannel board. It seemed like Jesus was dying right there. If I were the only person in the world, he would have died for me. Bitter tears fell when I comprehended the truth that my sin had caused his death and then joy as I received the gift of eternal life he offered. It was the most important decision of my life. I was eleven years old.

My father worked hard to provide for the family, eventually becoming an over-the-road truck driver. His physical absence was necessary, but when he was home, he was emotionally absent from both my brother and me. He simply didn't know how to impact our lives. Not once did I ever doubt his love—somehow I knew it was there—but I needed to see it demonstrated. When I started singing solos in church, he bragged to his friends about my "great voice," but never once did he hear me sing.

The day of my high school graduation Daddy broke my heart. Shortly before Mother and I left for the ceremony, he left the house. I watched his empty seat during the entire evening, hoping he would come. For weeks the ticket and his suit were left lying beside his bed—Mother wanted him to comprehend how he had hurt me.

When I graduated from Bible college, he had another excuse for not coming. However, much to my surprise (and joy), on the day of my wedding, decked out in his finest, he gently led me down the aisle. I think my mother (a normally meek, gentle lady) threatened him with......if he didn't show up. My brother was ready as a backup just in case. I'm glad my father didn't disappoint me that time.

He attended church off and on but to my knowledge did not make a profession of faith in Christ. When I wanted to go to college, he chided, "Why do you wanna do that? You'll spend all that money and then just get married anyway." But he (with Mother's urging) helped me through six long, expensive years of higher education. Of course, when I got married, he said, "I told you so." But I knew he was proud of me. I realized in later years that he felt so ill-at-ease dressed up, associating with "cultured" people that he just couldn't bring himself to get into that situation. Also, he was a creative genius. He could invent anything. If he had only had the opportunity for an education, how different his life would have been. Deep in my heart I loved this crude but gentle man with the bluest eyes I ever saw.

Mother and I, on the other hand, were flourishing spiritually and socially in the strongly evangelical Methodist church in our neighborhood. In my teen years I continued active in that remarkable church, even serving as president of our Youth Fellowship. But starved for male affection, from age thirteen on I always had a boy friend. During the week I chased around with non-Christians, bringing sorrow to my mother and to the Lord. God in his mercy kept me from gross sin that would have left scars for the rest of my life. During my senior year of high school, I invited my best friend, Sarah Rankin (later Lewis), to a Youth for Christ rally. I wanted so much for her to become a Christian. That night she received Christ as her Savior, but the Lord also challenged my heart about straddling the fence. *When will you live all-out for me?* he seemed to say. That night I surrendered all to him. *Whatever you want, Lord, I'll do!* I wept.

I enrolled at Moody Bible Institute in Chicago in 1950. Their rules stated a student was required to be eighteen years old during their first semester, so I had to wait to enroll. In retrospect, I think I must have been the most immature student to ever walk those hallowed halls. I couldn't meet the requirements as a music major since my classical background in piano was weak. I took as much music as possible along with the required Bible courses. Professor Don Hustad taught choral conducting and arranging, ear training, and introduced me to Handel's *Messiah* and other classics. My voice teacher, Guy Latchaw, remarkably guided my singing voice into adulthood. I loved it all, even graduating with honors, totally unaware that I would someday use everything I learned in future ministry.

In my spare time, I read volume after volume of missionary biographies, readily available in the girls' dorm. I heard missionary speakers tell of their love and service for the Lord in far away lands. I wanted God's will for my life and began to have a sense of his call to be a missionary. Time after time I knelt beside my bed and prayed, *Lord, I'll go where you want me to go!* But then I had to be honest. *Lord, YOU know that I really don't mean it!* for in my heart I was afraid the Lord would call me to some far away place all by myself. I just couldn't yield. But I did come to the place where I prayed, *Lord, I'm willing for you to make me willing.*

After graduation from Moody I returned to Milwaukee and worked as a secretary for a year. During that time I became actively involved in various ministries in Grace Methodist Church. God was in the process of preparing me to be a missionary but I didn't know it yet. But I did feel I should continue my education. One weekend a Gospel team from Taylor University in Indiana came to the church. As the men sang and shared their message, I was deeply moved by their strong love for the Lord. But I had never even heard of their school, and had already been accepted at another fine Christian college. But the Lord's still, small voice came again. Within a few weeks I was accepted by telegram and boarded a train for central Indiana. Not knowing how to contact anyone from Taylor when I disembarked in Marion, I took a taxi, using too much of my meager funds. After what seemed like an endless drive in the country, there it was—Taylor's high bell tower welcoming me. I had no idea what a life-changing experience lay ahead.

One of the first persons I met was another new student, Tark Tarkington. I kidded him about his "Nawth Cahlahn-ah" drawl, and we became friends. He seemed so mature in his walk with the Lord. Then I learned he had just returned from three years in the Philippines with the Air Force, where he had come to know the Lord under the ministry of Jesse Miller. Each morning as we waited for breakfast, he asked what I had learned from the Lord in my quiet time. "No Bible, no breakfast!" he challenged so all in line could hear. It didn't take long for me to determine to have the right answer. Then he presented me with a pack of memory verses to learn. That first semester I grew more in my walk with the Lord than ever before.

In the spring the school held a youth conference. Dr. Bob Cook was one of the speakers. During the final session he painted the most frightening word picture I had ever heard on the cost of being a missionary. "Young people," he exclaimed, "if you commit your lives to the Lord to be missionaries, you might even *DIE* on the mission field!" *I know, I know*, I agreed silently.

"But I want to assure you, dear young people, that if you will be obedient to the Lord, you will be safer in a far away land *all alone* in the center of God's will than in the biggest home in the best place in America outside of his will."

I did serious business with God that day. I counted the cost and from the depths of my heart said, *I will go anywhere, Lord.* At the end of the message Dr. Cook challenged those who had made decisions to be sure to tell someone. I found Tark and we wept, prayed and rejoiced. From that day I knew I was called to be a missionary.

Tark met Alma the following summer and they were married. Living in the married quarters on the campus, they invited interested students to come to pray for the work among the military in the Philippines. Through prayer, I felt intimately acquainted with people like Jesse and Nettie Miller, Tom Hash, and Chuck Hall. Then one night Tom came to one of our meetings. He was en route from Moody in Chicago to his home in Louisville, Kentucky. He shared a devotional message about how God lovingly purges away the dross in our lives so that we become like pure gold to shine for him. My heart was deeply challenged—I wanted so much to be clean for God to use.

Walking back to the dorm that night I recall praying, *Lord, this Tom surely seems to love you a lot. If you have a life partner for me, I pray it will be someone like him.* It was a genuine prayer, but quickly forgotten. I knew Tom was engaged to a girl at Moody.

The following summer between my junior and senior year I was working two jobs. Driving to the second job one afternoon, waiting to turn left, a large gravel truck failed to see my signal and hit my car from the rear. As I careened across two lanes of oncoming traffic, I could see two cars whiz by, but my car stopped safely on the left shoulder. I sat stunned, gripping the steering wheel, my turn signal clicking, the engine still running. People came from everywhere. "Are you okay?"

"I think so......yes, I'm fine," I stammered. One man opened the door.

"I think you'd better get out. The gas tank has burst and it could catch fire," he warned, easing me out of the seat. The back of the sedan was driven into the front seat, the passenger side window was broken.

Taken by ambulance to the hospital, I was examined and released but advised to see my family doctor. A friend took me home.

Later we drove to the doctor's office. On the way I leaned my head against the window and discovered a large lump near the temple. My legs were now showing bruises from the knees to the ankles. *How did that happen?* I wondered. I thought I had stayed behind the wheel during the impact. (There were no seat belts in those days.) Evidently, as the car swerved, I slid on the bench seat, hit the window with my head, scraped my legs on the dashboard, and tumbled back into the driver's seat. The doctor said I had a mild concussion, but my neck probably would have been broken had the window been open.

That summer before my senior year of college I was becoming very eager to know where the Lord wanted me to serve as a missionary. Surviving that potentially fatal accident made me more aware than ever before that he had a job for me to do for him. Those days of rest were spent thanking him for that and recommitting my life to be used for his glory in any way he wanted.

On Sunday morning as I entered church, the current copy of *POWER* magazine was handed to me. I couldn't believe what I saw. The feature story was about Jesse Miller and the ministry to military in the Philippines. I was so moved by the article and the sense of the Holy Spirit's direction that when I returned home I spent the entire afternoon in prayer. Was God leading me into that ministry? I was certainly willing but could see no place for a single girl in such a specialized work among men. Late that day, though, the Lord showed me through his Word that this was his will for my life. Through sobs of joy I prayed, *Lord, if you want me to scrub floors or work as a secretary in the servicemen's home in the Philippines, I'll do it. It will be a privilege to serve you at any task.* From that moment I knew I was called to serve in OCSC.

Chapter 6

"TELL ME AGAIN"

The following week thoughts of Tom Hash came to my mind. It seemed strange because we were only casually acquainted—our paths had crossed but two or three times. I did know, however, that his engagement had ended. My thoughts were disturbing. Were these embers of my own desire, waiting to be fanned into flame? Or was God giving further direction for my life? Finally I prayed, *Lord, if these thoughts are from you and Tom is the one you have for me, please show me through your Word. Otherwise, remove them from my mind.* All afternoon was spent with the Lord. Finally, emblazoned on the page of my Bible were these words: "...you have the mind of Christ." Deep in my heart I knew Tom was God's blessing to me and that we would serve him together as missionaries to the military. I thanked the Lord, praising him for his direction and then made a final covenant with him: *This is all your doing, Father, so I will have nothing to do with bringing it about. I'll just wait on you. And please, Lord, withhold any feelings of love until you give them to both of us.*

It would have been impossible for me to do anything—I didn't even know where Tom was. Within a week, however, I received a letter from the Tarkingtons, then missionaries preparing to go out under OCSC. I had invited them to our church to speak and present the ministry. The letter stated they were coming. Then a post script: *Oh, Tom Hash is traveling with us. And Dotty, we think you would make the perfect wife for Tom.* I chuckled, relishing my inside information.

The next few weeks were spent in feverish preparation for their arrival. They would stay at my parents' home with me. Can you imagine my excitement at the opportunity to observe the man I was to marry without his knowing? I wondered if those five days would bring us together.

The appointed day found me anxiously listening for the sound of the approaching car announcing their arrival. When they pulled into the driveway, I flew outside, eager to catch a glimpse of the passengers. Sure enough—there was Tom!

The following days provided opportunities to become acquainted as I accompanied him on the piano while he sang at the meetings and as we shared our goals. I was deeply impressed by Tom's quiet spirit and immaculately-ordered lifestyle. On the final day, sitting under the lilac tree in our front yard, I shared with Tom my sense of God's calling to serve with OCSC. As home secretary of the mission, he needed to know that. We had a time of prayer together. Then he was gone.

As the car disappeared down the road, I was overwhelmed by deep disappointment. Humanly speaking, I did not know when we would ever meet again. Satan's whisper, *You fool!* struck a responsive note, but then the assurance of God's promise flooded in again, bringing deep peace. *Well, Father, it sure is going to be interesting to see how you bring this about!* I whispered with a sigh.

I returned to college, plunging quickly into my final year of studies. One day I received a letter from the

Tarkingtons saying they would be in the area for meetings. I wondered if Tom would be with them. *Will this be your time to bring us together?* I wondered silently to the Lord, reinforcing my resolve to leave it in his hands.

They came, and Tom was with them. Again we sang together at meetings. One evening as I was studying, my roommate came to inform me that this "good looking guy" was at the dorm desk asking for me.

Dressing quickly, I flew down the stairs—to the landing, that is. Then pausing to compose my churning emotions, I ambled down the remaining flight, casually approaching him. "Hi, Tom, what a nice surprise!"

"Hi, Dotty, can we go for a walk?" We strolled out into the moonlight and for the next hour I listened as he shared his testimony—how he had received the Lord as his Savior while stationed in the Philippines. As he and others matured in their walk with the Lord, they won more to Christ. The group expanded until they rented a house in which to meet, asking the missionary to live in it. He shared his burden to continue this ministry and to return overseas to reach other servicemen for Christ. Finally he said, "Dotty, I just don't meet many girls who feel called to this unique work. I'm wondering if the Lord might be leading us together."

We sat down on a rock under a towering pine tree, the moon shimmering through the branches. Looking me squarely in the eyes, he asked gently, "Tell me, has the Lord shown you anything about all this?" In a surge of panic, I silently stormed heaven, *What do I tell him? I wasn't going to have anything to do with this, remember?*

Tell him the truth was the reply to my heart *After all, you can't lie to him—he's going to be your husband.*

Dropping any mask of pretense, I shared openly what the Lord had shown me. Tom listened intently and then said, "Let's pray." We did and then walked back to the dorm.

Two days later he asked for a date. I was so disappointed. It was homecoming weekend and the musical ensemble I led was scheduled to sing that evening. "That's okay," he said, "perhaps we can go out after the program." As he watched me lead the group, he wondered if the Lord was indeed bringing such a "talented" woman into his life.

Following the program, we drove through the Indiana countryside. Tom showered me with a kaleidoscope of questions, always returning to the central theme, "How did the Lord reveal this to you?" I repeated the story.

A hush fell, then, "Okay, tell me again...." I went over the details again. We stopped briefly at a drive-in for some thing to eat and then were back on the road. Eventually he turned into a secluded country lane. Stopping the car, we got out to walk in the moonlight. As we strolled along he asked, "Dotty, do you love me?"

"Not really," I replied softly. "You see, I asked the Lord to give us love together." We walked a little farther. He turned to me, smiling, "I think he's answering your prayer." There under the glimmering Indiana moon, he took me in his arms and gently kissed me. We drove back to the dorm, prayed together, and said goodnight.

The next few days were wonderful. The Lord gave us that love for each other only he can give. To our great joy, we discovered we had chosen the same life verse of Scripture: "Being confident of this very thing, that he who hath begun a good work in you will perform it until the day of Jesus Christ." (Philippians 1:6). When Tom left the following week for a long deputation trip, plans were in place for a June wedding eight months away.

While we were apart, the Lord gave Tom the same assurance he had given me that we were moving in the direction of his will.

During the Christmas holidays we visited our families and became better acquainted. Since Tom had already spent time at my home, there were few surprises for him. My family was "self-contained" in Milwaukee—Mom, Dad, and me. My brother and other relatives lived great distances away so we had little interaction.

But when we went to Louisville, well, that was another matter. Our first evening at Aunt Ida's she served her southern fried chicken—the kind that made the South famous. Of course, I was on my most prim-and-proper-Northern-city-girl-behavior, so I ate it as politely as I knew how, delicately separating the layers of meat with my knife and fork. After the meal Tom took me aside. "Honey, please don't *ever* do that again. They simply won't understand!" he said, gently but firmly. I didn't forget *that* one!

Then we drove out to the country where Tom had been born and where many of his relatives still lived. I was to travel to many foreign lands in years to come, but none affected me like rural Kentucky.

Arriving in the evening, we were warmly welcomed by Tom's dad and stepmother, Lou, into their country home. We sat around the wood stove in the kitchen while Lou brought Tom up to date on all the relatives. I listened intently as she spoke rapidly in her country dialect. First she filled us in on all of the other nine members of the immediate family, moving on to Uncle McKinley's. Of course, Aunt Bessie's were next and.... She talked about their "bakker" crop and how it had done, and the state of the "bottom" land. I tried desperately to translate this into something I could comprehend, but failed miserably. I was experiencing another world.

At bedtime Tom climbed the narrow stairs to the unheated attic. I was taken to the guest room where I quickly prepared for bed. Slipping between the flannel sheets, I promptly sank deep into the bowels of...*a feather bed!* After the initial surprise, I actually found it to be quite cozy and soon drifted off to sleep. But in the wee hours of the morning, my deep slumber was gradually penetrated by the aroma of bacon cooking and the sound of pans rattling in the kitchen outside my door. I flicked on the light, squinting at my watch. *Four a.m. ! What in the world?* I drifted back to sleep.

At 5:30 I was awakened again by a tap on the door and Lou calling, "Breakfast's 'bout ready. Y'all come naw!" I dressed quickly and stepped into the kitchen. The large table, set for four, was completely covered with food. Along with the usual (in my thinking) bacon, eggs, and sausage, were big, delicately browned biscuits, fried squirrel, country ham, corn relish, *peeled* tomatoes, fried okra, homemade jelly and jam, honey, and several items I didn't recognize. While Tom was in "hog heaven," I was in culture shock.

The next night we stayed with Uncle McKinley's family "down the road a piece." He and Aunt Mayme ran the local country store with a single gas pump in front. Entering the small shop, a plethora of sights and smells assailed my senses. The walls were lined floor to ceiling with shelves stacked with everything from canned goods to work gloves to "chawin' t'bakker." Piles of boxes and barrels filled the center of the room with only a tiny path of the dusty plank floor open to walk through. Several people stood at the counter waiting to make a selection from a wide variety of local snacks.

Uncle McKinley, rotund in his bibbed overalls, greeted us warmly. "C'mon, have some 'pikka dawg,'" he invited, reaching into a big glass jug and fishing out a large piece of pickled bologna. Recalling Tom's counsel, *they won't understand*, I accepted the strange offering. I watched Tom chomp into his, then nibbled a bit of mine. It was indeed "pickled." I ate it all!

We were led through a door at the back of the store to the family home. The kitchen area had a sink, kitchen stove, refrigerator and *long* table at one end. A worn linoleum covered the sagging wood floor. A wood-burning stove, couch and lumpy double bed filled the other end. A door on the side of the room led to the area where the children slept. There were two double beds for the four girls still at home and behind a partition, a bed where the two boys slept. That night I slept with the girls, Tom with the boys.

The McKinley Hashes, nine living children in all, were poor in this world's goods, but strong values and high goals were instilled in the childrens' lives. Aunt Mayme had been a school teacher, so education was important to the family. All of the children attended school even before compulsory attendance was required in Kentucky. Three of the children became valedictorians and two salutatorians upon graduation from high school. Six completed master's degrees or above, several becoming teachers. The family endured hard times, but Uncle McKinley and Aunt Mayme always encouraged their children to be the best they could be. And they did just that!

As we made our rounds to the other homes, some relatives insisted we visit the grave sites of departed relatives, including Tom's mother. The cemeteries were located beside little picturesque, if somewhat run-down, country churches. Those sacred grounds were lovingly groomed each year on Memorial Day. There I learned about even more of Tom's long-departed "kinfolk."

At the end of the week when we returned to Louisville and then on to Taylor University in Indiana, a sense of normalcy gradually returned to my befuddled mind. Before long, my journey to Kentucky seemed like a time-warp dream. However, years later, when we took our children there, they experienced the same culture shock I had.

Chapter 7

"'TIL DEATH DO US PART" OR SOMETHING LIKE THAT

In January Tom was to leave for California to attend to the duties of the home office of OCSC. He came to Taylor to attend my senior voice recital and to say goodbye until June. The thought of being separated for so many months from the one whom I had just come to love so deeply was more than I could bear. My tears of parting disturbed Tom deeply and I knew it. After he left my disappointment became a deep sadness.

Driving back to Louisville, Kentucky, Tom sensed the Lord's leading that we should marry right away. He asked the Lord to provide two things if that was his plan: a diamond ring for me and cash for our wedding. Because Tom had been on deputation for a year helping the Tarkingtons raise their support to go to the Philippines, he had no income or money. Day by day the Lord had provided his needs. But this was something different.

After the breakup of his engagement at Moody, Tom had given the engagement ring to Chuck Hall, who had it reset and presented it to his intended. But it was soon returned to him. When Tom got to Louisville, he received a call from Chuck. "I'm passing through Kentucky and would love to see you. By the way, I'm returning your ring."

Tom was staying with Aunt Ida. "I don't want to influence you," she mentioned one evening, "but I do intend to give you $100 as a wedding gift."

The Sunday morning after Tom left me at Taylor I was still very sad and didn't want to go to church. When I knelt to pray, the Lord rebuked my heart, *Are you going to sulk and mope and be of no use to me for the next five months?* I was so ashamed. How could I be so selfish after all he had done? With tears of sorrow I confessed my sin to him and the melancholy melted away into joy and peace. *Lord, I AM available to be used right here. Thank you for your forgiveness.*

The following day I called Tom to assure him that I was all right—that the Lord had taken the sadness away—I was willing for the separation. After talking for some time he asked, "Are you through?"

"Yes."

"Well, honey," he began, "sometimes the Lord wants us to be willing to do something for him even though he may not call on us to carry it through. He has shown me that we should be married a week from Saturday. We will go to California together—you can finish school there. What do you think?" I was stunned. It took a minute for it all to sink in.

Then I replied, "I'll have to call my folks to see if it's okay with them. I'll call you back."

"Hi, Mom. Is Daddy there? I have something to ask you." They knew, of course, that we were planning a June wedding.

"What do you think of Tom and me getting married a week from Saturday? We would like a church wedding, of course." Silence. Mom and Dad were whispering.

"Well, if that's what you want, I guess it's okay. But we don't have the money—we'll have to borrow some. I'll call the pastor and see if it's okay."

The plans were set in motion so I called Tom back. "I'll pick you up on Friday afternoon," he responded. I returned to my room with head and heart spinning. My first final exam was in the morning!

The next day I received a call from Mom. "Guess what! The insurance settlement on your accident just came. The check is for $800! We'll have a fine wedding."

I went to see Dr. Milo Rediger, president of Taylor, who listened intently to my story. Sensing God was at work in my life, he graciously gave permission for me to leave, take the two courses I needed, and transfer them back to graduate in June.

I had a full-length white fake fur coat—my pride and joy. (Mother always said I had champagne taste and a beer pocketbook!) When Tom saw me in it the first time, which happened to be in Chicago, he thought, *What woman in her right mind would wear a white coat here?* The girls in the dorm loved the coat too, so I had no problem selling it for $100. I wouldn't need that coat in southern California and I did need money to buy a wedding ring for Tom.

Balancing wedding plans with study that week was a challenge. But when Tom arrived to take us to Milwaukee on Friday, I was packed and ready. As we drove down the country road, I glanced back at the campus I loved so much and a tinge of nostalgia welled up. But when Tom pulled the car over to the side, opened a tiny box, slipped the gleaming diamond solitaire onto my finger, and then gently kissed me, I knew everything was all right. I was so happy I almost wept.

We arrived at my home in Milwaukee that evening. The next day we applied for a marriage license and chose our announcements (no time for printed invitations), wedding rings, a florist, a photographer and a wedding cake. Tom left the following day to return to Kentucky. The wedding was set for the following Saturday at 2 p.m.

The next days were a whirl of activity, including a bridal shower. I put the finishing touches on the wedding dress I had made during Thanksgiving vacation. Girlfriends from my childhood planned the reception. Gifts poured in—thoughtful gifts of large pans and practical items to be used in the servicemen's home ministry.

On Friday evening when Tom's sister Deloras (my matron-of-honor) and her husband Jim finished work, they began the drive to Milwaukee, stopping to pick up Chuck Hall, the best man, at Moody in Chicago. "I, Tom, take thee Dotty...uh...." Tom murmured as he desperately tried to memorize the vows we had agreed to recite during the wedding ceremony—something new in that day. Then he stuck his head out of the window to try to see the pavement lines in the dense fog. "For better, for worse, for...uh...." It was 4 a.m. when they drove wearily into our driveway.

Up by 7 a.m., Tom and I picked up the marriage license and rings and then rushed to the rehearsal.

Deloras and I dressed at the church while Tom and Chuck drove home to pick up their clothes. To their horror, the house was locked—my parents had left, not knowing Tom and Chuck were planning to return. Trying every opening, eventually they were able to get in through the cellar door. Within minutes they were back in the car for the twenty-minute drive back to the church. (On time, to Tom, has always meant being ten minutes early.) He glanced at his watch. It was ten minutes to 2 p.m. *I'm late for my own wedding*! he groaned.

At the proper time, the organist started the prelude. She had been informed that there might be a delay. Pastor Hovda was waiting behind a screen under the balcony for the groom and best man to arrive. His proper demeanor was augmented by his formal black tie and tails.

The men rushed in. When Chuck saw the pastor, he broke into a nervous, mischievous laugh. Having never seen long tails before, he was reminded of a penguin so began imitating one. Immediately, the pastor stepped out toward the altar. Tom followed with Chuck after him.

As the strains of the wedding march began, Deloras came down the aisle in her beautiful powder blue waltz-length dress, carrying red roses. But as she caught Chuck's eye, a smile formed on her lips and a twinkle came into her eye. *What in the world is he doing behind me?* Tom wondered.

I came down the aisle on my father's arm to stand at Tom's side. Other than a small delay, everything was fine now. What could go wrong?

After the proper preliminaries, the pastor said, "Tom, you may say your vows." We turned to face each other, clasping hands. Silence. A blank stare. Then Tom began to give his testimony—how he was saved in the Philippines and pledged his life to serve the Lord. He remembered a few things from the vows, so threw those in.

Pastor Hovda couldn't hear well so he just smiled. "Dotty, you may say your vows." I gulped. All I could do was repeat what I had memorized—nothing innovative from me. The same happened with the ring ceremony. We were pronounced man and wife, exiting up the aisle.

The receiving line formed at the back of the sanctuary. One woman remarked, "My, young man, those sure were the most unusual vows!"

"Yes, ma'am!" Tom responded. Our beautiful ceremony on February 4, 1956 with two hundred fifty attending was all I'd dreamed of. Of course, the church people did a great deal to help, as that dear family of God lovingly launched us into marriage and ministry. But that day should have been a sign that our lives would never be "normal."

After an evening away, we returned home to pack our belongings into the station wagon, and, along with Jim and Deloras, headed for Kentucky. Our honeymoon was the trip from there to California.

Our wedding on February 4, 1956
with Jim and Deloras Wilson

Chapter 8

BEGINNINGS

Our purpose for living in California was to establish a home office for OCSC and to make the mission known through literature and representation. We worked with a lawyer in Oxnard to complete the incorporation of OCSC and put out the second issue of *The Bulletin*, OCSC's official publication.

I registered at Pasadena Nazarene College for the two courses I still needed to complete my degree in music education, Tom got a job at a steamship company, and we moved into a little furnished apartment. Eagle Rock Baptist Church became our church home. There we became very active, singing in the choir. Dr. Clyde Narramore, the minister of music, asked Tom to join a male quartet for which I was pianist. We traveled locally, singing at a number of functions and churches.

As a new bride, I was eager to please my loving husband. While he was at work each day, I attended classes and worked diligently on my studies, OCSC work, and the usual household tasks. But I seldom seemed to get it all quite finished before he walked in the door in the evening. Often the house, though clean, was in some disarray. Night after night I watched him effortlessly move through the small apartment, adjusting the clutter into neat piles. At first I was threatened, sensing inadequacy, but soon I adopted his philosophy: "If you're going to have a mess, have a neat mess." Before long I learned his little trick, and our home has been neat and orderly ever since.

Because I had been a professional student (I was 24, Tom 26), I wasn't an experienced cook when we married but I was highly motivated to learn. Each day I carefully planned a perfect menu—salad, meat, vegetable, bread, and dessert. But coming from his Kentucky/Kansas background, he gently remarked, "Where are the vegetables, honey?" I spent quite a few meals trying to hide the tears welling up, dabbing them away with my napkin. Before long I would fix two vegetables, and he stopped asking for more.

I was a pretty spoiled woman at that time (probably still am) and hadn't learned to control my temper. One day during an argument, I stomped my foot. Tom grabbed me by the shoulders, put his face in mine, and very softly and lovingly said, "Honey don't ever do that again." I learned that day, as did our children to come, that temper tantrums were unacceptable behavior to this gentle man who practiced what he preached.

About three months after our wedding, we became aware that I might be pregnant. But before I could go to the doctor, while at home one night, I had a miscarriage. In those days before ultra-sound and abortion, we were much less aware of the fact that this was a real baby. As a result, though a little disappointed, we didn't grieve over the loss like we would now. But we do know we have a little one waiting for us in heaven.

The pay at the steamship company where Tom worked as a clerk was adequate, but the job required many hours of overtime. Tom wrote to Jesse Miller, "We desire so much to be in full time activity for the mission. We feel the full responsibility of the mission and have a great burden to travel, presenting the work and visiting the guys. But there are financial obligations here and the Lord has not yet led me to quit my job and start out on faith. So until he specifically says to do so, we cannot move."

Nettie sent wise counsel in a letter: "You sound busy, busy. Remember, don't let *activity for God* take the place of *effectiveness for him!* And don't let present demands on your time and activity keep you from your goal and the place you've consecrated to him."

Every young man longs for his first new car and Tom was no exception. The old station wagon was worn out so we traded it in on a new 1956 Ford Ranch Wagon. It was the least expensive model made—six cylinders with overdrive, only one sun visor, stick shift, minimal chrome and paint—absolutely nothing fancy. The payments of $75 a month and the $2000 we owed on it seemed huge to us. The day we drove it home we prayed, "Lord, this vehicle is dedicated to you and to the mission to be used in any way you see fit. And as long as we have an income, we will make the payments. But if you want us to step out on deputation and keep it as transportation, then we will trust you to pay the bill. If that doesn't happen, we'll return it to the finance company. It's yours and you may do with it as you see fit."

Before the first payment came due, we had an accident. Traveling home from work at rush hour in downtown Los Angeles, someone stopped suddenly in front of us. Tom hit the brakes, but it was too late. Just getting us off to the shoulder was quite a feat in the multiple lanes. When we did, we found the grill and right fender crunched, the other car only slightly damaged. Fortunately, we were able to drive the car home. It looked so pathetic sitting in our driveway, one headlight pointed awkwardly upward and the fender hugging the scraped tire.

"Well, Lord," Tom said out loud, "this car is yours. I guess I needed this lesson to help me realize it's only tin. I accept this from you and determine not to set my heart on 'things'." We paid the insurance deductible of $50 (the total bill was $140). The following day we received a $50 check in the mail—confirmation that the Lord was in control.

In a letter to the Millers, Tom expressed our deep feelings: "Dotty and I pray each day that we might be able to devote one hundred percent of our time to the work and are willing to step out in any direction the Lord leads."

I completed my college work and received a B.S. in Music Education from Taylor University, graduating *in ab sentia.* Having spent six years and thousands of dollars for that degree and not being able to walk the aisle to receive the diploma caused some sadness. But we simply didn't have the money to travel back to Indiana.

We continued looking for a suitable place for the permanent home office of OCSC, but every door seemed to be closed. With no money and no peace about pursuing anything we saw, we started to wonder if the Lord was leading elsewhere.

We had a strong desire to have a Bible conference in the U.S. like the ones the GIs had experienced in the Millers' home in Manila. So when Pastor Ivan Olsen from our Berean Fundamental Church in North Platte, Nebraska offered the facilities at Maranatha Bible Camp for the Labor Day weekend in 1956, we jumped at the opportunity. Invitations were sent to all of the people on the mailing list. Dr. Ed Spahr, missionary on furlough from the Philippines, agreed to be our speaker. Jesse Miller's mother volunteered to do the cooking. It was a grand reunion of many from the Manila home as well as relatives and friends. Sid Hendry brought a group of airmen from the Denver Servicemen's Center. The Bible teaching was deeply challenging, the fellowship warm and uniting. Most of us were poor in this world's goods, but all were rich in God's blessings. Before leaving, someone handed Chuck Hall, then a student at Moody, a ten-dollar bill. But Chuck felt Sid needed it more so placed it into his hand. Thrilled to have money to give, Sid felt burdened for our needs to get back to California so gave it to us. But Tark and Alma were heading for the Philippines soon and needed funds, so we passed it on to them. I'm not sure who finally kept it, but it didn't matter for that ten-dollar bill gave all of us the joy of both giving and receiving.

About that time, we received a letter from Howard and Cally Erickson, missionaries who had been at radio station DZAS in the Philippines and were now working at HOXO in Panama. They shared their deep burden for the military men walking the streets of Panama City, frequenting the bars and houses of prostitution. Could we send someone? Tom and I shared their burden, praying earnestly for someone to go. God answered that prayer. We were the ones! We were willing and began preparing for that challenge.

Jesse and Nettie Miller sensed God's direction to return to the U.S. to establish the home office of the mission since Tark and Alma Tarkington were available to replace them in the servicemen's home in Manila.

Tark and Alma arrived in Los Angeles the last week of September to prepare for their voyage to Manila. They stayed at the home of Joe and Annie Olsen, parents of Margaret Patty and Annette Mitchell (later Hendry). We helped pack their five crates, two foot lockers, boxes, and suitcases. Alma spent most of that time in bed, fearing she might be pregnant with the threat of a miscarriage—a serious complication on a freighter with no doctor on board. The day of departure we all had a fine dinner at the Olsens and then took the Tarkingtons to the ship and settled them into their cabin. They set sail on September 30, 1956 aboard the MS *Ingadi* of the Ivaran Line. The trip went well and thankfully Alma was not pregnant.

Part III

Stepping Out

Chapter 9

OJT

Two significant changes had occurred in our lives in the past months: God seemingly closed the door to establishing the OCSC home office in California, and he designated us to be the ones to open a Christian Servicemen's Home in Panama. Sid Hendry invited us to move to Denver to assist him in the Christian Servicemen's Center there in order to get some on-the-job training (OJT).

All of our earthly possessions were loaded into the red and white station wagon with *Reaching Servicemen for Christ* painted on one door and *Overseas Christian Servicemen's Centers* on the other. The OCSC home office was neatly packed in Tom's briefcase. We had his last paycheck, but that was all. There was no promise of support or of a place to live but there was a deep peace assuring us we were following God's will.

After the final farewells we went to sleep in our little apartment for the last time. Early the next morning we discovered an envelope inside the screen door. In it were five crisp ten-dollar bills and a farewell note from a high school student in Tom's Sunday school class. Knowing that young man had mowed many a lawn at one dollar each for that amount of money, we were deeply humbled. We were also greatly encouraged as the Lord whispered to our hearts, *See, I will take care of you and you will always be amazed at how I do it!*

When we arrived in Denver on October 15, 1956, Sid Hendry informed us that a Christian couple had invited us to live in their home.

After dreaming about being with the military men for so long, we plunged into the ministry at the Christian Servicemen's Center and were quickly surrounded by men in uniform.

Saturday night was the Youth for Christ rally and it was customary to take a group of the men to that evangelistic meeting. It was so exciting to have the airmen crowd into our station wagon. But the joy quickly left when several lit up their cigarettes. As the smoke filled the over-full car, Tom and I exchanged puzzled glances. How we hated to have that smell permeate our new car. (Smoking was acceptable in any situation in those days.) *Is it yours or mine?* the Lord's rebuke came to our hearts.

Yours, we acknowledged.

Then let it be mine, he responded.

We're sorry, Lord. You know that all we have is yours to use for these men, even the car. It was a promise we never forgot.

Sid, Tom and I spent all of our time at the center—from opening at 11 a.m. until closing at 11 p.m. The bond of Christian love between us was growing daily. None of us had any income because Sid had already taken his discharge from the Air Force. He had a new Oldsmobile and we had the new Ford, but usually there wasn't gas money for either. When some came in, we put gas in one car, leaving the other one parked.

People from local churches brought sandwiches, cookies and cakes to the center each weekend. It was God's wonderful provision for us, but at times I thought I couldn't swallow another sandwich (somewhat like manna). One day someone gave us some money for groceries. That evening everyone at the center shared in the hearty dinner I cooked.

The Lord blessed the ministry to the airmen from Lowry Air Force Base. During the week about fifty came and on weekends hundreds of men wandered in and out of the center. We usually took between sixty and seventy-five airmen to Youth for Christ on Saturday night and almost always a few received Christ as their Savior. On Sunday afternoons we held a GI Gospel Hour and some usually came to the Lord then. The rest of the time was spent one-on-one. We felt strongly that we needed to win them as friends rather than jamming the gospel down their throats the minute they walked in the door. We followed up their conversion by talking with them, giving them the Navigators' memory work, a quiet time notebook, and other materials.

Just before Christmas, Sid left for North Carolina for the holiday, leaving us with the responsibilities of the center. We made plans to take the airmen up to Evergreen for a day of ice skating on the lake. When eighty showed up that morning instead of the twenty-five we had expected, frantic calls to various churches to borrow their buses produced good results. Tom and I drove up to where we were to meet the park attendant. "The skates are in that building over there," he said, pointing over the lake. You can just drive over the ice."

"Uh...what?" Tom gasped, his heart jumping to his throat. But off we went—Tom's first experience like that. We got the skates and headed for Evergreen.

By the time we arrived, the buses were there. Soon everyone was fitted with skates. Most had never been on ice skates before. They looked like windmills in a stiff breeze. Tom and I had decided not to skate because we didn't have seventy-five cents for the rental, but the attendant loaned us two pair free for bringing all of the men.

The pavilion had a crude kitchen, so I prepared the beans, hot dogs and potato salad I had brought. After a hot lunch everyone gathered around and Don Whipple, director of Youth for Christ, gave a salvation message. At the end he did something we had never seen before: he asked everyone to keep their eyes open and heads up while he gave an invitation for the men to receive Christ. Several stood to their feet, giving their lives to him.

In November, to our great joy, I became pregnant. Since we were located in downtown Denver, I searched the upscale shops for ideas for maternity clothes. After many days at my sewing machine in a little room there at the center, I had a lovely new wardrobe.

On Sunday evenings we represented both OCSC and the center in local church services. Sid, Tom, Paul Lewan, and Warren Litynski formed a male quartet, and Sid, Tom and I sang as a trio. Those meetings sparked much interest in the servicemen's work. The free-will offerings helped meet our personal needs as well as the needs of the center.

Along with the center ministry, Tom and I were carrying on the business of OCSC. One day we received a letter from Harley and Miriam Dow, who were students in a Bible college. "We sense the Lord calling us to reach servicemen for Christ. Please send us an application." Well, we didn't have such a thing, so I gathered up some forms from other organizations and compiled the first OCSC application on my typewriter.

We were always torn between giving our time to the new believers and to the first timer who walked in the door. Both were so important. Before long we knew we needed a home as well as the center building downtown—a place where the Christian men could relax and stay overnight on weekends.

The Denver Servicemen's Center

We found a home for rent not far from downtown. It was a two-story turn-of-the-century mansion with an attic large enough for twenty men to sleep, six big bedrooms upstairs, a full apartment in the basement, huge living room, dining room, kitchen, plus two other rooms on the first floor. And it was mostly furnished. The rent was an awesome $250 a month, but before long enough people had pledged support to pay the rent. We moved in. Tom and I were the directors of the home and Sid of the center, but we all lived in the new facility. What joy to unpack our wedding gifts and use them. Meals in the dining room were a special joy, and though finances were very low, our needs were always met.

I held a women's Bible class for some of the girls who came to help. Eventually, quite a few marriages came from those friendships: Mel and Mary Lou Duke, who later served with The Navigators; as well as Harry and Doreen Horn and Larry and Lois Woodward, who served with OCSC.

During our time in the home, Harley and Miriam Dow, the first couple to be officially appointed as missionaries with OCSC, arrived with their two small boys. It was our desire to give them some practical experience in the ministry while they did their deputation in preparation for leaving for Alaska.

Jesse and Nettie Miller with Jimmy and Judy arrived in the spring and stayed with us while they looked for a home that would double as their residence and a permanent home office for OCSC. From all I had heard about the Millers, I envisioned them as the most incredible people on the earth. So when within an hour after their arrival Nettie had the wringer washer out in the kitchen, washing their clothes from the trip, I wasn't too surprised. Then when I awoke the next morning to find her scrubbing the kitchen floor, moving out the refrigerator, and cleaning everything in sight, I didn't know what to think. I learned later that was how she dealt with stress—it was my first exposure to her incredible energy, endurance, and determination.

Much later on our first furlough when we came to work in the home office, I had the courage to tell Nettie that I had no plans to try to keep up with her. She assured me she didn't expect anyone to do so, but many of the women in the mission felt obligated to try. Many years later, when the shoe was on my own foot and others were threatened by my God-given stamina, I remembered how I had felt and tried to assure the new OCSC women that they needed to be what God wanted them to be, not what I was. My tendency to compare has not prevented Nettie from being one of my dearest friends to this day.

Each month the Lord provided our car payments in remarkable ways. But there came one time when the money simply wasn't there. Remembering his commitment to the Lord, Tom was determined to follow through. A young army officer had driven a "delivery" car to Denver, heard about the home, and came to stay a day or two. Since he needed to get on to California, Tom asked if he would take our car and turn it in to the finance company. He didn't reply. The next morning he informed us, "I just can't do that; I'm sorry."

"Why?" Tom asked.

"I believe the Lord wants you to have that car," he answered, handing us a check for the exact amount of the payment.

Our baby was due to arrive the first week of September. On August 12th I was sent to St. Luke's Hospital for x-rays, assuming the procedure was routine. After many "takes," I was told I could go home but to call my doctor the next day. When I did so, I was informed that my regular doctor was away on vacation, but the senior doctor wanted to talk with me.

"Mrs. Hash, this baby will be born by C-section." he announced matter-of-factly. Shocked, I began to cry.

"Oh, many babies are born this way and it is very successful," he assured me. "Of course, if you want us to try labor, we can. But you have a fifty percent chance of survival and the baby has none."

"When must this be done?" I stammered.

"Well, there's no rush, but it should be this week." Conferring with Tom, we told him to schedule it as soon as possible.

From that moment on Tuesday until I entered the hospital Thursday afternoon, I worked like a mad-woman, baking and cooking so the guys would have food to eat. I cleaned the house from stem to stern, washed thirty-five sheets (by wringer washer, dipping and rinsing them all), hung them out to dry, folded them, carried them to the attic, and with the help of Tom, made up all the beds. It's a wonder I didn't go into labor!

Thursday noon we had enough change in our pocket for Sid, Tom, and me to get a pizza. Then we drove to St. Luke's Hospital where I was admitted. The next morning Tom arrived at the hospital just in time to pray with me and watch as they wheeled me into the operating room. He was told to wait downstairs until he was called. The senior obstetrician turned out to be famous for his sixty-second C-sections. I was given a general anesthetic and in one minute Lori was born. After several hours in the recovery room, by mid-afternoon I was taken to my room. "Where is my husband?" I groggily inquired of the nurse.

"Uh... Do you have a husband here? Oh, no!" She rushed from the room.

Tom had been patiently waiting for word for nine hours. Since he had no experience with such operations, he assumed it took that long, but admitted he was getting a little worried. When the nurse ran in he was greatly relieved. She apologized profusely and led him to my bedside.

We named our firstborn Lori Grace. In the room with me was a young woman also having her first baby. I had told her we were missionaries, and when she learned Lori's name (and spelling) she remarked, "Wow—a pretty fancy name for a missionary's child." The medical bill was $400, which we paid off in small installments during the following months.

Unknown to us, during that week-long stay in the hospital I picked up a staph infection which lay dormant until an illness weakened my body. It didn't have long to wait.

My mother arrived by train from Milwaukee about the time I came home from the hospital. A persistent muscle spasm kept me in intense pain for several weeks. I had been determined to nurse Lori (uncommon in those days, unheard of for someone with a C-section), but I persisted without any encouragement.

Tom, Sid, and the fellows were at Maranatha Bible Camp for our second annual conference and I had a nasty case of "baby blues." Mother tried to comfort me and took such good care, but it was a difficult time for me. When Tom returned, he informed us that we would begin our deputation immediately. With Mother's help on my first full day out of bed, we again packed up our earthly goods, loaded them into our station wagon, and headed for Louisville, Kentucky. Lori was two and a half weeks old. We were unaware how unwise this was, for it put my health into great jeopardy.

Chapter 10

TESTING AND TRUSTING

Mother and I stayed with Tom's sister and brother-in-law in Louisville while Tom made a survey trip to Panama that summer in 1957. I began feeling better but was told by the doctor to stop nursing due to abscesses—a real disappointment. Later I was to be very thankful.

While in Panama Tom determined that the need for a servicemen's home was truly great. Because the men were all stationed within the Canal Zone (an American controlled five-mile wide strip across the Isthmus with the canal running through it) we should be located there. But acquiring permission to locate in the Zone was almost impossible. The pastor of First Baptist Church was willing to sponsor us, but this would mean the ministry would be part of the church. We were unsure if this was a wise way to establish the work. The other alternative was to enter the Republic of Panama, locating in Panama City.

Tom met a host of wonderful Christians in Panama, including John and Leah Nitz. John, a physical therapist, worked at the American Gorgas Hospital. They fellowshipped at First Baptist Church. The greatest impression they made on Tom was how they handled their growing family—at that time one girl and four boys. He watched John play hard with the boys, attend lovingly to his daughter, and together with Leah discipline with a firmness and love he had never witnessed before. He determined he would emulate their godly example with his own children. Years later, when teaching my ladies' Bible studies, I always referred to Leah as my "Proverbs 31 lady."

Tom was invited to a single men's Bible study at the home of Dr. Roland and Muriel Icke. There he met a number of soldiers and airmen. When Tom and I moved to Panama, some of these men were the first we invited to our Christian Servicemen's Home.

As soon as Tom returned, our deputation began. For the next two months, we traveled to any church or individual who would allow us to present our slides and message, eventually ending up in Denver. It was great to be back at the home with Sid again. The first evening there, I felt like I was getting the flu—it came on so quickly. Hurrying downstairs, I prepared a batch of formula for Lori's bottles, then went to bed. By morning I was really ill. The doctor came, prescribed medication, and said to stay in bed. Two days later I could no longer get up. When he returned, his face grew pale. "We don't want to lose her," he warned. "She needs to go to the hospital, but her blood pressure is too low to make the trip." After administering an injection, he called the ambulance. Nettie Miller came to get Lori and lovingly cared for her for the next couple of weeks. As the attendants wheeled me out the door, the emptiness and fear I felt was overwhelming. Lori was not yet three months old, Tom looked so worried, and the doctor was deeply concerned.

At the hospital the room was swarming with medical personnel. They packed me in ice to bring down the fever of 105 degrees. Someone was at my side every moment. "You will need to have a private nurse tonight, " they informed me. "Shall we call someone for you?"

"I don't know what to do—we don't have money for that," I pleaded. I guess they decided to do it themselves, for they were there all night. Testing showed that I had had Asian flu, but a staph infection was now threatening my life which hung in the balance for several days. Eventually the tables turned, and on the tenth day I was released. The dear doctor (who had been a missionary in Asia for many years) did not send us a bill. We stayed with the Millers for two more weeks—until I was well enough to resume our deputation.

On the invitation of Pastor Carl Goltz, we spent a week at the Berean Fundamental Church in Torrington, Wyoming. Carl and Doris were a great encouragement to us. From there we drove to North Platte and stayed with Pastor and Mrs. Olsen, who again allowed us to take the pulpit to present our ministry to the military. Tom and I always sang at the meetings and were warmly received. And that Sunday we became members of the church. Through those dear saints, the Lord was challenging our hearts and drawing us closer and closer to himself.

With meetings scheduled en route, we were planning to head to Wisconsin for the holidays. We had three dollars to get there. A hole blew in the muffler on the car, making it sound like a truck, but a Christian mechanic told Tom it would be safe from fumes for the trip.

In OCSC's early years, we followed the financial philosophy of George Mueller—to tell only the Lord our needs. (It was also before the days of credit cards.) After speaking at the morning service, Pastor Olsen asked, "Do you have money to get where you're going?" Since we had the evening service in the Berean church in the next town and the three dollars would take us there, Tom replied, "Yes, we do."

Pastor Ivan Olsen and his wife Alice

"Oh, you young missionaries are all alike!" he chided. "You wouldn't tell us if you were starving to death!" Picking up the phone, he told the church treasurer to write out a check for twenty-five dollars which we could pick up on our way out of town. The rest of the love offering would be sent to us.

Stopping at the cheapest gas station on the edge of town, Tom told the attendant to put in three dollars worth. Glancing at our out-of-state license, he remarked, "Not much for where you're going!"

"Well, I'd put in more, but that's all the cash I have. I only have a twenty-five dollar check from a church here in town."

"What church?"

"Berean Fundamental."

"I'll take that," he shrugged.

We were on our way rejoicing. That twenty-five dollars got us all the way to Milwaukee. When we pulled into the driveway we had an eighth of a tank of gas and fifty cents. God had been faithful.

About this time Tom wrote to the Millers: "Today as I thought through the need for equipment, for passage, and for support, my heart was completely filled with the thought that Dotty's and my only real need is to be filled with the Lord. We are trusting the Lord to do this—that only he might be seen in these weak lives."

After spending the holidays with my folks in Milwaukee and having great fellowship with the people at Grace Methodist Church, our meetings took us to Kentucky, Indiana, Illinois, Minnesota, Michigan, Washington DC, Cleveland, then back to Nebraska and Denver.

While in Louisville, Lori had an acute case of diarrhea and was in the hospital for three days. After admitting her, the doctor asked us to stay in the waiting room while she was settled into her bed. When we walked into the room, I broke into tears. There was our little lamb, an intravenous needle stuck in the top of her head. It was a necessary procedure and a good place for it, for she could move freely without restraints, but it was tough on these new parents. She recovered quite quickly. Tom wrote: "Our hospital bill was $74.35 and we haven't received the doctor bill yet. The insurance policy we applied for went into effect right after this, so we have to pay for it ourselves. The Lord knows what he is doing. We don't mind, for he has supplied and it helps us to trust him all the more."

Tom had the privilege of speaking at the country church (in the "holler") of his relatives in rural Kentucky. It was cold, but the pot-bellied stove in the center of the room had been well stoked. Men in their bibbed overalls sat on their side of the room, the women on the other. Average attendance was about twenty, but that night over one hundred came. They heard that Howard Hash's son was speaking. They wanted to hear the moonshiner's son who had become a preacher. As the singing began, most of the songs were familiar, but my "refined" musical ear was assaulted by altered rhythms and peculiar sounding words. Once again I realized how vast was the difference between this world and the one from which I came. It wasn't that one was better than the other—just different. Tom gave his testimony with real liberty and many said his father and others were deeply moved.

That winter a trip from Peoria to Moline, Illinois, a distance of one hundred miles, took five hours due to a blinding snow storm. We got stuck on one hill and a truck towed us for about half a mile for a dollar. Another time we were on our way to meetings in a rural church in southwestern Michigan when the snow began to fall. Tom stopped at a station to put on chains. We continued on for an hour, then stopped to call the pastor. "Don't try to come any farther," he warned. "We're snowed in. Just try to get some place where you can stay."

Remembering the intersection an hour back, we started out. Tom stopped several times to help pull cars from the ditch since ours was one of the few with chains on. One of the drivers we helped glanced into our car and saw Lori. "You'd better stop helping people and get that baby out of this storm!" he warned.

Hours later we arrived at the intersection, but the motels were all full by now with buses and trucks filling the parking lots. "Could I just bring my wife and baby into the lobby for the night?" Tom pleaded with a motel attendant.

"No, we can't allow that. But we will call a hotel in the next town and see if they have a room." A room was promised, and once again we headed into the snow. Hours later we found the hotel, but the usual price had doubled. We carried Lori to the warmth of the room. Huddled around the old steam radiator, we thankfully ate the leftover chicken we had brought along.

The next morning when we called, the pastor told us to come back to the corner where we had called from the night before. A farmer was plowing the country road and would meet us there. We followed his plow to the pastor's home, but snow came again, stranding us for the next five days. It was the most snow I had ever seen.

Since our station wagon was our only home during that year, we developed efficient systems for Lori's care. She slept in a bassinet just behind the front seat (no seat-belts in those days). By getting on my knees, I could feed and change her. We had a bottle warmer that plugged into the cigarette lighter. We learned early to plug it in long before she awoke, for it took forever to heat. But it worked. Of course there were no disposable diapers then, so I had a brown paper grocery bag for her neatly folded diapers. A diaper pail with secure top held the soiled ones. Our philosophy "a place for everything and everything in its place" kept us from utter chaos. Her fancy little dresses, which I sewed by hand while traveling, hung on little hangers.

On the deputation trail
this car was our "home" for Lori's first year.

We kept her on a strict schedule. When we arrived at a church for an evening service, she was already in bed for the night. We simply picked up her bed, carried her into the church, and let her sleep. After the service, we carried her back to the car. She slept in a bassinette until she was seven months old. After that we got a small crib and sawed off the legs. That worked until we left for Panama just before her first birthday.

Our support came in slowly, but by spring of 1958 we were nearing $200 per month. In those early years no support level was established so when a missionary couple felt they were ready, they left for the field.

We returned to the Berean Church in North Platte once more, this time to do a visitation program for the church which might possibly result in more financial support. We left Denver in the morning with eight dollars—enough for gas and lunch. When we stopped for lunch, I noticed that Lori was feverish. I took her temperature—104 degrees. We gave her some aspirin, praying for the Lord's protection as I held her in my arms all afternoon. When we arrived in North Platte that evening, Pastor Olsen took us up to the missionary apartment. He was about to leave but asked, "Is there anything else you need?"

I replied, "Yes, Lori is very ill. Do you know of a doctor?"

"I sure do!" He went to the phone to call a pediatrician friend.

"I'll meet you at my office in five minutes," the doctor said. Upon examining Lori he said she needed some antibiotics and proceeded to write a prescription. Our hearts sank. We didn't have money for the medicine. Leading us from the office, the doctor glanced at his watch.

"Oh, there isn't a drug store open this late," he remarked. He went to his cabinet and handed us some samples. Our thanks to him and to the Lord were many. Lori cried day and night for several days (making for great visitation!), finally breaking out in a horrendous rash—she had roseola, a form of baby measles.

During this time in North Platte, the Berean Council met with Tom to determine whether he would qualify for ordination. The full day of questioning was successful and he passed. The formal service that followed was both an ordination for Tom and commissioning as missionaries for both of us. As we knelt before that host of godly pastors and deacons who placed their hands on our heads and shoulders commending us to the Gospel ministry, we wept softly as someone sang,

So send I you to labor unrewarded,
To serve unpaid, unloved, unsought, unknown,
To bear rebuke, to suffer scorn and scoffing,
So send I you, to toil for me alone.
As the Father hath sent me, so send I you."
(Margaret Clarkson, John Peterson, Singspiration/Zondervan)

We received word from the Canal Zone that our application to enter would not be considered until fall. Taking this as an indication that the Lord would have us enter Panama City to begin the work, we investigated the matter of passports and visas. (They were not necessary for the Canal Zone.) We learned it would be best to enter on visitors' visas, then apply for permanent ones upon arrival. The least expensive transportation we found was to ship our household items from Mobile and fly from Miami. We planned to sell the car because we didn't have funds for freight or customs. We would pay off the balance due and try to buy something on arrival.

Returning to Denver, we began the packing and crating process. We didn't have any furniture to send so the crates consisted mostly of books, kitchen items, linens, and personal belongings. My mother had purchased a large set of stainless dinnerware and given us most of her fancy things for entertaining.

One morning when Tom went to the post office, he received a letter from Chaplain Merritt Dayton. We hardly knew him but were aware that he had recently served a tour of duty in Panama and had become extremely concerned for the needs of the military men there. Sitting behind the steering wheel of the car, Tom tore open the letter. *Dear Tom, he read. We are going to purchase a new station wagon soon and feel the Lord wants us to give you our old one.* The letter went on to describe it: a 1954 Ford station wagon, nine passenger (ours was six), four door (ours had two), V-8 (ours was a six cylinder),

Fordomatic (ours was a stick shift), plush inside and out (ours was the most stripped down model made), no rust, undercoated, without a dent. The mileage—60,000 miles (Tom looked at the odometer on ours—60,000).

Tom located a dealer's car to be delivered to New York City to which we hooked a trailer containing our crates. We dropped off "our" Ford wagon in North Platte to the Buttermore family, who generously offered to buy it and drove to Louisville in the dealer's car. From the sale we were able to pay off the remaining loan with enough money left to ship the "new" car and crates, pay customs, and purchase some furniture in Panama. Tom and his brother-in-law, Jim Wilson, drove the dealer's car to New York and then took a bus to Ft. Bragg, North Carolina, where the Daytons lived. They graciously placed the keys and title for the shiny forest green Ford wagon into Tom's hand and the next day he and Jim headed back to Louisville.

Soon we were loaded again with a trailer attached to the "new" Ford, ready to leave for Panama via Pensacola and Miami. Our promised monthly support was about $200. God had indeed done the miraculous. Tearful farewells to Tom's Aunt Ida and other family members were made even more sad by the fact that Lori had a 103-degree temperature. A trip to the doctor allayed our fears, for he assured us it would be safe to travel with her. We stopped for the night in Bowling Green, Kentucky, and settled into a motel. About midnight we were terrified when Lori's fever soared to 105.4. In those days there were no medical facilities where you could just drop in—you called your family physician or pediatrician.

Then Satan, the enemy of our souls, really moved in. *Fools! What are you doing to this baby, dragging her off to some foreign place when she should be at home where you can care for her.* My motherly heart sank in agreement. Tears fell, not because we doubted God's leading but because we felt so utterly helpless. But immediately the Holy Spirit reminded us that he was in control and would care for us as we recalled I Peter 5:7, "Casting all your care upon him; for he careth for you."

We bathed Lori's feverish body with cool water and gave her aspirin. Then we knelt beside her crib, pleading with the Lord for healing. Before long she fell asleep and so did we. The next morning her temperature was almost normal and remained that way for the rest of the trip.

The car and crates were shipped from Mobile. We boarded the train in Pensacola at midnight. The next morning when we changed trains in Jacksonville, we discovered, contrary to what we had been told, we needed reservations. The train was over-booked. After manhandling our heavy bags into an overflowing luggage compartment, we found a table in the club car. Soon we were asked to leave. Then I spent several hours holding Lori in the ladies' lounge, while Tom roamed the train searching for a place for us. Eventually we slumped wearily into some vacant seats in a coach. When the train chugged into the Miami station the next day, two very tuckered missionaries disembarked. But the Lord had a special surprise in store for us. We learned that one of the five-star beach front hotels was offering off-season rates at "missionary" prices. Soon we were soaking up the Florida sunshine in the Atlantic ocean.

That night, settled comfortably in our lovely room, we thanked the Lord for watching over us for that part of our journey. As we drifted off to sleep, I thought, *By this time tomorrow we will be missionaries in Panama.*

PART IV

PANAMA

Chapter 11

SO NEAR BUT SO FAR

The Aerovias Panama Airways prop plane lifted off from the Miami airport at 7 a.m. on August 7, 1958 for a non-stop flight due to arrive in Panama City, Panama, at 1 p.m. My heart beat wildly with excitement: this was my first trip abroad and my very first ride on an airplane. Lori had just settled into a good nap when the stewardess informed us we would be landing in Havana, Cuba, and everyone must deplane. "But my daughter..." I protested.

"I'm sorry! *Everyone* must deplane!" was her brusquc reply. Tom and I knew that the situation in Cuba was unstable, for the rebel commander, Fidel Castro, was fighting his way to the capital to take control. We were told to form a group on the airplane stairway (no jetways then). When the entire crew and passengers were assembled, our picture was taken. Then we were led into the terminal where our travel documents were examined. "Proceed this way!" an authoritative uniformed man barked in English and Spanish as he herded us into a waiting room. We sat like sticks, afraid a move might cause an international incident that would keep us in Cuba forever. My imaginations and fears ran rampant. An hour or so later, with hardly a word, we were led back onto the aircraft. A sigh of relief went up as the plane lifted off the runway bound for Panama. The reason for that stop remains a mystery to us to this day.

Several hours later we were told to prepare for landing at Tocumen Airport in Panama City. As we deplaned, we could see Howard and Cally Erickson, Conservative Baptist missionaries serving at radio station HOXO, waving at us from the observation deck—a comforting sight! In the car on the way to the city, a kaleidoscope of sights and smells assaulted my senses. The moist tropical heat; jungle foliage; roads teeming with buses and people; noisy, totally out-of- control traffic; shanties with grass roofs; vendors peddling their wares; and little children in rags all speaking a language I didn't understand put my mind into sensory overload.

By that evening we were nicely settled into the Ericksons' apartment, asking hundreds of questions. We learned that our tourist visas were good for only 90 days. Permanent visas cost $150 each and we would have to go to Costa Rica to get them. Housing was going to be expensive. We could see our meager funds coming to an end long before the expenses. But we knew God had brought us this far and would not abandon us now.

With Howard's help we located a small house, new and clean with rent of $70 a month, including water. It was located on a main bus line but about five miles from downtown which was seventeen miles from Fort Amador, the U.S. Army headquarters. The distance concerned us, but married servicemen lived nearby and traveled it every day. We were able to purchase basic pieces of used furniture for $250.

We moved in on August 16, Lori's first birthday. After helping us unload, Howard shook our hands warmly, wishing us the best in the Lord. We were on our own and suddenly felt terribly lonesome. After Lori went to bed that night, Tom and

I got into an argument. We were twenty-two miles from the GIs we loved, had no transportation, were unable to speak Spanish, had no church family, suffered from the heat, and had heard rumors of pending riots. I wanted to go home! If I had been anywhere in the U.S. I probably would have. We laughed about it later, concluding that more marriages would survive if young couples were far away from refuge. They would learn, like we did, to resolve their problems and move ahead. But that night was awful!

We began attending First Baptist Church, the largest evangelical church in the Canal Zone, loosely affiliated with the Southern Baptist Convention. Before long I was asked to become the interim choir director. Our car and household goods arrived safely requiring minimal customs fees. We started inviting a few soldiers out to our home—men Tom had met at Dr. Icke's singles Bible study when he was there on the survey trip. An embryonic ministry was emerging.

One morning we awoke to the news that a riot had erupted at the border between Panama City and the Canal Zone. We rushed to the scene to find cars burning in the street, an overturned bus, stones flying, and people running everywhere. Our hearts sank. The soldiers were confined to the Canal Zone—we to Panama City. We suddenly felt isolated from the very ones to whom we had come to minister. We needed to be in the Canal Zone.

The Panama Canal Zone, we were learning, was a community like no other in the world. It was an area about fifty miles long, ten miles wide (five on each side of the canal) reaching from the Atlantic Ocean to the Pacific Ocean across the Isthmus of Panama. The building of the canal was begun by the French and completed by Americans. It was a manmade waterway cutting through Central America, linking the two oceans enabling ships to travel between them without sailing around South America, saving 7,800 miles.

The land was owned by the Republic of Panama, but the 1903 treaty between the U.S. and Panama gave the U.S. the right to construct a canal and to govern a designated area as if it were sovereign. The Panama Canal Company, a U.S. government corporation, operated the canal and the Canal Zone government provided the various services such as schools and the fire department. There was also a large military presence. Each branch of service had one or more bases in the Zone. While military personnel came and went, the Panama Canal employees and civilian employees of the military were a stable community, some families dating back several generations to when the canal was completed in 1914.

The governor of the Canal Zone had traditionally been a senior officer of the U.S. Army Corps of Engineers, appointed by the President of the U.S., confirmed by the Congress, and served for a term of four years.

In the 1950s the Zone was totally self-contained with American and Panamanian schools, commissaries, hospitals, postal system, police, movie theaters, bowling alleys, churches, and clubs. The government-owned housing areas had look-alike buildings and immaculately groomed yards; the entire Canal Zone was a tropical garden. Panama was a land of perpetual summer, always green, with little violent weather.

Panama City, the capital of Panama, was located across the street from the Zone on the Pacific side. Balboa was one of the townsites in the Zone, with Balboa Heights being the center of Canal Zone government and headquarters of the Panama Canal Company. The Canal Zone and Panama were separated only by a street, Fourth of July Avenue, but the distinction between them was clearly felt and seen by all who passed from one side to the other. There were no fences or check points dividing the Zone from Panama. The Panama Canal Company employed 15,000 workers of whom approximately 11,000 were Panamanians. They were employed in all aspects of the work, though the over-all control was exclusively by Americans.

Americans who worked for the Panama Canal Company received a salary somewhat higher than the average U.S. wage in consideration for living overseas in the tropics. But the cost of living was relatively low when compared to Panama, where custom duties drove up prices. Panamanians hired by the U.S. received salaries generally higher than their counterparts in the Republic.

By God's divine appointment, we were introduced to Philip Steers, who was the principal financial officer, a general officer of the Panama Canal Company and Comptroller of the Canal Zone Government. He and his family were believers, active in the Christian community. We shared our dreams for the Lord's work with him. Phil was very sympathetic and agreed that our ministry needed to be in the Canal Zone, and if possible in an area of easy access for the soldiers without transportation.

He pointed out that the governor received many legitimate requests from religious and humanitarian organizations wanting to establish a presence in the Zone. He noted, however, that our work was different in that it was directed to the military in order to provide the men with a desirable option to the streets of Panama. "I will help you," he said. "You will have to make a formal request and there is no guarantee that approval will be forthcoming. And it could take some time." He offered to introduce Tom to the governor, but first he suggested that we prepare a letter formally requesting authorization to establish our mission in the Zone. In addition, to our surprise, he said, "You will need a building. Before you do anything else, let's look around to see if any are available."

At the housing office we learned that four large buildings were empty with no plans for their future use by

PanCanal. The first three had some potential but also serious drawbacks. Either they were unsuitable for a home atmosphere, would require too much renovation, or were poorly located. Somewhat disheartened, we drove to the last address. When we turned into the immaculately groomed street lined by majestic palms leading to Corozal Hospital and then up the drive to building 548 in Corozal townsite, we knew we were "home."

As we entered the stairwell of the large wooden building, the odor of mildew and cockroach droppings assaulted our nostrils. Then we heard wings flapping. Horrified, we watched bats fly around us, angry that we had disturbed their sleep. Little piles of termite dust lay on the wooden stairs. We walked slowly through the former nurses' quarters, closely examining the sixteen rooms, four bathrooms, two stairwells, and eight carports. There was no kitchen—we would need to build one. But other than cleaning and painting and the removal of some walls, it was perfect! Our hearts beat wildly as we returned to the car. There, we bowed our heads, asking the Lord to make this the Christian Servicemen's Home.

We drafted a letter to Governor Seybold, requesting permission to establish a ministry there. Then Mr. Steers arranged an appointment for Tom to make the formal request directly to the governor. Tom will never forget that day.

> Phil accompanied me into the governor's office. I had never seen such a massive desk! The governor, in his immaculate white suit, looked awesome. My knees knocked; my palms were sweaty. After reading my letter and asking many questions, the governor said, "There are all kinds of religious groups wanting permission to locate in the Zone. Why should I authorize *your* mission to do so?"

At that moment the Lord reminded me that even though the governor was dressed in civilian clothes, he was still a two-star army general and a soldier at heart.

"Sir," I said, "you know that when the soldiers get off duty they usually head for the bars, casinos, and prostitutes there at 'the limits' in Panama City. Our mission wants to provide an alternative—a home away from home—where the welcome mat is out, where they can get a home-cooked meal and have Christian fellowship in a loving atmosphere."

"Just where would this home be located?" the governor asked. I handed him the second letter requesting the use of the former nurses' quarters now vacant and apparently scheduled to be torn down. The governor carefully read the letter and handed it back to me with the comment, "Take it to the executive secretary. He will make arrangements."

I thanked him, we left his office, and went to the executive secretary's office where we delivered the letter and summarized our conversation with the governor. "I'll take care of it for you," was his abrupt reply.

As Mr. Steers and I returned to his office, he said, "Tom, do you know what really happened just now? In those few minutes your mission received the governor's approval of housing your ministry in the Canal Zone. This is unique, as no other mission has that privilege! You will have your Christian Servicemen's Home in the Zone as soon as the papers can be processed. Praise the Lord!"

The rent was assessed at $100 a year but later reduced to $10 with the stipulation that we maintain the building to PanCanal standards.

After reading II Corinthians 1:16-24, Tom recorded in his quiet time journal on October 27, 1958, "It is because

God has promised to seal us for himself that he establishes us. He is the fullness of all promises since he alone can faithfully keep them."

Less than two weeks before our visas were to expire, we were given official residence in the Zone. This included a U.S. post office box with stateside postal rates and no customs, buying privileges at the Panama Canal Company commissary, and medical privileges at the American Gorgas Hospital. We moved into temporary quarters in the little Canal Zone town of Gamboa, headquarters of the dredging division thirteen miles west of the home, until our building was habitable.

The Christian Servicemen's Home in Panama

Chapter 12

"FILL THESE ROOMS"

Three families from the Baptist church caught our vision for the ministry: Duane and Kay Arnold, Ed and Cleo Kinnett, and Wally and Shirley Brian. Day and night we worked as a team. Every wall, floor, and ceiling had to be scrubbed with bleach to remove the mildew and then painted twice with oil-based enamel paint. The floors of beautiful mahogany were riddled with termite holes which had to be treated. The outside walls were single boards—one side was the inside, the other the outside. Diagonal boards were nailed over them in places on the inside. Light showed through some of the cracks, but it wasn't a problem for large overhanging eves protected the building during the heavy rains in rainy season. Air conditioning was rare at that time.

Money for paint and supplies was scant, but whenever we needed something, the Lord provided. The kitchen project was going to be the most expensive. One day Tom learned that a building was being torn down in Curundu. He rushed over to find kitchen cabinets strewn out on the ground. "What will you do with these?" he asked the workman.

"We'll junk 'em if no one wants 'em!"

"May I have them?"

"Sure. Just haul 'em away."

Wally Brian made them fit and with a fresh coat of white paint they looked like new. Chet Bockus, a missionary from the interior, needed a place to stay for awhile and we invited him to stay with us. He just happened to be a carpenter. Soon new Formica topped the base cabinets. At surplus on base, Tom found a brand new sink with a small chip in it for $15.

When the kitchen was usable, we received permission to move in. This made life easier, especially for sixteen-month-old Lori. She had learned to play among the paint cans and scrub pails, but now she could sleep in her own room and I could prepare meals instead of carrying sack lunches. And the money spent on rent and utilities in Gamboa could be put toward the renovation.

Our biggest project was to remove walls in the center of the first floor which would open up a large lounge and dining room. The PanCanal contractor wanted $460 to do the job and it required endless red tape. We then learned we could hire one of the carpenters to supervise the work in his off-duty hours with us supplying the labor. The electrical work was contracted out.

Each night when Tom and I dragged our weary bodies up to bed, we knelt together and prayed, "Lord, thanks so much for this wonderful building and for all we accomplished today. Now please fill these rooms with soldiers who need you so desperately."

We were working on the last room one evening when we heard a motorcycle roar into the driveway. In sauntered a leather-clad guy, who in moments let us know that he considered himself God's gift to women. He was reared on the streets of Detroit and had joined the Army to get away from the gangs. All evening he told about his exploits in the bars, brothels, and casinos downtown. When he roared away on his motorcycle, I was relieved! I hoped he'd never come back.

Again that night Tom and I bowed, held hands and prayed, "Lord, thanks so much for this wonderful building. Now please fill these rooms with soldiers who need..."

"Oh, no, not him!" I wailed. "I can't stand him! I hope he never comes back!" Then I wept softly as the Lord reminded me of my commitment to him and the love he had given me for servicemen—and not just the "nice" ones.

Gene did come back, and before long he received Christ into his life. What a change! His conversation changed from talking about the girls downtown to wanting to know what a Bible verse meant. His sneer became a sweet smile. His nicotine-stained hands became soft and white. I loved to watch him play gently with Lori.

Eighteen months later Gene's tour of duty was over and we took him to the flight line to see him off for the U.S. Walking up the steps to the plane, he turned and waved. Tears streamed down our faces. I wept openly. Our first-born son was launched. Later we learned he was attending Bible college.

Tom learned that furniture was available for bids at a navy surplus warehouse on the Atlantic side. He selected a china cupboard, eight dining chairs, a large desk, floor lamps, a small work table and a brand new gas stove, and he bid $36 for the whole works. Miraculously, the bid was accepted.

We worked hard to get the home open for Christmas. When the Christmas trees from the States arrived at the commissary, we set ours up in the unfinished lounge. All decked out with lights and tinsel, it looked so lonely—the only thing in the room. But by working right up to Christmas eve, everything was in order for the special time. We were pleased when about fifteen singles and families came. Then sixteen men came for dinner Christmas Day and fourteen the following Sunday. Six to eight came every day during the holiday season.

First Christmas at the Home—1958

The Sunday after Christmas, Tom gave out ten sets of the Navigator "B" rations (basic Bible verses on little cards) for the men to memorize. They followed through well, many proceeding to learn the entire 108 verses in the program. They came regularly one night a week to share the verses and report on their quiet time and the books they were reading. We saw definite growth in the group of eight to ten who came.

"We are leaning hard on the Lord these days as we begin our work with the fellows," I wrote to the Millers. "How we do pray that he will just completely indwell us and win the fellows to himself. We are very happy and content here. I wish you could see this place—what a perfect provision from the Lord. Everything about it was arranged by him. We are amazed at his plan and graciousness. What a privilege to be his servants! How we pray that we may be so yielded to him that he can fulfill his plan for this place. We are beginning to see the Lord start touching the hearts of the guys to help with the finances—just the faintest indication, but it's starting. Pray that they might take hold, not for the sake of money, but for their own spiritual growth."

Trips to the interior to visit mission stations were particularly fruitful. Getting away from the Zone and witnessing the work of the Lord among the nationals became a turning point in many of the men's lives. Though wearying on us and taking a heavy toll on our vehicle, the trips were well worth the effort. In August of 1959, Tom made his biggest trip to the interior. The night before the trip began, the men had packed the non-perishable food, appropriate clothing and sleeping equipment, insect repellent, cameras and film, an outboard motor, and those all-important fifty gallons of gas into the station wagon. Tom made the 100 mile round trip to Chepo, where Mr. Martz, the New Tribes missionary lived, and dropped off the supplies. At 4 a.m. the next morning, he and the six fellows were up, shaving, and packing their personal items. I served them a big breakfast knowing it would be a long day.

They drove the trip to Chepo, arriving there at 8 a.m. Mr. Martz and the national guide who would go along were there to meet them. At their first look at the dugout canoe, the men wondered if they had made a terrible mistake. It was two feet wide and fourteen inches deep, a real tippy thing that required everyone to sit deathly still. Much to their surprise, everything fit, and before long they shoved off into the Bayano River bound for Indian territory in the Darien Gap. The river looked smooth, but they soon realized how deceiving it could be. They fought hard to get upstream, then held their breath as they shot the rapids. The responsibility of continually bailing water was passed from man to man. Eventually the Indian village appeared in the distance.

Tom required that all the men on the trip be Christians, for the tribe they were to visit had only recently been reached by the missionary and the first seeds of the

Gospel sown. Until then, Mr. Martz was the only outsider ever permitted to stay overnight in the village.

Then a near-tragedy happened: the guide indicated to go one way, but Mr. Martz failed to see his signal and started the other way. The canoe got into the cross-current, the rudder wouldn't respond, and they plowed straight toward the island. Quick thinking on the part of the guide and one of the men enabled them to grab some low-hanging branches. Grinning from ear to ear the guide asked, "Que paso?" "What happened?" By then the villagers were lining the high bank to investigate.

Heading down the Bayano river in the dugout canoe

After fighting the swift current for some time, they finally landed, tied down, and climbed out of the canoe. Mr. Martz approached the chief, asking permission for the men to visit. Nodding, he indicated they should take their things to the "guest house." With the Indians watching in fascination, they made their way to the hut, which turned out to be the "council building." Soon a fire was glowing and they cooked their supper of rice and stew.

Mr. Martz had warned the men not to take pictures while in the village because the Indians might think they were capturing their spirits. So most of that trip was recorded only in the men's memories.

Soon the entire male population of the village convened in the council building. The chief graciously allowed the foreigners to observe their meeting. They couldn't understand a word, but the proceedings, the people, the building, and the dimly lit fires fascinated them, holding their attention. They couldn't help but think how different the situation would have been if these Indians knew the joy of salvation in Christ. The stark contrast between dark heathenism and the light of the Gospel gripped each man's heart.

When the council meeting finally ended, the soldiers strung their hammocks from the poles that held up the thatched roof of the building. Between the continual parade of visitors—human and non-human—and the various men flipping over in their hammocks, it was a somewhat sleepless night. In the morning when they retreated to the river bank for devotions, the missionary challenge was very real. The need for someone to bring the Gospel to those Indians and thousands of others in the jungle didn't seem far removed. Boarding the dugout for the return trip, the men had a new understanding of the people who lived beyond those miles and miles of river bank. The trip left an indelible mark on each one.

We were able to hire two Panamanian maids part time to help with the heavy housework. I did all the laundry and cooking, they did the ironing and cleaning. We paid one $15 a month, the other $19 a month—expensive for our meager budget, but we couldn't do it all ourselves.

Jettie was an older black lady of Jamaican descent who lived in one tiny room with one bare light bulb in Panama City. She begged to work for us because she wanted to be in a Christian home. We simply didn't have money to hire her, so we worked out a plan: she would come on Sunday mornings and prepare dinner for everyone while we were at church. As pay, she could take home the leftovers. From those she cooked up a big pot of "stew" and sold it on the streets.

While shopping at the commissary one day, Lori interrupted my thoughts. "Look! Look, Mommy! There's Jettie!" Sure enough. She had spotted a box of Aunt Jemima pancake flour. The picture looked just like Jettie. When we returned home, she showed the box to Jettie. "Oh, honey," she purred. "Ah ain't nearly that purty." We really grew to love that dear Christian lady.

In the tropics, creepy crawly creatures thrive in abundance. The only ones that really bothered me were cockroaches. I could detect their odor a mile off. Even now I shiver at the thought! We cleaned and cleaned but never really got rid of them. When the babies were small and needed a bottle in the middle of the night, I stood at the door of the kitchen, closed my eyes, flicked on the light, and waited until the roaches scattered. Otherwise they sounded like popcorn crunching under my slippers. We never went anywhere at night with bare feet! Snakes were abundant also. One day one of our kittens was missing. Soon we spotted a boa constrictor behind the home, immobilized while ingesting the poor thing. We called the snake patrol who came to try to capture it, but it quickly spit out the dead cat and slithered away into the brush.

But the snake hideout was eliminated one day when the tall grass in the field behind the home caught fire.

Standing in the kitchen window on the second floor, we watched the flames leaping above us, perilously close to the building. The fire department arrived quickly to put out the fire, but the incident remains a vivid memory in Lori's mind.

Missionaries have their stories. One of them is that you can tell first-term missionaries because when they see bugs in the flour, they throw it all away. The second term, they carefully sift out the bugs. By the third term, they just cook 'em and eat 'em. The story has some truth.

Several times we were given a box of wonderful chocolates from the U.S. only to discover they were crawling with ants. We quickly learned to pop the box into the freezer, wait a few hours while the ants crawled off and froze to death, and then enjoy the delicacy.

More riots and Panamanian elections caused concern for the Americans who lived in Panama City and the interior. We were quite safe, but missionaries who came in from the provinces to care for business were vulnerable. There were no mission guest houses in that day so our home became the substitute. How the missionaries loved our attractive, clean, safe home where we spoke English and ate American food. It became a haven to many—too many. I wrote to Nettie Miller, "Our dear friends, the Pruntys with New Tribes Mission, and their Indian man stayed with us for a week; three Mennonite fellows were here for five days; then five more New Tribes missionaries waiting to go to the U.S. came for four more days. A family with two children waiting to get into their apartment avoided the trouble by staying with us." We loved the fellowship and providing hospitality, but the increase in laundry, cleaning, cooking, and expenses took a heavy toll. When the burden became too heavy, we turned it over to the Lord. "Please help us with this problem," we prayed. "We simply don't have the heart to turn anyone away." Soon the unrest died down and the flood became a manageable trickle.

Glen and Billie Prunty became dear friends, staying with us whenever they came from their mission station in the Darien Gap, the virgin jungle between Panama and Colombia. Their first Indian convert was Hombreo. His first visit to our home was memorable. "Did you have a good sleep?" we asked him the next morning.

"Oh, no," he responded with Glen interpreting. "I tried to sleep on that bed, but the mattress got so hot. I kept turning it over and over, but it didn't help. So I just slept on the floor."

Lori had a little quacking duck pull-toy. Hombreo was so fascinated with it that he ran round and round the ping-pong table pulling it behind him, laughing and laughing.

One morning at breakfast I took some bread from the freezer, put it on a plate, and set it on the table, because I knew in a few moments it would be thawed. But Hombreo happened to pick up a slice. "Oh, mui frio!" (very cold!) he shouted, tossing it into the air. He had never experienced anything frozen before.

But the kicker was when I went into the bathroom in the bunkroom to clean. I saw a rag hanging over the shower door. Thinking I should probably throw it away, I asked Tom about it. It was Hombreo's g-string. He would not think of going into the shower undressed! I carefully put it back.

On December ll, 1959, the Lord brought David Thomas Hash into our family. My mother came to help, a once-in-a-lifetime trip for her, a godsend to me. The week of rest in the hospital to recover from the C-section was what I needed. Someone loaned us an air-conditioner which provided cool dry air when David and I came home. With the holidays upon us, I went from the hospital to the grocery store to stock up on necessary food and supplies. Because I felt really good, I plunged into the work immediately.

One afternoon, when David was five months old, he had a slight fever. I wasn't alarmed because I thought he was cutting teeth. But the next day he was worse and by evening his temperature was over 105 degrees. I thought he might go into convulsions. We rushed him to the hospital. The doctor took him into the examining room and soon returned saying, "It looks like David has meningitis. We've had another case today. It could be a viral strain, therefore not crippling. But he is a very ill baby." Sensing our deep concern (my tears were a give-away), he held our hands and prayed for our baby. What a comfort that dear Christian doctor was to two hurting parents. David was in the hospital for a week and recovered completely. But since that was a new strain of meningitis, we took him every month for a year to the Middle America Research Unit for blood tests so they could do research.

Dinner at the Home

The group of guys increased. We were excited to see them growing in the Lord. The place just seemed to buzz with happy Christians. Many came to know the Lord, the regular guys were reaching out inviting others to the home, and most were responding to Tom's discipleship training. But Satan, the enemy of our souls, was preparing an attack that would send us reeling.

Chapter 13

INTO THE DEPTHS

Many of our trials during those Canal Zone days came as a result of trying to integrate our ministry with the local churches. Jesse Miller, our leader, did not have experience in this area to be able to give us counsel. By our next term we determined that working within the military chapel program was best for OCSC and this later became our official mission policy. But we simply had to learn the hard way, making serious mistakes in the process.

We enjoyed attending First Baptist Church. It was strongly evangelistic and many people came to know Christ. They had a full program for all ages, including the servicemen, so were not happy when the men became involved in the activities of the home.

Then Phil and Maria Steers invited us to the Curundu Protestant Church. Pastor Milton Leidig was a godly man, but to us his messages seemed somewhat scholarly. Therefore, we mistakenly thought he wasn't strongly evangelical. We were welcomed warmly, became involved in music, and were grateful when the home was included in the church's budget. We enjoyed going but were concerned for the guys who went with us. We felt most of the sermons were over their heads.

While we lived in Panama City, Tom was granted a pass to come and go on the military bases in the Zone. But when he went to have his pass renewed, the chaplain's first comment was, "Well, I see you sneaked into the Zone while my back was turned. You should have stayed in Panama where you belonged." He then sent a messenger to scrape the base sticker off our car. We knew he could recommend that the home be placed off limits to the servicemen. Thankfully he didn't do that. But the incident brought deep sadness to our hearts.

Then the men entered into deep spiritual battles. Tom wrote to the Millers. "One man is gone for good by his own choice for he preferred to continue his deceptive way rather than admit his wrong before God. Nearly half of our regular group has, in some degree, fallen backward in their walk with the Lord. One soldier left the home saying he will never be saved because of the type of people we are. We tried to lead him to the Lord, but he refused to give up an adulterous relationship with a girl while his wife is home. He has turned a number of the young Christians against us...."

I also wrote, "We don't know how we could ever carry on without the help of our prayer warriors at home. Never before have we felt so helpless and useless in our lives. Satan has been permitted to turn on the heat from within and without, leaving us somewhat desolate—except for God. We do know that he is on the throne and his hand is over all, giving a deep assurance and some peace. The two fellows, one an adulterer and the other calling God a fool, have drawn the majority of our regular fellows away. Instead of thirty men, we now have around ten. Many of our regular fellows are now speaking against the home. This breaks our hearts. We can see that their unwillingness to surrender all to him is the source of the trouble. We are becoming so terribly tired and exhausted. Sleep doesn't seem to help. It has been so hot."

During that difficult time, PanCanal requested that we paint the outside of the building which was covered with moss and mildew. The contractors wanted $400—out of the question for us, so we did it ourselves at a cost of $110. Since we could buy gray paint for $1.25 a gallon while white was $4.00 a gallon, we decided on gray with white trim. But what an endless and dangerous mess it was! We used scaffolding and "sky hooks" to reach under the eaves. Ninety-six big windows with six little panes in each had to be marked, screwed loose, laid on the grass, painted and put back up. In the midst of the project, most of the men deserted us, leaving it all to Tom.

Next door to the home, sharing the same driveway and parking area, was the building belonging to Alcoholics Anonymous. Knowing their strong desire for anonymity, we avoided having meetings the nights they had theirs, even closing the windows and enduring the heat to keep the sound from traveling across the driveway. But they were unhappy to have us there. And the neighbors up the hill complained when we sang and threatened to call the authorities.

I wrote, "Today is Saturday—a depressing day.... We rejoice though sorrowful, for in the midst of the desert the Lord sends his spring, his manna. One day, the Lord willing, we will write a letter void of heart-breaking accounts of what Satan is doing, but full of what the Lord is doing. Then we will have traveled through the valley having learned just a taste of what it is to trust. I'm sure we will consider it well worth it." I had no idea how prophetic that statement was to become.

Our first time of rest came when Tom was invited to be the speaker at a retreat for the missionaries of the Gospel Missionary Union. He spoke each morning for three days and we provided the special music in the evening. The rest of the time we were free. Restful nights, good fellowship, and ample time with the Lord restored our weary bodies and souls.

But as we drove into the front yard of the home, the sense of oppression returned. I wrote, "We have been in a terrific battle with the enemy for two months now and sometimes the going seems awfully tough. We have about twenty men in our regular group, but one by one Satan has struck them out until there is only one who has stood all the tests. Some others still come, but there isn't any growth in their lives. Two came forward in the Curundu church revival the other night. Tom was the song leader and dealt with them. The battle is a spiritual one and can only be won by prayer. We question ourselves every day to see that we are in a right relationship with the Lord, and as much as we know we are walking as he leads. The Lord knows and has an answer."

Seven months after David arrived, we discovered I was pregnant again. I was devastated. I could barely handle the work load now with two little ones. How could I go through another pregnancy and C-section so soon? I had been graciously endowed with considerable stamina and a strong work ethic, so when David joined the family, instead of letting some of the work go—like ironing our underclothes—I simply worked harder and longer. I was to pay dearly for such irresponsibility.

One time, after praying all week for grocery money, truly believing the Lord would supply, I made out my menus and grocery list as usual. On the way to the store, we stopped at the post office, hoping a check would be there. Nothing. So we bought food for three meals with the $2.50 we had. After the last meal on Saturday noon, we called the men together, explained the situation, and then reluctantly said, "We're sorry, but there will be no more meals this weekend." Before long three of them came to us.

"I know my money belongs to the Lord, but I held back for some reason," Don Tetamore said humbly, handing us money. Another fellow said that just before payday he usually had about $5 left but today had $18. He gave us $10. Another fellow gave $5. So the Lord provided, and the men were moved to a new responsibility. It was also a lesson in humility for us.

Several weeks later, I entered the kitchen one morning, opened the deep freeze, stared at the trays of ice cubes, and then at the one solitary soup bone. It clunked as I placed it on the counter. I knew there was nothing else to make into soup. "Honey," I called, "we'll have to go to the store." Pooling the coins in Tom's pocket and the ones in my purse, we had a grand total of thirty-seven cents. At the vegetable counter we carefully selected an onion, a carrot, some cabbage, a stalk of celery, and a potato.

Back at the home, I chose my biggest soup kettle. Clunk—in went the soup bone. Chop, chop, chop— the veggies. A few seasonings and then water to the brim. On went the cover and I put it on the stove to simmer.

Several hours later I called the family for lunch. Daddy held one-year-old David's little hand and I held three-year-old Lori's between us as we bowed to pray. "Dear Heavenly Father, " Tom began, "thank you for this food...." His voice broke. I looked up—his lashes glistened with tears. A lump was growing in my throat. "Father, you know we're not thankful for this at all," he blurted. "We came here as missionaries, trusting you to meet our needs. But we have nothing. Why have you failed us?" The sobs of self-pity I had been smothering broke loose.

Tom continued, "Before we left the States, you gave us that promise in Psalm 81:16 that you would 'feed us with the finest of the wheat, and with honey out of the rock....' What's wrong, Father? Why have you failed us?"

We cried and prayed, and the Lord seemed to be speaking to both of us. I haven't failed you. *I have given you just what you trusted me for— no more, no less. You didn't believe that I would provide your next meal, did you? I want you to learn to trust me for more than a meager provision.* Right there we confessed our lack of faith to him and promised from that day forward we would trust him for the abundance he wanted to give us.

After lunch we put the children down for their naps. There was contentment within our hearts that could only be explained as a supernatural work of God. We knew the filling of our cupboards was now the responsibility of God—we were depending, in a new way on him to take care of us.

Soon we heard cars coming up the driveway—lots of cars. "Anybody home?" voices called from below. I ran to the window and watched as several women from the Curundu Church unloaded their car trunks and brought in bag after bag of stuff, plopping them on our kitchen counter.

"We thought you might need some groceries!" they chirped and were gone.

We looked into the bags—all kinds of food—items I had *never* been able to purchase—a cake mix, nuts, chocolate chips, meat—the finest of the wheat, honey out of the rock. Our cupboards were full.

This incident was one of transition in our five-year journey of learning to trust God for our needs. No longer would we be content with lack, pretending to be grateful for meager provision. On this day in 1961, our faith took on a new dimension and was to develop from bud to fragrant flower as we availed ourselves of the abundant provision God holds out to every one of his children.

Our discontentment with the churches continued to grow. A new Conservative Baptist missionary couple arrived in Panama with the goal of starting an English-language church in Panama city. Eager to find an acceptable way out of our difficulties and knowing our beliefs were compatible with theirs, we began to lay the plans for joining hands in their endeavor. Tom taught a Monday night Bible study for couples that met at the home of Phil and Maria Steers. Several of the couples were folks from the home whom we had led to the Lord; others were from the church. We discussed the new church idea with them, and some were definitely interested in working with us.

Couples' Bible study group.
Phil and Maria Steers are second and third from the left, we are in the middle.

The Hashes are trying to split the Curundu church! the rumors screamed as they spread like wild fire through the close-knit community. We were stunned! We felt perfectly justified in encouraging "our" people toward a church where we felt their needs would be met. The people in the church, on the other hand, were strongly opposed and deeply hurt.

Tom went to the pastor, approaching the matter as kindly as he could, but soon perceived that he was deeply hurt and thought our actions were a cruel betrayal. "I think you should just leave the church quietly," he said sadly.

Then our dear friend, Phil Steers, informed us by letter that he felt he could no longer serve on our board or be associated with our mission in any way. In our sincere desire to do what was best for the ministry we had wounded our dearest friends. We thought our hearts would break! The next days we entered the darkest valley of despair we had ever experienced.

One morning Tom and I drove up to an overlook of the canal where we had often gone to have our quiet times. We wept before the Lord, confessed every sin the Holy Spirit brought to our minds and then waited on the Lord as we individually read his Word. Soon that still, small voice whispered in my heart, *You have wronged Pastor Leidig, my faithful servant, by judging him. The damage caused is very deep and has hurt many of my people. You must make this right.* I wept quietly as the truth sunk in.

To Tom he cautioned, *I want to remove a word from your vocabulary—MY—my men, my fellows, my servicemen's home, my ministry. They are not yours, but mine. You must give them to me. I will take care of them even as I gave my disciples to my Father. By trying to protect them, you have caused hurt to my body, the church. You must make this right.*

The magnitude of our sin came like a flood. We admitted to the Lord what we had done, asking his forgiveness. *How can we make this right, Lord?* We soon had an answer: *Go to the pastor and confess, asking his forgiveness.*

Pastor Leidig was loving and kind and gently forgave us for the dissension we had caused. "However, " he said, "I am reminded of the story about the feather pillow that was torn and the feathers went flying into the air. What you have done is like those feathers. Can you pick them all up and return them to the pillow ticking? Of course not. The discord you have sown has scattered through the entire congregation. You need to go to them also." We agreed.

The congregational meeting was called. Without trying to justify our motives, we confessed how we had maligned Pastor Leidig, causing dissension in the whole church. We pleaded for their forgiveness. Tears flowed freely on many faces, especially ours. It was the most humbling experience of our lives.

We returned to fellowship at the church, but without our critical attitude. Years after we left Panama, Pastor Leidig had to temporarily step aside from the ministry due to illness and stress—we have always felt partly responsible and wish so much we could relive those days in a more Christ-like way. In his years at Curundu Church, Pastor Leidig was instrumental in seeing more than ten of the young people enter Christian ministry and he built the missionary budget to more than $10,000 a year, much of it going to the Christian Servicemen's Home. A faithful servant, he is now with the Lord.

Phil and Maria Steers also lovingly forgave us. Many years later when their son, David, was in the military stationed in Panama, he found good fellowship at the Christian Servicemen's Home under Mike and Rachel Paulson's leadership, as well as Crossroads Bible Church, the new name and location of the Curundu Protestant Church. And for as many years as OCSC/Cadence has continued the ministry in Panama, there has been a strong relationship between the church and the home. Thankfully, the pain we caused was forgiven and did not cause long-lasting dishonor to our Lord.

After that painful experience, Tom began a prayer meeting at the home at 6 a.m. on Sunday mornings. A handful of men knelt together asking God to work in their hearts and lives.

God answered. Don Tetamore became our keenest fellow and most active in his witness. Don brought out Roy Rogers, a young black soldier, who was saved at the home. Don Cerney was growing spiritually. Wally and Shirley Brian continued faithfully by our side. We learned that Gene, the first one to surrender fully to the Lord, was in a Christian college preparing for future ministry.

Four months into my pregnancy I was admitted to the hospital for five days with back pains and pleurisy—but the main reason was exhaustion. The doctor warned that I must slow down. I tried, but simply didn't know how. It was almost Christmas—a very busy time. Every Monday morning there were linens from ten bunks to be washed and hung out to dry; pillow cases and all the clothing we wore on the outside had to be starched, sprinkled, and ironed. Each day there were extras for meals. The mahogany floors and furniture needed dusting every day, because all the windows were open at all times. And there was never a time when two small children didn't need attention. I was wearing out.

My physical and emotional health declined rapidly during the last two months of my pregnancy until I was dangerously close to collapse. Since depression was new to me, I didn't know how to handle it. At each visit to the doctor, he warned me to get more rest. We stopped serving meals on weekends. The faithful men fully understood. David was fourteen months old and had been in the hospital four times for high fever from unknown causes. He was such a tiny little lamb, with the sweetest disposition a mother could ever want. Lori was a bright, darling three-year-old, but very demanding. We had to keep her in line constantly or she'd run the whole show, including the guys.

The baby was to be delivered by elective C-section on April 10. Three weeks before, the doctor shook his finger at us and warned, "I want you out of that servicemen's home today! Not tomorrow, *today*!" We knew he was right, but where could we go? Then our friends, Dr. Bob and Linda Hall, a fine couple looking forward to serving as missionaries, offered to switch homes with us. It took a week to make all the arrangements. Leaving the maid behind, we moved to their little apartment. The guys loved the Halls and things went well at the home without us, even though Bob worked long hours as an intern at the hospital.

Tom and I both "knew" this baby was a girl (no ultrasound back then) and had agreed on the name of Susan Kay. It wasn't that we particularly wanted another girl—we just felt it would be one. On April 10th I was wheeled into the operating room. As before, Tom stayed in the waiting room, since husbands were considered unnecessary items during childbirth in those days.

The room was full of doctors and nurses—all friends of ours. The atmosphere was friendly, but professional. The spinal anesthetic was given and surgery began. I was wide awake. "It's a boy!" the doctor announced as loud cries filled the room.

"A boy?" I said in disbelief.

"Shall I put him back?" the surgeon asked, laughing.

"I'll take him!" the anesthesiologist announced eagerly. Good natured banter continued all during the suturing process.

I didn't see Tom for twenty-four hours after the delivery because I was in the recovery room. When he came to see me the next morning, he quipped, "I hope you like the name Daniel Bruce. I already sent out the announcements."

I had been told by the doctor to plan to stay in the hospital for ten days—mostly for rest. It was a very refreshing time for me, but tough on Tom. David came down with his usual 105 degree fever so was admitted to the hospital again. Gorgas Hospital was a sprawling facility of several buildings, connected by covered walkways. So while caring for three-and-a-half year old Lori, Tom visited sixteen-month-old David in pediatrics and then ran to the building where the maternity ward was located to visit Danny and me. The same pediatrician cared for both boys. One day she asked, "Can we keep David for a few extra days? We really would like to find out what is causing his frequent fevers." They kept him and eventually determined his body made insufficient amounts of gamma globulin, so his immune system was weak. Shots of the missing ingredient made an amazing difference for the next four years of his life. He still got sick, but not as terribly ill as before.

By the time I went home to the little apartment, I was feeling quite well. I had been warned not to lift anything heavier than the new baby for six weeks, but with a sixteen-month-old still in diapers it was a difficult order. After awhile I grew lax. One day Dr. Hall came to visit and saw me lift David. "Dotty, you simply must not do that! It's very dangerous for you." I tried to be obedient after that.

It was good to return to the home and to the guys. Leaders like Frank Smucker, Tom Garrett and Dave Fleth had grown during our absence; others hadn't. A few had stopped coming, but there were also some new guys. I plunged into the work again. In a few weeks Danny broke out in a full body rash. "I don't know what color hair this one will have," the doctor said matter-of-factly, "but he sure has a red head's complexion!" From then on we had to keep Danny upstairs in the only air-conditioned room. There were no baby monitors back then, so I made the trip up and down stairs umpteen times a day. We were amazed how much one more baby affected our lives.

Before long the depression returned with a vengeance. One night, after the children were in bed, I sat at the kitchen table sobbing uncontrollably. I simply couldn't stop. Tom put the guys in charge and we went for a drive all over the Zone. For hours I cried. Then standing on the Miraflores bridge holding me tightly in his arms, Tom prayed for deliverance. The episode (and others to come) convinced Tom that something had to be done or his wife's health and mind might be ruined forever. So furlough plans were set into motion.

A few months earlier, Jesse Miller and Gordon Gustafson had come to the Zone to speak at the Bible conference for the men. Gordon had served as a missionary in the jungles of the Philippines, but health problems prevented his return. While Gordon was in Panama, the Lord gave him a deep desire for the work among servicemen. Therefore when Jesse asked the Gustafsons to replace us, they were eager and willing. Of course, they needed to raise support.

Trips to the interior, bad roads, heavy loads, and the tropical climate took their toll on the Ford station wagon. By 1960 it needed a complete overhaul, the ceiling head liner had fallen down, and the back fenders and tailgate were badly rusted. Tom pushed, walked, and did without the car so much that he began to wonder if he should sink any more money into repairs or just try to hold out until we could get something better. Then a large family offered to purchase it. We began a car fund with the money from the sale. We were loaned cars by people who would be away. After much looking, we decided a new Chevrolet Greenbrier van would best meet our needs. The following year we ordered it from the U.S., costing $2381.

In August of 1961 the new red and white mini-bus arrived. The regular guys had made a big financial push, many of them giving sacrificially to help pay for the shipping. What a joyous day as we all went to the dock to pick it up. Nine people could fit in it comfortably. Before the trip home, sitting in the odor of new vinyl, we bowed to thank the Lord for his provision. Within four weeks we would leave Panama and not see that vehicle again.

The '54 Ford loaded with men on one of the grueling trips to the interior of Panama.

One morning before breakfast Lori was being particularly difficult. After being corrected several times, we had to spank. After the sobbing stopped, she took both of our hands and pulled us to the bedside. "I want to ask Jesus to take my sin away. Please pray with me," she said matter-of-factly. We knelt together and she invited Jesus into her life. Four days later she turned four. We noticed a definite change in her little disposition.

When the men rotated back to the U.S., it was our custom to go to the flight-line to see them off. With mixed joy and sadness, the group stood in a circle, held hands, and bowed in prayer, committing the departing one to the Lord's keeping. They boarded the plane and flew up to the States. In preparing for our furlough, we considered returning to the U.S. by ship. When Lori heard us discussing that possibility, she broke out in tears. "No! No! We can't get *up* to the States in a ship. You have to go in an airplane!" She was greatly relieved when we decided to fly.

The Gustafson family of six arrived on September 1, 1961. God had marvelously provided their financial support in just a couple of months. It was Labor Day weekend, so a trip to Santiago had been planned. Gordon and his sons made a quick start into the ministry by packing and boarding the new van for the trip. Three of four unsaved guys received Christ that weekend, and two of the Christian fellows made things right with the Lord.

I helped June and the girls settle into life in the Zone. Our understanding was that the Gustafsons would relieve us for just one year—then we would return to Panama. So we left the home intact with all of our things (including all of our wedding gifts and my mother's antique dishes) as well as those acquired for the ministry. The next twelve days remain a blur in my mind, as we bid farewell to all of our wonderful friends and especially the servicemen whom we had grown to love so much. By the time we planned to return, most of them would be gone. We felt we were leaving the ministry in very good hands and were trusting the Lord to bless the Gustafsons in their new venture.

In retrospect, we know that during our first term as missionaries, God took us through the refining process of boiling away the dross, skimming off the waste, seeking the fine gold. He took us to Panama not necessarily for what we could do for him, but for what he would do in us. He was gently preparing us for many years of fruitful ministry to come.

The family in fall 1961
just before departure from Panama

We are troubled on every side, yet not distressed, we are perplexed, but not in despair; persecuted, but not forsaken; cast down, but not destroyed.
(II Corinthians 4:8-9)

In this ye greatly rejoice, though now for a season, if need be, ye are in heaviness through manifold temptations, that the trial of your faith, being much more precious than of gold that perisheth, though it be tried with fire, might be found unto praise and honor and glory at the appearing of Jesus Christ.

(I Peter 1:6-7)

PART V

FURLOUGH

Chapter 14

NOURISHED BY GOD'S PEOPLE

On September 13, 1961, we boarded the plane for Miami. It was quite a trip with the three small children—Lori just 4, David 21 months, and Danny 5 months. Just before landing for a stopover in Kingston, Jamaica, David (who was potty-trained and in training pants) had diarrhea. It went all over him and Tom's light blue suit. When the plane landed, Tom went to the plane washroom to clean up. I grabbed David and the diaper bag and headed for the terminal bathroom. I quickly got his clothes off and stood him in the sink when the call came over the intercom: *Last call for flight....* "Oh, no!" I was panic-stricken.

"They won't leave you, but you better hurry," a flight attendant assured me. I got David dressed and rushed from the terminal onto the tarmac toward the plane. Horrified, I realized the engines were running and the ramp had been taken up. "Wait!" I shouted over the roar of the engines. I ran even faster. Then the door opened and a stewardess emerged and ran toward me, grabbed David, and screamed, "Come on!" In the meantime, the attendants had been going up and down the aisle counting people.

"My wife and son are in the terminal," Tom told them when he realized what was happening. That's when they opened the door and sent the girl after me. The rest of the flight was uneventful.

We had eighteen boxes of stuff to clear through customs when we landed in Miami. Tom was carrying David, I was holding Danny, and Lori was squirreling around, tired from the flight. When the boxes came up on the ramp for the customs officer to inspect, he said to Tom, "Open 'em up!"

"All of them?" Tom asked incredulously.

"All of 'em!" Tom put David on the floor, who promptly ran out through the automatic doors and onto the taxi driveway, Tom and I after him. We brought him back in Tom's arms and returned to the customs agent. "Never mind," he sighed. We were out the door in minutes. We paid $7.50 in overweight charges for all of those boxes.

We had made an agreement with Gustafsons to trade vehicles for the year we planned to be on furlough. We picked up their one-year-old white Rambler and began our journey to Louisville and Milwaukee. Stopping in restaurants was interesting. We asked for two highchairs and a booster chair. Other patrons would look at us, shake their heads and whisper. I am sure they were wondering if we knew there was a way to stop having babies so fast.

At each home where we stopped, Lori asked, "Is this where my grandma lives who has my new bed?" So when we entered the driveway of my parents' farm house near Milwaukee, we were all ready to stop. My parents had lovingly remodeled the upstairs for us. Our bedroom had a comfortable sitting area and the children's room had two cribs and a single bed. There was a small half bathroom. Everything was fresh and new. It was an incredibly safe, secure haven for a very tired missionary couple. My nerves were threadbare. Every time we were in a situation that caused stress, an escape mechanism kicked in and I became very, very sleepy.

When we arrived in Milwaukee, the weather was forty degrees and rainy—but it felt like zero to our tropically acclimated bodies. The next day we took the children to church wrapped in blankets. David had been given a pair of long pants and Lori a sweater on the trip. After the evening service, everyone went to the basement for refreshments. There, to our surprise, were tables and tables with lovely used or new clothes spread out on them; snowsuits and warm pajamas and sweaters for the children; and a lovely, almost new coat for me—everything we needed. Then they called Tom to the front of the room and presented him a check to purchase a new suit and overcoat. About $600 was given to us by people in that congregation in the next several weeks. Even today tears come as I think of those dear saints at Grace Methodist Church (now Redeemer Evangelical Free Church) who lovingly cared for a rather fragile family of missionaries. May their tribe increase!

Leonard Lovdahl, one of the men in the church, called us one day. "I would like for you to use my car for your long distance deputation trips. It is heavier and more comfortable for your family than the Rambler. And I also want to pay for your gas." His car was a new Oldsmobile convertible. We did have a little difficulty explaining such a luxurious car to people we visited on deputation.

One day Tom drove to Great Lakes Naval Training Center for a meeting with Chaplain Dave Meschke and some other chaplains. Tark, who was on furlough too, met them there. As Tom got out of the Olds, he pressed a button and the trunk flew open (innovative in those days). Not to be outdone, Tark quipped, "Well, I'll tell you one thing! My car sure uses more gas than yours!"

It was at Grace Church at age four that Lori sang her first solo and we began singing three-part trios with her.

We went to a missionary doctor for physical exams. After thorough checkups, I was declared fit to return to the field, but Tom needed a surgical procedure for back problems. I told the doctor how close to collapse I was, but he indicated I must deal with that spiritually (a common philosophy in that day). I was devastated. But through my parents' and Tom's loving care over the next eight months, my emotional health returned. Spending hours at my sewing machine making new wardrobes for all of the children and myself while Mother helped with the children was very therapeutic.

In that era, when missionaries came home it was called a "furlough." All who have experienced that phenomenon will testify that it was anything but a vacation. Most of the next eight months were spent visiting friends, supporting churches, donors, and of course, the many fellows who had been in our servicemen's home.

Duane and Kay Arnold, who had been so dear to us in Panama, now lived in Michigan. They offered to keep Lori and David during one of our trips to the East Coast. On that trip we stayed in a home where the children had chicken pox but didn't think much about it. On our way home, we stopped in a motel for the night and Tom became very sick. I drove to Michigan the next day while he lay in the back seat feeling miserable. At the Arnolds' home, we saw a doctor who said he had strep throat and put him to bed for five days. Then I drove us all back to Milwaukee. The next day he broke out with chicken pox. He was a mighty sick man for two weeks. Two weeks later, all three children came down with it the same day.

Just before we were to leave on our next trip, Danny became ill. When he didn't respond to the doctor's medication, he was admitted to Children's Hospital. Should we cancel our trip? But after a few days on IV fluids and medication, he was much better. Since he was to be released the following day and Grandma Keeler would care for him during our trip, we set out for the East Coast. He did just fine.

David was sitting on the potty one day when he passed a big worm. Horrified, I called the doctor. Being from Czechoslovakia and still having a strong accent, she replied, "Bring me de boy and bring me de verm." After examining him and the specimen, she asked,

"Vere haf you been wid dis child? Ve don't have verms like dis here!" We explained, and subsequent treatment eliminated the problem. I remembered the times in Panama when I had stopped David from putting his hands in the water on the driveway and then in his mouth, but evidently I had missed a few.

God was blessing the ministry of OCSC. New missionaries were being appointed to serve. As a result the Millers' workload in the home office was now overwhelming. During those years the entire cost of running the mission was carried by the Millers. Consequently, Jesse was on the road promoting the mission a good deal of the time. He was in great demand as a speaker and God used his biblically-applied stories of the war to challenge many hearts.

The Gustafsons were extremely happy running the servicemen's home in Panama. Schooling for their four children was going well and men were responding to their ministry. They wanted to stay. As a result, the Board of Directors asked us to assist the Millers for at least a year before returning overseas, taking over the promotion and publication department. We took this before the Lord in prayer and he gave peace of heart.

That summer we spent several weeks in another visitation program in our Berean church in North Platte. The plan was for us to visit in the homes of people "on the fringe" who were not giving to the church with the hope that they would catch the vision for missions and become involved. If it resulted in personal support for us, that was fine. We were to have lunch and dinner in a different home each day, six days a week. We loved doing this. It certainly was Tom's cup of tea, but with three pre-school children it was a challenge. Of course, we wanted them to be perfect: to eat with good manners, not touch things, sit still and be quiet. Quite an order as we look back! Our posture on this was to have negative consequences for Lori, but nevertheless it went quite well and the Lord blessed our ministry in the lives of people.

The church had a one-bedroom missionary apartment upstairs. It proved to be a cozy haven for the times we could spend there. Thinking Lori would like a little privacy, we fixed up a large closet as her bedroom. Many years later we learned she was terrified in it and to this day is fearful when alone at night.

The Hash family in 1962

On Sundays Danny attended the church nursery. During one service he pitched his glass bottle onto the floor where it smashed into a thousand pieces. The attendants politely asked us to bring plastic bottles after that. That incident should have been a harbinger of things to come with Danny.

In the middle of the visitation project, we attended OCSC's annual Bible conference in Denver. On the way Lori started vomiting. It didn't stop. Arriving in Denver in the middle of the night, we called a pediatrician. "Give her tea and call me in the morning," he said. When he examined her the next day, he exclaimed, "What have you been doing with this child? She has an ulcer!" The subsequent baby-food diet cleared it up, but we knew she was paying dearly for our lifestyle. Returning to the church, we asked to visit in only one home a day.

Chapter 15

NEW ASSIGNMENT

Planning to return in a year, we had left all of our household goods in Panama. Now we needed to set up housekeeping in Denver. God met this need through the dear folks at the Berean church who gave us a household shower. I felt like a new bride! Now all we needed was a home, furniture, and appliances.

OCSC was growing. Dick and Margaret Patty's ministry at Subic Bay in the Philippines was bearing precious fruit. Sid Hendry went out to help them. Tark and Alma Tarkington moved the original Manila home to Cavite City to be nearer the troops. Harley and Miriam Dow opened the Christian Servicemen's Home in Anchorage, Alaska. A growing group of Christian airmen pleaded for someone to come to start a ministry at Clark Air Force Base, also in the Philippines. Sid responded by going over weekly from Subic to teach a Bible class, and in 1960 the Lord led Chuck and Jane Hall to be the first directors of that ministry.

From 1957 until 1961 the home office of OCSC had been located in the basement of Jesse and Nettie Miller's home. As the mission grew, volunteers and some paid staff were added as well as new equipment. The space was filled to overflowing. All in the mission prayed for God to provide a larger facility. God answered that prayer when Lawndale Baptist Church donated their building to OCSC. With some renovation it was usable in a very short time. Since the basement already had a kitchen, that area was made into a small apartment for visiting missionaries. We were the first to occupy the freshly painted rooms. When it was needed to house others, we looked for a more permanent home.

With our meager income, the only affordable place we could find was a three-bedroom apartment of the Denver Housing Authority. With the few pieces of furniture we purchased and those loaned or given to us, our apartment was comfortably furnished. But we certainly were unique to the community. Not only was Tom the only resident father in our row of apartments, but he also drew much attention as he left for work each morning in his shirt and tie, carrying a briefcase. By painting the concrete floors, purchasing an area rug for the living room and linoleum for the kitchen, and covering the open closets with curtains, the place looked quite homey. Our little apartment soon became the "showcase" for others to see how they could fix up those sparse quarters. Opportunities to reach out to others were on our doorstep each day. God used us in the lives of several families.

A friend paid for Lori to attend kindergarten at a Christian school, and two dear Christian ladies offered to care for the boys so I could work in the office two days a week. I was also asked to teach music at Western Bible Institute one day a week, including directing the choir. One of the classes I taught was "song leading," a required course for all future pastors. What fun to see those grown men (several veterans out of our OCSC ministries in Asia) waving their arms trying to figure out what to do. Years later we spoke in several of their churches where I played the piano while they led the singing.

Having sung in the Moody Chorale years earlier, I convinced the school leaders that a choir tour would be profitable for the students as well as for the school. They weren't very confident but agreed to let us go. The tour was set for the Easter holiday week; the president would travel with us to do the speaking; a student would drive the school's Greyhound-type bus. However, at the last moment the president decided he couldn't go, so I (at age thirty-one) was the only faculty member on the tour. We gave concerts each night and all day Easter Sunday throughout Nebraska, Kansas, and Colorado. Hearts were blessed, we all grew in learning to trust the Lord (especially when the bus broke down), and we brought back generous offerings to help the school.

During that furlough we began meeting with a group of friends for fellowship. The outgrowth was the founding of the Berean Fundamental Church of Denver (now Lakewood Bible Church) with Tom serving as temporary pastor. The Lord blessed that little group and they were soon able to call a full-time pastor.

Even though we stayed in the States for two years, our hearts were never far from the servicemen we loved. Chuck and Jane Hall had started the Christian Servicemen's Home at Clark Air Force Base three years earlier but needed to leave the Philippines due to her allergic reaction to the burning of the sugar cane. When we were asked to take their place, Tom was excited. What joy for him to return to the place of his spiritual birth. I wasn't sure.

Although I had completely recovered from my previous near-breakdown, I was fearful it might recur when I got back into a busy ministry. Dr. Ray Buker, member of our Board of Directors and Director of Personnel for the Conservative Baptist Foreign Mission Society (CBFMS), allayed my fears. "We have found that those who have recovered from a breakdown sufficiently to return to the field do not allow it to happen again. They know the warning signs and are more careful." I hoped I would be wise enough to follow the advice.

In August we broke up housekeeping and moved back to my parents' home in Milwaukee where Lori began first grade. Before we left, the student body at Western Bible Institute (now Colorado Christian University) presented us with a gift of $400 toward our passage. Our date of departure would depend upon securing visas.

For several years we had prayed for the Lord to provide a vehicle for the ministry at Clark, not dreaming we would be the ones to answer that prayer. We were able to sell the Rambler and purchase a used 1963 Corvair Greenbriar van. We drove the van from Milwaukee to Oakland, California, arriving at the Home of Peace, a guest house for missionaries, on November 21, 1963.

The next day Tom worked in the shop crating our belongings and loading them on a trailer to take to the ship. At about 11 a.m. we received the shocking news that President John F. Kennedy had been shot. All activity came to a standstill as we awaited further word. Then came the announcement: our president was dead! When Tom arrived at the dock, he was informed that all the dock workers had gone home, the ship's departure delayed indefinitely. Returning to Home of Peace, he found everyone in a state of shock. It was Tom's 34th birthday and a party had been planned during the dinner hour in the dining room. They had made his favorite dessert, lemon meringue pie. But no one wanted to celebrate anything—we just ate the pie and went to our rooms.

We didn't have enough money to stay at Home of Peace beyond that day. We recalled that a man who had come through our servicemen's home in Panama now lived in Oakland, so we called him on the phone, explaining our situation. He was a single school teacher with a nice home. "I'd love to have you come and stay here," he responded. So all five of us moved into his typical bachelor home for the next week. He had a TV, which we, along with all of America, watched day and night as the assassination was replayed, as well as the subsequent shooting of Harvey Oswald by Jack Ruby. Our time there was reciprocal, for we did a thorough cleaning of his home and I cooked meals. It was a special provision from the Lord.

We left our Greenbriar van with friends in San Francisco until we could make arrangements for its shipment to the Philippines. Our crates were at last stowed on the ship and we settled into our cabin for what was to be an eventful voyage.

Chapter 16

DEAD IN THE WATER

The U.S.S. *President Jefferson* slipped away from the dock in the early morning hours of December 1, 1963. Even with a wool blanket and Tom's arms wrapped tightly around me, the biting, cold wind chilled us to the bone as we stood on the deck watching the Golden Gate Bridge disappear into the distance. We wondered what adventures lay ahead.

Within a few hours, our captain informed us that one boiler was not functioning properly so our speed had been reduced. We plodded slowly onward for 760 miles. Just after retiring one evening, the captain bolted into our rooms. "Secure those children! We're adrift at sea!" The engines had been turned off and dismantled while we waited for parts to be sent from Los Angeles. I soon learned that a ship "dead in the water" is at the mercy of the ocean—lying in the trough of the swell, rocking constantly as the waves rise and fall. For the rest of the night, with each roll a chair or suitcase slid across the room. We could hear dishes breaking in the galley. Eventually the movable items were secured, and all became strangely quiet.

The next morning we gingerly made our way to the galley. I, along with four-year old David, had been assigned to sit at the captain's table for the voyage, while Tom, Lori and Danny were at the other end of the dining room. I put David into the high chair beside me, but with the first roll of the ship, his chair slid across the room. Panicking, a steward jumped to catch him, and then promptly tied his chair to mine with a dish towel. We bounced around with the waves for two days.

Then the captain received a radio message that a plane had been chartered and the engine part would be dropped into the sea for our lifeboat to pick up—it would appear in seventeen minutes! It was dusk—about 5 p.m. The ship pumped thick, black smoke from the stack to identify our location. No plane. As darkness came, every light on the ship was turned on—even our stateroom lights shone brightly from the portholes. Our hearts jumped as we saw the flashing red lights of a plane coming into view. But it just flew past—a regular flight from Los Angeles to Hawaii.

We scanned the skies again. Each twinkling star now looked like a plane. Then—definitely flashing red lights. As it came closer, the plane flashed a white light in our direction. The anticipation was even more intense. All was in readiness: the men in their life-jackets ready to be lowered into the lifeboat. But again the plane flew off into the stars. The vigil continued for hours with everyone hoping it would return. Then hope was gone. Via radio we learned that a pilot of a passing commercial plane had talked with the pilot of the one coming to us. He circled for fifteen minutes but couldn't locate us, and then returned to the coast. His location indicated he was within sight of our ship.

Our captain carefully contemplated our situation. Soon he learned there was a stationary Coast Guard weather ship in the area 225 miles away, but they could not go beyond their perimeter. Should the engineers try to patch up the disabled motor with the old part and have the ship "limp" to the weather station? If so, what then? Yes, he would do that and hope for the best.

After several hours of clang, clang, clang below, the ship started slowly forward. I awoke at 2 a.m. to feel the vibrations of the engines and the splashing of the water. After fifty-two hours of stillness, it was a welcome sound.

The ship hobbled along for twenty hours; then flashes appeared on the horizon. The captain hurried from the bridge to the radio shack. Beep, beep, beep—over the radio came the wonderful news that we were approaching the Coast Guard ship and they had our long-awaited bearing on board! This being an emergency, a Coast Guard plane had delivered the part.

The engines quieted, we stopped moving. The small Coast Guard cutter made a quick circle around us, let down a little motor boat with six men aboard, and before we knew what was happening, the part was lifted by rope aboard our ship. In moments the cutter was gone—the only words spoken had been by the coast guardsmen (young servicemen stationed in the midst of the sea) "Hey, you guys, what in the world is in this thing—sure must be important stuff!"

"Just motor parts," was the reply, and the little boat was off into the choppy, dark waters.

Sleep didn't come easily during the next seven hours as the crew made the long-awaited repairs. But as the sun arose the next morning, the ship began to move, slowly at first, then a little faster. We were once more on our way. Total time lost—five days! Total cost—$20,000! We were due in Guam on December 13th and in Manila on December 21st. Now we would probably have Christmas at sea.

Due to the five-day delay, the ship's fresh water supply was depleted so we were told to take "navy showers." The ship was old and blew black smoke all over the deck. Now they could no longer hose it down with fresh water. With the slightest touch, a dark smudge appeared on our clothes. With three young children, keeping clean was a challenge. We changed their clothes many times a day. The only washing machine was in the crew's quarters below, and I was not allowed there, so Tom took a load of clothes down every day. The only time I got seasick on the entire voyage was when I did the ironing. When we entered tropical waters, we let the boys run in short pants and no shirts to save laundry.

Other than the five Hashes, there was just one passenger aboard, a retired English and speech professor from a well-known university in New York City. She was a very cultured New Englander on her way to visit her son who worked for the U.S. Embassy in Cambodia. We came to enjoy her very much. One night we were sitting with the children in our deck chairs, singing and reading stories before putting them to sleep. She heard the singing and asked if she might join us. She seemed enthralled with it all, especially the stories the children clamored for—David and Goliath, Paul and Silas in prison, Daniel in the lion's den. After telling about Daniel, she laughed quietly.

The next day, while talking on the deck, she mentioned how cleverly I had adapted the story of Daniel to make my own application. (I had told it exactly as it appears in the Bible.) She told me how the story is actually written: Daniel had met a lion in his youth and had relieved it of a painful brier in its paw. It just so happened that when he was thrown in the lion's den, it was the same lion and upon recognizing Daniel, he didn't harm him. She was shocked when I told her my story was the true Bible account. I told her where to find it to read it for herself. I couldn't believe that a professor of English literature didn't know the accurate account of such a familiar Bible story.

After putting the children to bed, Tom and I often walked on the deck, watching the stars. They seemed so close and friendly—personally ours for those nights at sea! It seemed strange to be heading to the Philippines. The only reason we would ever leave our home, our loved ones, and the security of our homeland was because our Heavenly Father had said "Go!" In obedience to his call, we had loaded up all our earthly possessions, taken our children from home and school, and headed for parts unknown. But for him it was worth it all. He left his home for us—left all that was dear, and came to those who hated him, eventually killed him! Was it worth it? A thousand times, yes. But we wondered again what lay ahead.

"Tomorrow is my birthday! David chirped excitedly to the captain one morning.

"Oh, no," the captain exclaimed. "December 11th?"

"Uh, huh," David replied nodding his blonde head, "and I will be four years old." He held up four little fingers.

"Oh, my, that's really too bad," the captain replied, looking sad. "You see, we skip tomorrow. That's when we cross the international date line."

Then seeing David's countenance fall, he quipped, "Oh, well, we won't skip tomorrow—let's skip the next day. Okay?" David's face brightened as he shook his head.

The next day at dinner, the cook brought out the biggest (and ugliest) birthday cake I had ever seen. It was four thick layers high, about fifteen inches in diameter, covered with an awful blue frosting. On top were four candles. David thought it was wonderful, grinning shyly as all in the dining room sang "Happy Birthday, dear David."

We turned our clocks back a half-hour each night to accommodate the passing time zones, relishing the extra sleep. Days were wearing, for we had to watch the children every moment. The captain was apprehensive about their safety since a ship with less than twelve passengers has no doctor on board. He didn't know much about children—he was a seaman who seldom saw his own. We played parlor games with him in the evening, graciously declining his offer of cocktails. He knew our stand as Christians and accepted it, even though he didn't agree.

Lori had school each day. All of the children made friends over the railing with the crew on the deck below. Lori drew pictures with her crayons, then "sailed" them down to the waiting men. They loved it. They, in turn, made kites and flew them as the children watched excitedly. When Tom went down to do the laundry he saw Lori's pictures displayed on the bulletin board.

We landed at the island of Guam on December 19. Within minutes after docking, the cargo doors were opened, emitting the pine fragrance of hundreds of Christmas trees destined for the military families stationed on the island. Is it any wonder the captain was a nervous wreck when the ship was delayed? After Christmas his cargo would be worthless! By 7 a.m. the following morning, all had been sold to eagerly waiting families.

We were met at the ship by Norm Wetther, Conservative Baptist missionary who worked with servicemen there. We stayed with Don and Geneva Bengtson, from the original Manila home, who were stationed there with naval intelligence, enjoying the fellowship together.

But the biggest thrill was the "coincidence" that the plane Erv Meyer (fellow OCSC missionary) was on en route to Okinawa landed there the same night we arrived. A typhoon had recently devastated Guam. The terminal was a make-shift table near the flight line with one bare light bulb dangling overhead. The shock on Erv's face when he saw us approaching him on the tarmac soon turned to great joy. His first thought was, *Either they are in the wrong place, or I am!*

The two days went by quickly, and soon we were back at sea. We had a lovely little Christmas tree in our lounge. While on Guam we had purchased a gift for each of the children and the Bengtsons had also gotten some for them. On Christmas Eve, the captain gave a delightful Christmas party for the children. When all were assembled in the dining room, the radio man rushed in with an "urgent" message for the captain. He read the marine radiogram out loud:

> *To USS President Jefferson 6:30 pm, December 24, 1963. Rush NR 1 from the North Pole.*
> *Dear Ancient Mariner,*
> *Unavoidably delayed. Unable to locate the three Hash children, Lori, David and Daniel. Are they with you? If so, shower them with presents and wish them the merriest Christmas ever. Santa Claus.*

In came the first mate, a bulging duffle bag over his shoulder, shouting "Ho, Ho, Ho!" He presented each child with gift after gift, mostly candy from the ship's store, but a few other gifts purchased by the lower deck crew members on Guam. Refreshments were served—Christmas goodies lovingly prepared by the cook. A delightful surprise!

After the party we went to bed. Then the officers and the lady passenger had their party with champagne and other libations, lasting on through the night. We appreciated their respect for our standards, excusing us from the festivities. When we landed in Manila harbor the next morning, we wondered how the crew successfully maneuvered that ship through the Philippine Straits in their condition. But we were indeed thankful for a safe trip.

Part VI

Clark Air Force Base

Chapter 17

ADAPTING

The ship pulled up to the dock in Manila Bay at 7 a.m. on Christmas morning 1963. What joy to see Chuck and Jane Hall, Ben Cady and a few of the fellows there to meet us. By 10:30 we had cleared customs with our cabin baggage and were on our way to Clark Air Force Base, three hours away. Christmas dinner was waiting at the Christian Servicemen's Home when we arrived and was followed by a reception for us in the evening. With couples and single men, the group numbered around sixty, many of whom were new believers.

The ministry at Clark was actually begun by an Air Force sergeant and his wife who had been challenged during the Bible conference at the Manila home in 1956. As a result, Cecil Allen, his wife, and six children opened their home at Clark to the servicemen for fellowship and Bible study. The normal tour of duty for servicemen overseas was two years, but the Allens extended for an additional two years in order to serve the Lord in this way.

After Sid Hendry arrived to assist Dick Patty at Subic in March 1959, he rode a motor scooter the fifty miles to

Clark on Mondays to teach a Bible class and to challenge the growing group. He wrote to the home office, "The group of Christians is growing in number and in the Lord.... There are some seventeen in attendance. Each one is praying specifically for someone to come.... Such hungry hearts I have never seen! They are like sheep without a shepherd."

It was during this time that Ralph Porter, an airman stationed at Clark, came to know Christ as his Savior. Ralph and Wilma later became missionaries with OCSC and serve faithfully to this day.

Chuck and Jane Hall were God's answer to the prayers of that little group. They arrived in the Philippines on August 2, 1960, shortly after the Allens rotated back to the States. The group had rented a house for them, paying the rent for two months in advance, had hired two house girls, and even bought a few pieces of furniture.

The Halls were virtually on their honeymoon when they arrived. Their first meal in this, their first home was eaten on packing crates covered with a cloth, a romantic candle glowing in the center. Later Jane admitted the reason for the elegant atmosphere was to disguise the steak she had burned. But Chuck was duly impressed.

In a short time they knew the house was too small to carry on a growing ministry. They found a location in Embassy Court, a secure compound along the perimeter fence, just outside the main gate of the base. There were about fourteen homes in the compound, surrounded by a barbed wire fence. There was an entrance gate into the compound, where guards on twenty-four hour duty checked everyone coming through. Dispersed among the homes were three guard shacks where armed men watched throughout the night hours.

The Clark Christian Servicemen's Home

The Halls negotiated with the owner of the compound to have a home built, customized to fit the needs of the ministry. The two-story, 1900 square foot building had four bedrooms, a *sala* (sitting room) and bath upstairs, with a kitchen, dining room, living room, and small office downstairs. Within a year of occupancy, the Halls realized it was simply too small, so at their own expense (the building was rented) and with the help of the airmen, they added a large screened-in porch on three sides. When we arrived, the construction was complete, but it still needed interior finishing.

For the next week Tom and I followed Chuck and Jane around like puppy dogs, eager to learn as much as we could. The most confusing to me was shopping—bartering for everything, knowing where to get this and that and what to look out for. Angeles City, the town near us, had 90,000 people but no paved streets. It was full of open shops, *calesas* (colorful horse-drawn carts for hire), jeepneys (World War II jeeps converted into colorful taxis or buses), and pedicabs (tricycles with seating for two people on the back).

The climate and culture were similar to what we knew in Panama because both countries had been under Spanish rule for many years in the past. The cost of living was inexpensive compared to the States. I could have my hair done for thirty-five cents. Anything imported was very high, so we lived solely on local goods. Tropical fresh fruits and vegetables were available in abundance and cheap. Jane, a wonderful teacher, was very patient with me.

I experienced some cultural adjustment, especially when buying food. In Panama we had privileges to buy all American products at the Panama Canal commissary. Now I was learning the art of bartering. I learned that you could never just run into a store, make a purchase, and run back out—everything took so much time. How many times I muttered under my breath, "Boy, if they were in the U.S...." Sensing my impatience, Tom gently but wisely counseled, "Honey, we are the foreigners. If we don't like the way they do things, we can go home." I never forgot those words. Many a time they echoed in my mind, calming my simmering intolerance.

We inherited such fine house help. Rosie, a precious Christian about ten years older than I, did all the cooking and washing. When the Japanese attacked the Philippines at the beginning of World War II, Clark Air Base had been devastated. Rosie and her American military husband lived there. Her husband retreated to Bataan Peninsula with the other airmen and Rosie never saw him again. When the Japanese soldiers came, her life was in danger because she was married to an American. She fled into the hills and joined a guerrilla band for whom she cooked and cared for the sick throughout the war. The guerrillas helped prepare the way for the American forces when they liberated the Philippines. In my thinking, she was a true hero.

Purita was responsible for light cleaning, dishes, folding clothes, and helping with the children. Felix, the houseman who was a dedicated Christian and soul-winner, came twice a week to do the heavy cleaning (waxing floors) and the yard work. Flora came one day a week to iron. We could have all of them for about $30 a month. They needed the work and our financial support was now at $287 a month so we felt we could keep them on.

We had a large yard where David and Danny loved to play. Lori, always slower to adjust to change, was restless and fearful, not wanting to go to school. The school on base allowed us to enroll her into one of the eighteen first grade classes for tuition of $306 per year. The bus came right to our compound and she carried her lunch.

As a farewell gift, the Halls had promised all of the house help they could attend the Bible conference at Camp John Hay in Baguio in January. Since Lori was to start school, it was determined that I should remain at home with the three children. Not knowing how secure we actually were in our compound, I was terrified to stay alone. Therefore, Jane arranged for a Filipino girl to come to stay at night. (Looking back I see how silly it was. What could one young girl do to protect me?) The first night was fine, but the next day the girl called saying she couldn't come. I was panic stricken. I knew I wouldn't sleep a wink. I prayed earnestly for the Lord to do something! About dusk I heard motorcycles in the driveway. Rushing to the door, I saw two leather-clad men getting off their bikes, faces covered with dirt. I could tell one was Filipino but wasn't sure of the other one. I stood at the door wondering what to do. One of them spoke to me. "Are the Halls here?" I knew he was American.

"No, " I responded, "everyone has gone to the Bible conference in Baguio." Instantly I realized how foolish I was to let them know I was alone.

"Well, my name is Jim Irving. I usually stop here with the Halls when I am traveling."

I remembered hearing his name, and asked, "Are you Dr. Jim, the missionary from the Good News Clinic in Banaue?"

"Yes, I am," he replied. Relieved, I invited them in and prepared supper. In the conversation I asked whether they would go all the way to Manila that late in the day.

"Well," Dr. Jim hesitated, "I usually stay here overnight and then go on in the morning." Instantly I remembered the verse in the Bible about "entertaining angels unaware" as well as my very recent prayer.

"Oh, I'd love to have you stay," I urged. They did. I slept well, knowing I was the recipient of a very quick response from the Lord to my panicky prayer. Years later I shared that incident with Dr. Jim. He had no idea he had come as an "angel" that night. The next evening the Filipino girl returned.

The three weeks we overlapped the Halls were hectic and the day we drove them to Manila to board their plane for the U.S. I was fearful. The ministry was thriving and healthy. Chuck and Jane were dearly loved. Could we really carry on in their place?

After the Halls cleared immigration, the group of friends who had come to bid them farewell sat in the lunch room at the airport, talking. Wanting desperately to squeeze out every bit of helpful information from Jane that I could, I solemnly asked, "Jane, if it were possible, what is the one thing you would change during this term in the Philippines?"

Not missing a beat, she quipped, "I'd raise up perfume supporters—someone to send me a new bottle of perfume every month!" That was Jane. I loved and admired her greatly and was deeply saddened when the Lord took her home years later after a long bout with cancer.

Chuck had helped us get base passes through the chaplains' office; but having had some problems with one of the chaplains, he warned us against participating in his service. The first Sunday night we were unsure what to do. The guys got into their cars and roared off to the evening service; we sat at home alone. We knew it wasn't right. Memories of the difficult days in Panama plagued us. By the next Sunday we had resolved to attend the chapel services, no matter what. It proved to be one of our best decisions. When we arrived at the chapel, that same chaplain greeted us warmly. "I'm so glad you have come to Clark," he said, pumping Tom's hand.

Several months later the room where Tom's single men's Sunday school class met became unavailable. "I know of a perfect place to meet," one of the men said. He led them to a room that was comfortably air-conditioned without any windows. They had a great class. The next morning officers from the OSI (Intelligence) were at our door.

"Come with us, sir," they told Tom. "You have broken a security regulation." It sounded ominous. Tom then learned that the room where they had held the class was the "ready room" for the pilots flying to Vietnam. On the blackboard was the plan for the next bombing run.

The chaplain was contacted immediately. "I will take all responsibility for this incident," he told the investigators, boldly putting his arm on Tom's shoulder. "This man was working for me when he was in that room." The incident was cleared up, and Tom was eternally grateful for that kind chaplain.

But our decision to serve within the chapel program wasn't all rosy. The chaplain who later led the evening service was a man of liberal theology with a serious drinking problem. One night when he didn't show up for the beginning of the service, Tom started the singing. I was at the organ. Just about time for the offering, he staggered in. His clothes were rumpled, his pants wet up to the knees from falling in the rain. When the ushers brought the offering plates to the altar, he stumbled and almost fell. We were horrified! His "sermon" was a slurred disaster. All during the remainder of the service Tom and I tried to think of what we would say to the men who had come with us. We didn't want to be identified with the man but didn't want to blow the whistle on him either. The next day, having heard about the incident, the installation chaplain called Tom into his office. "I want to apologize for my chaplain's behavior last night," he said. "Be assured that this will never happen again." Soon the alcoholic man was sent back to the U.S. for rehabilitation.

Before we met, both Tom and I developed the practice of giving to the Lord. We continued this after marriage even though at times it was difficult. We knew the remaining money would stretch to cover the month's expenses if we gave to the Lord first before any other bills were paid. We also realized how difficult it was to carry on a ministry when our support level fluctuated every month. Because we were tithing our support to the Tarkingtons every month, it made theirs irregular also. Therefore before leaving the States, we determined before the Lord to send thirty dollars each month no matter how much we received. However, after paying the first month's bills at the Clark home, we had only forty dollars left and a whole month to go. Fearfully we sent off the check to Tark. That month, without knowing our financial situation, the men at the home gave more than ever before.

By now we had been missionaries with OCSC for eight years. The Lord had taken us through "Trusting 101" in Panama, especially in the area of finances. We must have passed the test because we didn't have to take that course again. There were incidents of trusting him for money for specific projects, but on a day-to-day basis, our support remained strong. As our income increased, we discovered more and more the great joy of giving to others. We learned from the Lord that if there was an abundance, he wanted us to pass it on to someone else. We adopted the verse, "Freely you have received, freely give." (Matthew 10:8b) In the process, we also discovered that if we freely gave, we also freely received. It was fun trying to out-give the Lord. Of course, he always won. The finances for the ministry were adequate, sometimes abundant. The men who came to the home were faithful in supporting the ministry that was impacting their lives. One day near the end of our time at Clark we were on the way to Manila for supplies when to our amazement we realized we had more money than time—an awesome experience for missionaries.

Clark Air Base presented endless opportunities for ministry. There were 6,000 to 8,000 air force, army, and navy personnel stationed there when we arrived; with dependents and civilian workers from the U.S. the number was above 10,000. Just a two-and-a-half hour flight across the South China Sea was the Republic of Vietnam, a country torn apart by communist aggression. The U.S. was sending in military advisors to help the forces of South Vietnam resist an all-out invasion. Clark became the staging area for the upcoming war.

The ministry at the home continued to build with many people coming for supper and "Victory Hour" on Friday night, Sunday school class on base, the Monday evening Bible class, jail and hospital services, and the women's Bible class. Someone joined us at our table for most meals during the week. Our faithful house help worked long hours to provide good meals and keep the home clean and attractive. Rosie, our cook, had the uncanny ability to prepare a delicious meal for just a pittance of money. She shopped in the open market for all of our fruits and vegetables at a price much better than I could have gotten. Of course, the morning she served scrambled eggs with canned whole kernel corn mixed in we did a double take. But we actually learned to enjoy it.

Having house help was a mixed bag. Although we knew we couldn't get along in that ministry and climate without them, it wasn't always a positive experience. One time after running through some fresh tar on the road, Tom told our houseboy to clean it off the car. A few minutes later Tom saw him scrubbing the paint with steel wool. Another time after we had been to the beach, Tom told the boy, "Please clean the sand out of the van." Soon he had all the carpets and seats out and was spraying the inside with the hose.

We learned by trial and error to be very careful to allow our helpers to "save face." If we wanted an honest answer to a question, we asked it so they could reply positively. Instead of "Do you understand?" which would always evoke a positive response, we sometimes asked, "Do you not understand? to which they could reply, "Yes, sir." Sometimes we were able to interpret a "Yes, sir" that really meant "No, sir" but not always. We learned to love our Filipino friends— dear, gentle people who had a genuine love for Americans.

It was necessary for the sake of our health that all fruits and vegetables be washed in chlorine bleach to kill bugs to which we had no immunity. Our kitchen helpers considered this strange. We watched continually to be sure they filled the dish pan full of hot, soapy water, or we would find them washing dishes for seventy people in a teacup of water. We insisted that each dish be rinsed in hot water containing chlorine bleach. My frustration over this subsided when I realized that most of them came from the barrios where they carried every ounce of water for long distances and had learned very young to conserve. Our flagrant use of water and soap must have seemed like the ultimate extravagance to them. Actually, we were very conserving of potable water because we had to haul all of it from the base in five-gallon containers. This was used for food preparation and drinking. Our tap water was used for everything else. The children learned very young never to get a drink at the sink. Actually, the only illness we experienced from bad food or water was from a fresh salad Tom ate at the officers' club on base.

Being able to eat at the restaurants on base was a special treat to us. We always ordered a glass of cold milk. Even though it was reconstituted by the dairy on base and put into bottles, it was far superior to the powered milk we bought off base. The children called ours "blue milk." They loved the base milk, but most American children thought it was awful. I guess it's a matter of perspective.

We experienced many typhoons in the Philippines, learning how to "manage" them to where they eventually became adventures. But our first one happened to be "Typhoon Winnie," our worst. I recorded the event like this:

5 p.m. The phone rang. "Hi, this is Dave. I won't be at Bible study tonight. We're on typhoon alert." Our first and only warning of the approaching storm.

7 p.m. Raining and windy now. About fifteen out for Bible study. I went upstairs to put towels around the windows. (Instead of glass windows, the house was built with wooden louvers, most of which had warped preventing them from closing tightly.)

8:30 p.m. The folks leave; the storm is increasing. Moved Lori out of her room and placed pans and bowls under the windows.

11:00 p.m. Electricity and water go off. Placed shower curtains over the windows, for the wind was driving the rain across the rooms. We heard a terrible banging on the roof as the wind rattled the aluminum shingles. We were mopping continually; the children awakened.

1:00 a.m. Two inches of water covered the kitchen floor. Moved to the bunk room as water dripped through the ceiling of our room.

1:30 a.m. The winds shifted—the rain came in David and Danny's room. The roof banged even louder. We could see debris, pieces of roofs and trees flying through the air outside. We were truly frightened by now. Huddled together, we pleaded, "Lord, please keep this place together." We learned later this was the height of the storm and most of the damage occurred at this time.

3:00 a.m. Checked the office downstairs—water was everywhere. We moved books, files, and the desk to the center of the room. Water was now dripping from the chandelier in the living room.

4:30 a.m. The rain and wind let up so Tom stepped outside to examine something lying in the yard—a piece of roof. He was amazed to see stars shining above. We learned later that the eye of the typhoon was passing over. Exhausted, we moved everyone into the guest room, the only dry one by now, and soon fell asleep.

7:00 a.m. Awoke to rain and high winds, with water coming in all the places it hadn't before. We could see that three houses next to ours had lost their roofs—the rubble lay in their back yards. The roof was leaking everywhere now. We piled up the bunk beds and resumed mopping.

11:00 a.m. The storm lessened some, so Tom went outside to determine the damage, expecting to see our roof in shambles. To our surprise, only the very top cap was gone. Tom scouted around the neighborhood and found the pieces.

4:00 p.m. The winds died down, but heavy rain continued. Tom climbed up to replace the roofing. It was several days before the electric and water service were restored. We praised the Lord for his protection!

Other than this first one, all in our family have fond memories of typhoons. The gate to the base was usually closed so we had unexpected time together. We usually had a day or so of warning, so the anticipation and preparations mounted gradually. Then as the storm surged in, we all moved from window to window wringing out towels and mopping up puddles. The electricity always went off, so candles added to the fun atmosphere. Some of the servicemen who happened to be at the center when the gate closed have fond memories of those special times too, and to this day our children look forward to stormy days.

Driving into the carport in a downpour of rain one night, Tom and I felt bad to be arriving late from Manila for the Monday night Bible class and a P.T.A. meeting which I was supposed to attend at Lori's school. While waiting for us, many of the folks had gone to the west windows to watch the storm. Suddenly someone called out, "Look at that ball of fire!" Then an incredible boom. A plane had crashed. As the first news was confirmed, the Bible class became even more serious. Then throughout the next few hours as the tragedy unfolded, word was released that all the passengers (more than 70) had been killed. Only the five crew members survived when the nose of the plane had blown free of the wreckage and fire. The plane was bringing new troops to Clark Air Base. Some of the victims may have been future men of the home—now the opportunity was gone forever. A taxi driving on the road from town to the base happened to be at the end of the flight line as the plane came in. A wheel of the plane caught the taxi, killing one man and seriously injuring the other man and the Filipino driver. The young men were on their way downtown to drink. Had we gotten home on time, I might have been on that road to the P.T.A. meeting. Sobering thought! "For he shall give his angels charge over thee, to guard thee in all thy ways." (Psalms 91:11)

The Philippine postal system left much to be desired. Our post office was located right in the center of Angeles City. Since there were no numbered boxes, our address was simply, "General Delivery." Each time we stopped to get our mail, the postmaster sorted through random piles of mail. We urged people in the U.S. not to send money or packages since their delivery to us was at the whim of the postal clerks.

One time we received a box of Florida oranges, lovingly sent by friends for Christmas. "The duty is 150 pesos," the clerk informed us. We tried our best to barter for a fairer price but failed.

Finally Tom said, "We can't afford that much. You keep them!" As we drove away we could visualize the clerks having a yummy *merienda* (snack) at our expense.

Chapter 18

ALL FOR A VEHICLE

Major Julian Sleeper and his wife Idabelle were active at the home when we arrived. I was totally unaware of the following incident until just a few years ago when Julian recounted it for me:

> Having been raised in a church that did not teach the security of the believer, I grew up with a "hope-so" religion. I heard the gospel and received Christ as Savior when I was twelve but was never sure of my salvation. After Idabelle and I were married, we attended liberal churches, but we knew they didn't teach the real Christianity we longed for. I doubted creation, the miracles, the account of Jonah, and even the deity of Christ. But God was faithful and wouldn't let me go!
>
> While at Ft. Leavenworth, Kansas, in the Command and General Staff College, I received orders for Germany. I knew this choice assignment would put my career into high gear. Then it happened—just a few weeks before graduation I broke my ankle. It was a serious break requiring three operations and steel pins to repair. I received a

delay in my orders to Europe and was assured that when I was well I could proceed to Germany. Finally, after months of casts, hobbling on crutches, and medical leave, the doctors gave me a green light to travel.

I called the placement desk in the Pentagon. "I'm ready to go to Europe," I announced firmly.

"Haven't you heard? You're going to Clark Air Force Base in the Philippines!"

I kicked and screamed and talked to all the bosses but to no avail. Finally a colonel told me in no uncertain terms, "You're going and that's that!"

"Yes, sir!" I responded, much more optimistically than I felt inside.

When we arrived in the Philippines, we looked for a church of our denomination, but there was none. We attended a Sunday school class on the base and met some servicemen from the Christian Servicemen's Home. They invited us out. We enjoyed the fellowship, wondered why everybody was so happy about their religion, and joined in where we could. We *looked* like we were one of them.

One Friday evening we came out to the home early. I was hanging around the kitchen and overheard Dotty talking to an airman. "Are you certain that if you were to die tonight, you would go to heaven?" I was eager to hear his reply—I knew what mine would be.

"I sure hope so!" he responded. *Great answer,* I thought!

"Why do you call God a liar?" Dotty responded.

"I would never call God a liar!" he replied defensively. "Read I John 5:10 to me," she said to him, handing him her Bible. "He that believeth on the Son of God hath the witness in himself; he that believeth not God hath made him a liar, because he believeth not the record that God gave of his Son." I hung on every word.

"Now read verse 13," Dotty replied. "These things I have written unto you that believe on the name of the Son of God, that ye may know that ye have eternal life, and that ye may believe on the name of the Son of God."

A light turned on in my heart. I could really know for certain that I would go to be with the Lord in heaven! And this knowledge wasn't based on feeling but the fact of God's Word. Right there in Dotty's kitchen, I received assurance of salvation and my life changed forever!

Now the Bible made sense. I knew every word was true—creation, the miracles, the virgin birth of Christ, and especially the resurrection of Jesus from the grave! I have not doubted my salvation since that time.

What if someone had shown me these verses (and others) from the Bible when I was twelve years old? How different my Christian life would have been. But what if I hadn't overheard that conversation that evening at the home? But God saw that I did!

While the Sleepers were with us, we invited a missionary with Child Evangelism Fellowship (CEF) to come to the home and chapel to introduce the work. As a result, several of our families began Good News Clubs in their homes. The Sleepers were one of those families. Several years later God used that introduction to eventually lead them to retire early from the U.S. Army and enter full-time work with CEF—first as a local director in Oklahoma City and second as USA Director. We still count them among our dearest friends.

For many months we carried on the ministry without a vehicle, praying for some affordable way to get our Greenbrier bus there. Then we received word that it could be shipped at no expense to us via Operation Handclasp, a U.S. Navy service which took unsaleable goods (mostly new) from manufacturers, shipped them overseas on Navy ships, and placed them into the hands of reliable nationals or missionaries who would see that they were distributed properly. Chaplains were usually the custodians of the process.

When we learned the bus would arrive at Subic Bay fifty miles away we were overjoyed. We held an evening of prayer, asking the Lord to be honored in the process of receiving the bus and getting it through customs into the country. We were unaware that this was the beginning of a small miracle. Several men went with us to Subic late on Sunday evening. Tom and I stayed in the newly finished guest room at the Subic Service Center, which Dick and Margaret Patty were in the process of building. Bob and Dorothy Bingham were assisting them in the ministry.

The ship arrived on Monday but remained in quarantine for some reason. We waited all day for some news, returning sadly to the center. That night the Lord gave us a special promise from II Chronicles 20:17 regarding the customs process we were entering: "Ye shall not need to fight in this battle; set yourselves, stand ye still, and see the salvation of the Lord." We slept peacefully that night, totally unaware of the battle that lay ahead.

On Tuesday Tom and Bob Bingham looked up the Christian officer on base who was handling the paper work for us. He had no word. They drove around to Cubi Point where the ship was docked. There was the bus, parked on the dock. A quick inspection showed absolutely no damage. Approaching the gang plank of the ship, they saw the chaplain, grinning from ear to ear. "I have requested the public information office to do a story and pictures as I present the keys to you," he said.

Soon the ship's captain arrived in his launch. Everyone snapped to attention. After being introduced by the chaplain, the captain led Tom over to the area where the ship's name, plaque, and medals were displayed. With flashbulbs popping, the captain dramatically handed him the keys to the bus. When they got into the bus to drive away, they were surprised that the chaplain had even filled the tank with gas.

Driving to the office of the Christian officer, they were disappointed to learn that the bus must remain on the base until the customs paperwork was completed—two or three round trips to Manila. Reluctantly they made arrangements to leave it at a chief's home. Tom was deeply disappointed, for he felt bringing the bus home would be of such encouragement to the folks at the home. Just as they were getting ready to board the local bus back to Clark, a Christian legal officer who had just returned from being with Tarkingtons on Okinawa, rushed up. Learning of the situation, he said, "I can check the bus off the base in my name until you complete the paperwork." With great joy we drove the bus to Clark.

That night, Tom composed a letter to the Philippine customs division, requesting a tax exemption on the freight charges, since it had come over free. When checking on the duty earlier, he had been told it would be classified as a truck costing about $450. At 11 p.m., Major Julian Sleeper came by. "Do you have cash to pay the duty?" he asked. Tom admitted he had only $100.

"Well, I want to give you $300," Julian said, sitting down to write the check. But when he handed it to Tom, it was made out for $350. Surprised, Julian responded, "Well, the Lord must be leading."

The next morning Tom and three of the men made the hot, dusty three-hour drive to the customs office in Manila. To their deep disappointment, the Bureau of Internal Revenue classified the vehicle as a car with duty of $1,500. Dejected, they returned home.

The following day, with many at the home earnestly praying, Tom and Dick Conrad returned with a letter of request that the vehicle be classified as a truck. "This cannot be!" seven different officials told them, one becoming very angry. But then one of the officials softened, seemingly wanting to help. "This has never been done before," he informed them cautiously, proceeding with the paper work.

"But you will need a deposit," he said.

"I only have money for the duty, not for a deposit," Tom replied. The agent angrily tore up the papers. Dick, who was waiting outside the counter, was appalled and began to pray earnestly.

Then Tom recalled the account of Balaam in the Bible, when he tried to pronounce a curse on God's people. *Lord,* Tom prayed silently, *please don't let this "Balaam" be able to pronounce a curse, but rather a blessing.* After about ten minutes, the official murmured, "If I get hung, I get hung," and began filling out new papers without the deposit.

"Do you have the owner's manual?" he asked. Tom handed it to him and he studied it carefully. "This vehicle was assembled on a truck chassis in the Chevrolet truck plant!" he exclaimed. "We can declare it a truck." Keeping the manual to support his action, he set the duty at $450!

As Tom and Dick joyfully left the customs office, Tom said smiling, "You're welcome to the manual. It was worth a thousand dollars to me!" He laughed.

Victory Hour that night was a time of rejoicing as Tom and Dick recounted their contest between the Lord and their "Balaam." It was a strong encouragement to all of us. Little time was lost getting the bus into the ministry.

Chapter 19

"HERE AM I, SEND MY SISTER"

Tom took a group of airmen on a week-long trip to visit missionaries working with tribal people in the northern mountains. They drove the six-hour trip north to Baguio and then boarded a local "Dangwa" bus bound for Banaue. As always, the bus was crammed with people. So Tom, Freddie Kerr, and Ken Kruzan decided to ride on top in the luggage rack along with the boxes, goats, and chickens. As the bus lurched along the narrow mountain road, they enjoyed the view, taking lots of pictures. Then they rounded a corner and Tom spotted a small village below. Smoke curled from the cooking fires in the thatched roofed huts. He remembered.

"Hey, Fred and Ken, see that little village down there? Fifteen years ago when I was a young GI, Chuck Hall and I made this same trip with a missionary, Jesse Miller. Jesse showed us that village and said, 'Maybe the Lord will call one of you to be a missionary there someday. They have never heard of Jesus.' Chuck had responded, 'Nooooo, not me!'

"'So it's, *Here am I Lord, send my sister?* Jesse jibed."

They got the picture. (Chuck did return to the Philippines with OCSC, but not to the tribes.)

Earlier that year, Ken had attended our servicemen's Bible conference. He had received Christ as his Savior back home, but now, far from home, he felt God's call for missionary service. After discharge, he attended Moody Bible Institute and eventually returned to the Philippines as a missionary with JAARS, the flight organization of Wycliffe Bible Translators.

Freddy wasn't called to return to the mountains of the Philippines but rather to the mountains of northern California where he has served faithfully as a pastor for many years.

Freddie Kerr, Bob Miller and Lucky Sargent experiencing missions first-hand

We made two types of trips. On Saturdays we took short trips to see points of interest. It was our desire to give the military folks an opportunity to see the Philippines and meet Filipinos who were not located near the base. It is sad, but the worst element of the nationals seemed to surround the base, lurking like vultures to relieve the GIs of their money and virtue. Most Filipinos were gracious, friendly, kind people who loved the Americans. We wanted our folks to see that side of the Philippines. We took them to visit mission stations, orphanages, and historical sites for that purpose. Those trips built positive memories in their hearts and minds. Not only did we see a lot, but the fun and fellowship were long remembered too.

About twice a year Tom took a select group of men on a week-long trip to visit remote mission stations in the tribal areas. One of the favorites was to the Good News Clinic run by missionaries of Far Eastern Gospel Crusade (later SEND International) located in the area of the Ifugao tribe. While there one time, a very ill man from a remote tribal area was carried in on a makeshift stretcher. Dr. Eliezar Sarmiento examined the patient, but shook his head. "He is gravely ill," he said. "He desperately needs a blood transfusion, but we don't have blood here." The doctor explained the situation to the relatives who had come with him, asking if they would donate blood.

"Oh, no! We can't do that!" they responded, fear filling their eyes. "If we do, we will die!" Even with all the explaining by the doctor, he could not convince them to put aside their tribal superstition.

"Then he will die," Dr. Sarmiento told them sadly.

When our fellows learned about the situation, they all volunteered to donate blood. Quickly Dr. Sarmiento checked their blood types and found one with a satisfactory match. The two men were placed on cots side by side and a direct transfusion begun. The Ifugaos watched wide-eyed, wondering why this foreigner was giving his blood for their relative.

When the man's condition stabilized, Dr. Sarmiento explained: "These foreigners believe in the true God and in Jesus Christ, his Son. Because of this, they love you and are willing to give their blood for you." Then he explained how their sin was condemning them to eternal death, and that God loved them so much he sent his only Son to give his blood and die for them so they could be forgiven of their sins. Just like the dying man received the airman's blood to save his life, so they could receive the shed blood of Jesus to have forgiveness and eternal life. We didn't learn the outcome of that witness, but know those Ifugaos saw a vivid example of Christ's love.

Tom and David on the Dangwa bus bound for Banaue

Tom and the airmen had ridden the Dangwa bus over Mountain Trail to get to the clinic—a rough, perilous, all-day journey. The return trip was to be via the Mission Aviation Fellowship (MAF) plane with pilot Don Berry.

They left the clinic piled into an old jeep with a couple of the men riding on the fenders and hood. Chugging up the trail to the landing strip, they noticed that part of the mountain was covered with a cloud. To their surprise, Don was waiting there in the little plane.

Bob White was one of the passengers in the first trip out. As Don began revving up the motor for take-off, Bob was terrified. All he could see of the landing strip was a few feet—he thought it just dropped off the mountain there. *He can't take off on that little postage stamp,* Bob reasoned. "Uh, Don, could we maybe pray before we take off," Bob asked timidly.

"Sure," Don replied, and bowed his head and asked the Lord for a safe trip.

During the short prayer, a whiff of wind blew the cloud away and there was the rest of the runway. *Thank You, Lord!* Bob breathed, and off they went.

Even at its best, that runway was something else. We took a navy pilot up there one time, a veteran of many aircraft carrier landings. When he saw the "runway" he gasped, "These missionary pilots do landings we would never try!" His appreciation for bush pilots rose about 100 per cent that day.

Bob White was a new believer when he came to Clark. His spiritual growth there was of great encouragement to us, and his commitment to the Lord refreshing. After his discharge from the Air Force, he attended college and seminary and became an army chaplain under the Christian and Missionary Alliance. After serving twenty years, he received his doctorate and was appointed a vice-president of Nyack Missionary College in Nyack, NY.

Tom had planned to baptize five of the men on one of the mountain trips. Bob White was one of them. A national New Tribes missionary, along with some of the Ifugao believers, agreed to lead them to an appropriate place. The rapid pace set by the tribesmen soon had the Americans puffing. After hiking for many miles through the famous Banaue Rice

Bob and Mattie White

Terraces, they came to a pond at the base of a small waterfall. In the rugged beauty of that remote stream, those five airmen gave testimony of their faith in Christ, all of which was interpreted to the Ifugaos by the missionary. Then Tom lowered them into the cool water.

Just as he finished, the missionary said, "This man is a believer too and would like you to baptize him also. Will you do it?" Tom led the man into the water, where he told of his faith in Jesus, the missionary interpreting. As before, Tom gently lowered him into the water. But before Tom could bring him back up, he jerked loose and disappeared. Startled, Tom searched the pond. Soon the man burst out of the water, smiling broadly, grasping a large wiggling fish. In a flash he popped the fish's head into his mouth and gave a quick bite. The fish was dead! Later the Ifugao told Bob White, "Now we are brothers!"

One of Tom's eventful baptisms

One November there were thirteen men ready to go on a mountain trip—the largest group yet. The first day they drove in the rain 100 miles to mile-high Baguio City. They checked in for the night at Camp John Hay, the military rest and recreation area, before boarding the local bus the next morning. During the night a typhoon blew in; by morning the roads were closed in all directions. The men spent the next five days sweeping the torrents of water that blew in across the room and out the door on the other side. One evening, Obe Hokanson, who had driven his Volkswagen van, decided to move it from the street in front to the back of the barracks. An hour later the men heard a loud crash. Looking outside, they saw a large tree fallen on the exact spot where the van had been.

Huddled around the fireplace to keep warm, Tom taught the lessons he had prepared for the trip and the group sang every song they knew and spent many hours in prayer. God did a mighty work in the lives of those men during that week even though they didn't get to the tribes.

Toward the end of the week the men realized they would not be able to return to the base by surface transportation before their leaves expired. After many phone calls to Clark, the Air Force agreed to send a plane for them. But it didn't include Tom, a civilian. Not willing to leave him behind, the men negotiated until the Air Force agreed to let him fly, provided he sign away any responsibility to the military. It was several weeks before the two vans could be retrieved.

Just before one of the mountain trips was scheduled, Tom discovered a large lump in his thigh. Checking with the doctor on the base, he was informed it had to be removed. Thankfully it was not malignant. After two days in the hospital, he was sent home for the two-week recuperation. At $45 a day for the hospital, we appreciated that consideration.

Captain Jim Stewart, one of our faithful men, offered to lead the men on the trip since he had previously gone with Tom. The plan was to drive Jim's Volkswagen van the first leg of the journey, ride a local bus for some hours, and then go by missionary aircraft into the jungle station they were to visit.

With Jim's van fully loaded, they headed out. Just as they arrived at the local bus stop, another bus hit them from behind, rolling Jim's Volkswagen van onto its top. Obe Hokanson, who was in the right front seat, hanging from the "ceiling" by his seat belt, called over his shoulder, "Chins up, youse guys!" No one was badly hurt so they all climbed out, checked the damage, rolled the vehicle back on its wheels, and drove back to Clark. Three of the fellows went on to the mountains, four who had slight injuries did not. About three weeks later we learned that one of the men had actually fractured a vertebrae in his spine. Due to rotate to the U.S. soon, he was placed in a cast and air-evacuated home. The van was fixed and amazingly the traffic court ruled in Jim's favor.

One summer while vacationing at Doane Rest in Baguio, Marge Haack, missionary with Christian Missions in Many Lands (CMML), invited Lori and me to attend a ladies' meeting with her at the nearby gold mine housing area. When we arrived at the house, the Filipino ladies welcomed us warmly, giving us honored places. When refreshments were served, we received a plate of *pansit*, a familiar vegetable and noodle dish. I loved it and ate heartily. In that culture if a person cleans his plate, it means he wants more. So when they brought a second serving, they and I were pleased.

After the second bite, I happened to glance down to the plate on my lap. My stomach did a quick flip-flop, for there, lying on its back minus the wings, furry legs sticking up in the air, was a giant rice bug (looks like a big cockroach). A second quick look revealed it wasn't alive, but deliberately cooked in the dish—a real delicacy. Since cockroaches are the one tropical bug I absolutely cannot abide, I couldn't touch another bite. Very slowly, I crumpled my paper napkin, placing it over my plate, covering the bug. Smiling broadly, I purred to the hostess, "Thank you so much. It was delicious. I am fully satisfied." She graciously removed my plate.

Chapter 20

BOARDING SCHOOL? NEVER!

Danny was growing into a more mischievous little redhead each day. One day I heard him singing at the top of his lungs, "Praise the Lord, praise the Lord, let the earth hear his voice!" only to discover he was tossing his best shoes into the plastic swimming pool in the yard!

While teaching my ladies Bible class at the home one morning, I noticed that the ladies were restless, even agitated, whispering to one another. Then someone shouted, "There's a fire out there!" We ran to the porch to discover the nearby guard shack on fire, the guards frantically stomping to put it out. Just then David and Danny came running around the corner, guilt written all over their faces. When the culprits finally admitted setting fire to the shack, (and two others in the compound I soon learned), I knew discipline was due.

Marching them to the kitchen, I gathered a candle and some matches. "I'm going to teach you boys that fire is very dangerous and it can hurt people!" I threatened. Up the stairs we marched. In their bedroom I lectured on the dangers of playing with fire while striking the match and lighting the candle. "Fire can hurt you!" I warned. The two little guys sat trembling on the edge of the bed, their eyes as big as saucers. "Now, give me your hand!" I demanded. Not daring to defy such a determined mother, each reluctantly extended a trembling little hand. They were absolutely sure I was going to burn them. Holding their hands tightly in mine, I lifted the burning candle, then tipped it, dropping a little wax on each one. They jumped in terror, screaming. I knew the wax wasn't hot enough to burn them and in a few moments they discovered it too. But they got the message.

One night I shooed four-year-old David out of the utility room and told him to go upstairs to prepare for bed. Being busy for a moment with other tasks, I noticed he hadn't obeyed but was again heading for the utility room. Irritated, I scolded, "David, go upstairs!"

"But Mommy," he responded, "I gotta get dat kitty otta da fijerator!" He was pointing to the deep-freeze. I rushed over and jerked open the door. Inside stood the tiny kitten, shivering and prancing for all he was worth, trying to keep its tiny paws off the ice. I shudder to think what could have happened if Rosie had discovered the prank the next morning! We might have had more than a dead kitten!

Tom and I were invited to a very special reception for one of the chaplains—a full dress affair. Important people from the States were to be there. I had my hair done at the beauty shop off base. Since hair pieces were stylish, the operator suggested I purchase one.

"I'd love to," I responded, "but I can't afford one."

"Oh, I'll put one on, you can try it tonight, and if you like it you can purchase it later," was her prompt reply. It was a deal I couldn't resist, so I was elegantly coifed that night.

Unable to return the hair piece the next day, I put it on my dresser. That afternoon when David and Danny spied it, the temptation to play barber shop was just too great. Once again they had a lesson to learn.

As the ministry grew, becoming more demanding of our time and energy, I recalled daily the advice we had received from seasoned missionaries: If you want to be good missionaries, you *must* take a siesta (nap) every day! Of course I wanted to be a good missionary! So for weeks after our arrival at Clark, following lunch I faithfully trudged upstairs to our air-conditioned bedroom. The moment I laid down, my mind raced round and round, reminding me of all the undone things waiting my attention downstairs. Sometimes I got a bit drowsy after about an hour, but by then it was time to get up. Or just as I was about to drop off, I heard this tiny tap, tap, tap on the door. It was Rosie saying I had a phone call. My attitude was not one of rest. After about a month I chucked the siestas, aware I would never be a "good missionary."

As the workload increased, I did have one or two times when depression closed in, but remembering my fiasco in Panama, I simply withdrew from society for a day or two to rest and spend extra time with the Lord. It worked. The advice I had received from Dr. Buker was sound—I knew how to read the signals and was wise enough to obey them.

Lori had been in the Clark school for a year and was now in the middle of second grade. Aware of her growing unhappiness and poor work, we went to see her teacher. "I just can't help Lori," she said sadly. "I am here in this Quonset hut with forty students; it's almost Christmas and I still don't have any textbooks; and by afternoon it's over 100 degrees in here. I don't even have a fan that works. I'm sorry. I just can't help her." (Improvement in the base infrastructure could not keep pace with the rapid influx of personnel at Clark due to the war in Vietnam.)

We went to the school counselor. "Well, we have two options here: we can have Lori finish the rest of second grade, fail, and then repeat it, or we can put her in a class of slow learners." We all knew neither option was what Lori needed.

That weekend we held a two-day Bible conference at the home. Our speaker was Dr. Everett Boyce from Faith Academy, the school for missionary children three hours away in Manila, While he was there, we shared our concerns for Lori. "That's simple," he said. "Send her to Faith."

"You mean put our seven-year-old in boarding school?" I responded emphatically. " No, I just couldn't justify sending our little girl away for someone else to care for when I am alive and able to do so myself. I just couldn't do that!"

"So... what are you going to do?" he asked matter-of-factly.

In the next few days we weighed all the options. (Home schooling was virtually unknown then and returning to the U.S. was not a consideration.) We knew Faith Academy was the best one for Lori, and she was eager to go. But I struggled inwardly, agonizing with the Lord. There must be another way. But I knew better. We made our decision.

After classes resumed I went to withdraw her from the military school. While waiting, I sat down under a banyan tree. *Lord, I just can't do this!* I sobbed. Then Satan hit me with his big guns! *See, you're such a crummy mother that even GOD won't let you raise your own children,* he screamed in my heart. *You are so impatient, you get mad at them, you don't spend enough time with them....* In a flash all my maternal failures crashed into my consciousness. *Yes, yes,* I sobbed, *I know, I know!* It was awful.

Then quietly the Holy Spirit reminded me of a verse I had learned long ago: "Trust in the Lord with all thine heart, and lean not unto thine own understanding." (Don't try to figure it out your own way {parenthesis mine} .) "In all thy ways acknowledge him, and he shall direct thy paths." (Proverbs 3:5-6)

Give me Lori, the Lord was saying. *Trust me. I love her more than you do. I'll take care of her.* As the reality of his Word crept into my soul, the inner turmoil was replaced with sweet surrender and then precious peace.

Lori went to Faith Academy. By putting her back one year, she gained the confidence she had lost and did very well academically from then on. Her brothers followed, all going to boarding school in first grade. But it was never an easy road.

By age four, David was again getting sick regularly, always with high fevers. An American doctor in Manila once again administered the gamma globulin shots, and we saw some improvement. But gradually the illnesses returned. At Faith Academy we could mark the calendar that he would be sick every fifth week. Finally an American missionary doctor recommended we have his tonsils removed and so he was admitted to a hospital in Manila for the procedure. After that, he was remarkably better.

Though he only attended one year, Danny left his mark on Faith Academy. This article appeared in the Faith Academy newspaper, The Mikifa:

> The first grade started off the year in a rather original way—with a funeral. It all started when the class's pet mouse died. Danny Hash set out with the serious responsibility of burying it, and of course, he knew that every decent grave had to have a tombstone. Since he couldn't write it himself, he trotted over to Mrs. Musgrove and had her print on a white paper, THIS IS A MOUSE. THE MOUSE IS DEAD. The funeral service was held during recess. They had pallbearers, but for some reason, none of

the first graders would agree to be the preacher. Mark Sharp's comment about the funeral was, "It was just like burying a man or a woman or a little boy or a little girl or a baby. Only it wasn't. It was a little mouse."

One Friday as we arrived at the dorm to pick up the children for the weekend, the housemother came running out. "I wanted to see you before school got out!" she declared excitedly. "Your son had a little accident."

"Let me guess which one," I replied laughing a little, but concerned.

"Yes, Danny was riding his bike down a steep hill. He hit a rock and pitched headlong over the handlebars. He has a broken arm." Sure enough, here came seven-year-old Danny, proud as punch, holding up the cast for us to see. We learned that the bone had been broken for three days before the housemother took him to the doctor. They were so used to his accidents that they assumed it was just another bruise.

After having all three children home one weekend, we drove back to Manila on Sunday evening, arriving at bedtime. We lovingly helped them undress and then tucked them into their beds. After kissing the boys in their dorm, we walked toward the car. Lori's housemother came running out, "I can't find Lori! She's not in her bed!" We rushed back to the dorm, searched everywhere, but she simply wasn't there. Then Tom went to the car. There huddled on the floor in the back seat, sobbing, was our precious little girl. Tom pulled her from the car, we hugged her, kissed her, assured her of our love, and then forcibly released her arms from his neck and handed her to the housemother. Hot tears streamed down our faces as we drove home.

"Lord, why must we be separated? Will this leave scars on their lives forever?" we wept. As we prayed and talked, we again counted the cost. The only other option for us at that time was to leave the mission field. But we knew God had called us. Anew we committed ourselves and our children to him.

From then on we brought the children home each weekend. I often made the hot, exhausting drive to Manila to pick them up each Friday. We arrived home just as 100 people were coming for Victory Hour. On Sunday nights we put the children to bed before 6 p.m. then arose at 4:30 on Monday mornings to make the journey back to Faith, arriving just before classes began. They handled this much better, their school work improved and they seemed happier. It was well worth the extra effort. But the day we picked them up the last time was one of the happiest of our lives—no more painful separations

As I went to God's Word for comfort and guidance about the children, he showed me again the story of Hannah in I Samuel 1-3. Human logic would have told Hannah she was a fool to give the only son of her barren womb to a fat old priest to rear. After all, his sons were not even "Christians" but immoral men posing as God's servants. But she was obedient to the promise she had made. I am sure as she went up each year to visit her son, she was appalled at what she saw surrounding Samuel. Scripture doesn't record how she felt, but God honored her obedience and gave her three more sons and two daughters. And he took her most precious possession and conformed him into the image of his Son, making history for his name.

Sending our children away was like placing them on the altar of sacrifice in obedience, and God blessed that offering. Faith Academy leaders have conducted a number of studies over the years and have found that a large percentage of former students now serving the Lord were at one time boarding students.

Years later we sat around the dining room table reliving those days. The children were mature adults, two of them serving as missionaries with our organization. Lori remarked, "You know, Mom, I think the reason we are such a close family today is because of those years of separation. We learned to love and appreciate our family unit."

Placing our children in boarding school brought some of the deepest agony of our lives. We have known many other missionaries who have chosen this route. Some of the children have not become committed Christians in their adult life. Some are bitter against God and their parents, some have psychological handicaps, some are nominal Christians. But most are just the opposite—strong believers who are obedient to the Lord, bringing honor to his name. As I compare those families with the average evangelical church family, I strongly believe that the averages may be about the same or somewhat better for the missionary kids.

We worked very hard to instill in our children the fact that we loved them and that we loved God too. We tried to teach them that the path of obedience was sometimes very difficult, but extremely rewarding. They also knew that we deliberately chose to be with them whenever we had the opportunity. For example, one time we found ourselves able to leave the ministry for a weekend when a couple offered to stand by for us. We quickly packed up our things, headed for Faith Academy, and checked the children out of school. They were totally surprised and thrilled beyond words. We drove to a resort area south of Manila and spent two wonderful days just being together. That spontaneous event remains a fond memory to the children.

When we went abroad as young missionaries, I had no idea the price the grandparents of our children were paying. They didn't see their grandchildren for four or five years. In those days we only called home in life or death situations.

Mail came and went at a snail's pace. We didn't have camcorders to record the children's growth.

Now we are the grandparents. We stand at the airport waving goodbye to our precious little ones. Our eyes puddle; a lump comes up in our throats! It's painful! I don't like pain! But God takes our offering and brings honor to his name! What greater joy is there?

The children, during their formative years, had the privilege of interacting with some of the finest Christian young men America was producing. And they learned that obedience to the will of God, even though difficult, was his plan for his children and resulted in great blessing.

Chapter 21

OPEN HOME, OPEN HEART

The ministry of hospitality is different from that of entertaining. When you entertain, you invite friends into your home—people you enjoy being with. But hospitality is an open home, open heart concept. People come whom you would never invite on your own. Some you really love having there, others you rejoice at their departure. But the purpose is to love them into the kingdom of God, or love them into greater maturity in Christ. If you truly love them, they will come. They know whether your love is genuine or whether you're just being nice.

It seemed like there was always someone in our home. At times we grew weary. We tried hard to observe our day off. One time we even put a sign on the front door: *Closed today. Please come back tomorrow.* Not a soul came in that door that day, but eighteen came around to the kitchen door. All felt they were special—the sign didn't apply to them.

As a mother of preschool children, I had to decide moment-by-moment whether to talk to them or to the ever-present adults. The little tap, tap, tap on my arm and the tiny voice saying, "Mommy, *Mommy,* ***Mommy***" seemed constant. We tried to teach the children good manners, such as don't interrupt when people are talking. But what should they do when Mommy (or Daddy) is *always* talking? Sometimes we made good choices, sometimes poor ones. Many times I became impatient with the children. The prayer constantly echoing in my heart was, *Please, Lord, don't let my sin leave scars on my children.*

One bedtime episode was a disaster. I knew I had lost it. Trying to comfort Danny after shouting at him, I hugged him, saying I was sorry. "Mommy," he said, his blue eyes searching mine, "Is it a sin to get mad?"

"Yes, it usually is, honey," I replied, feeling some guilt. "Mommy, is it a sin when you get mad?" Big guilt!

"Yes, it is," I admitted. Holding him close, I told him I was so sorry for sinning. Then I prayed, confessing it also to the Lord.

Danny kept our lives interesting. His insatiable love for dogs, cats, frogs, and geckos (small lizards whose tails he tied with strings and led around) was rapidly developing. But when he found a nest of baby mice in the back of our piano and wanted to keep them, we had a little talk about the animals that could be pets and those that could not. It didn't help.

Determined not to let David get ahead of him, at age four Danny resolved to ride a bike without training wheels. We learned of this when we heard his screams in the back yard—he had crashed into a post, gashing his upper lip and gum which was bleeding profusely. Rushing him to the clinic, we were informed that the wound would heal by itself. It did, but he has a scar there to this day.

One day Danny cut his finger. I led him to the bathroom sink where he stood in front of me while I washed the blood away. He slipped lower and lower in front of the sink. I pulled him up, but he just slumped down again. Finally, I gave a jerk and said, "Danny, I can't fix this if you don't stand up!" Then I glanced at his face. His bronze freckles were stark against his ashen face. He was out cold! It was his first time to faint at the sight of blood but certainly not his last.

One day when we returned from Manila, Rosie rushed out to us in tears. "I'm so sorry, sir," she wailed. She showed us the severely damaged electric typewriter. David and Danny had played in the "off limits" area when her back was turned and had made the typewriter stand a tent to crawl into. You can visualize the rest. The cost of repair to that valuable piece of equipment was excessive because parts had to be ordered from the U.S.

We were also learning the value of "things." When you freely open your home to guys in their late teens and early twenties, anything can happen. And it usually does. Even though we tried to teach them to be careful, something always got broken.

Trying to maintain an "American" home for the military in a foreign culture was a challenge. With the funds available, we decorated the home as attractively as possible, and carefully set pretty tables. One time I shopped all over Manila to find a punch bowl, but the only one I could find was imported. The price was exorbitant but it was worth it. (The same item was available in the military exchange for about three dollars, but not to us.) One evening after Victory Hour, someone came to me saying, "Rosie is crying in the kitchen." Alarmed, I rushed in to see her leaning over the dish pan weeping.

"Oh, ma'am," she sobbed, holding up pieces of broken glass, "I broke your punch bowl!"

Comforting her, I tried to allay her fears. "It's okay. It's only glass."

"But, ma'am, I know you looked so hard to find it and you liked it so much," she sobbed.

"Oh, Rosie," I said softly, hugging her tiny stooped shoulders, "We don't cry over broken glass. We cry over broken *people*, but not over broken glass." That has been my policy to this day. I'm sure we got another punch bowl.

I invited all of the regular guys to come one evening to learn about table manners. Sitting at the end of the dining room table, I had placed around me an elegant setting of china, crystal and silverware. I proceeded to demonstrate how to use each utensil, explaining that when you have lots of them, you simply work from the outside in. It seemed quite logical. Then I explained that instead of taking a knife to a whole piece of bread or roll and slathering butter all over it, you should gently break it into four pieces and butter each piece individually before eating that piece. After the session was finished, I asked if there were any questions. Tom Tarvin, looking puzzled,

Etiquette class—"It's just too much trouble!"

asked in his southern drawl, "You mean when I want to dunk my cornbread in my buttermilk, I have to break it in four pieces first?"

Lonnie Williford spoke up, "Wow! Now I know what to do when someone asks me home with them for dinner after church. I'll just say, 'No thanks! It's just too much trouble!'" So much for the etiquette class. But years later various men have remembered that evening, thanking me for what they learned.

Holidays were difficult times for military personnel stationed overseas far from their loved ones, so we tried to make them very special. Each Thanksgiving we served a traditional meal with the wives providing the items we could not purchase locally. I made elaborate table decorations and place cards for the sit-down dinner.

Our first Thanksgiving at Clark I was feeling really rushed setting up the tables and getting everything ready. In the door walked a couple with their two preschool children who were coming for the dinner later in the day. "We are going downtown to shop," they said cheerily. "We brought our children here to play with yours." Out the door they went before I had a chance to respond. Resentment began to build as their two and our three raced through the house, having the time of their lives. *How can anyone be so insensitive. I wonder how she'd respond if I brought my kids to her house when she was expecting sixty for dinner!* I mumbled under my breath. After simmering for sometime, the Lord spoke to my heart. *Are you going to let this incident ruin your opportunity to be a blessing to many on this special day?* Immediately I knew I was wrong, and the Lord got the victory. But it did help me set a precedent in the ministry; from then on I didn't babysit under any circumstances. With all families having maids, it wasn't necessary.

While we were at Clark, Dick Patty was completing the monumental task of constructing the Subic Service Center. Olongapo, the town outside the Subic Naval Base was located about fifty miles from Clark, an intense two to three hour drive. On May 23, 1964, we loaded up a large group of our folks and went to Subic for the dedication of the center. What a memorable day it was as a great host of people gathered to celebrate that monument to God's faithfulness and provision! We sang songs and gave testimony of praise to the Lord. Then Chaplain Dave Meschke, who was to become a board member of OCSC and then General Director, gave a stirring message. Dick and Margaret Patty hosted a delightful dinner followed by tours of the 8,000-square foot building. We had no idea we would someday direct that great ministry.

By the mid 1960s, Clark Air Force Base had 17,000 military personnel plus dependents, American civilians, and temporary personnel often amounting to entire squadrons. There were four major town sites in the Clark area, each the size of a small city. Because of the escalating war in Vietnam, the base operated on a three-shift schedule. Eight chaplains, most of whom were sympathetic to our ministry off base, served that huge community.

Air Force personnel stationed at Clark were not kidding themselves into thinking that the Vietnam War was a remote headache! Some of the saddest memories of my life were the endless processions, day and night, of hospital buses loaded with stretchers two high, filled with injured men, snaking their way from the flight line to the Clark hospital.

Women and children were being sent home because Daddy didn't come back. A regular fellow at the home would come in one evening and announce, "So long! See you in four months, the Lord willing!" Sometimes he returned; sometimes he didn't. We had a sacred responsibility to minister to these folk while there was time.

Four days each week, Bible classes were held for both men and women on the base and at the servicemen's home, reaching a varied group of people. God was at work in these classes.

The buffet supper before Victory Hour was a "calling card" for new folks to come to the home. Many were unsaved. Later some told us they came the first time "for the home-cooked meal, but found the *Bread of Life*." Even though a trip to the grocery store was a hard, hot two to three hour drive each way to Manila, it was well worth the effort.

The book room at the home provided good Christian literature in English for all in the greater Clark area. It also gave opportunities for service, as our faithful people, like Wayne and Esther Railsback and Bill and Chury Bennight, cared for sales and inventory each week. Many young servicemen learned the joy of reading as a result of this outreach.

On Sunday afternoons, Paul Kemp, Harold Glass, Nate Robinson, and some of the other men drove to the nearby town of San Fernando, Pampanga, where they held a service for the inmates of the local prison. Rudy Delez, a Filipino Conservative Baptist pastor, came from Manila to interpret for them. They taught Bible lessons, gave awards for Scripture verses memorized, and befriended the convicted criminals there. They were appalled at the conditions in which the men lived. No clothing or food was provided by the prison system—families were responsible for these necessities. Often the servicemen took used clothing and other items they needed. Several of those inmates received Christ as their Savior and began an earnest walk with him. The growth in the lives of the airmen was significant as well.

Working hand in hand with the chaplains, we taught Sunday school and other Bible classes; I played the organ and directed choirs; Tom and I led music in the evening service; and we both served as leaders in the Protestant Men of the Chapel and Protestant Women of the Chapel groups. I had the privilege of leading the choir in six presentations of "Messiah." And during this time, the choir received the coveted *"Best Choir in WestPac"* award. The installation chaplain and Ken Thompson, chaplain in charge of music on the base, were quite thrilled the day the official photographers came to take our picture holding the special plaque. The award also looked impressive on their efficiency reports.

One time just prior to one of our presentations of "Messiah," I was asked to speak at a PWOC (Protestant Women of the Chapel) retreat up in Baguio. The timing was perfect, because I would return just in time for a big dress rehearsal with soloists and instrumentalists we had hired from Manila. The day before we were to return to Clark, feeling rather mischievous, we women cooked up a prank. I put in a call to Chaplain Thompson. "I really have some bad news," I said, sounding miserable. "I have the chicken pox! I can't leave here for a week." Silence.

"Oh, no! What am I going to do?" he groaned.

"I don't know. I'm really sorry," I replied, trying to sound sympathetic. We hung up. We could visualize him sitting with his head in his hands, maybe praying, probably crying. After about fifteen minutes, I called again.

"It's a miracle! I'm well!" I cried. Then I started laughing, as did the women behind me who were listening. I won't quote his response, but you can be sure he got even in the weeks to come! That prank was the talk of the base for weeks.

One night while rehearsing the passion portion of "Messiah," my heart was deeply stirred. We were singing the chorus, *Surely he hath borne our griefs and carried our sorrows, and the Lord hath laid on him the iniquity of us all.* The extremely significant message combined with the inspired music gripped my heart. Abruptly stopping the rehearsal, I asked earnestly, "Do you understand what you are singing?" Then I simply explained the way of salvation so clearly expressed in the music and invited anyone who did not know Christ personally to receive his gift of salvation. Then we continued on with the rehearsal. Many years later we received a letter from an airman who was singing in the choir that night. He had come to Christ at that invitation and was continuing in his walk with the Lord.

Serving in a music ministry in the chapel gave us high visibility in the community. A number of folks came to the home and were ministered to because they met us in one of the choirs.

One of the ladies in my choir was Mary Sofield, one of the most dignified, elegant, godly ladies I have ever known. She was at Clark because her husband, Norm, was employed in communications by the U.S. State Department. They had a lovely home up in "officers' country" and two children they had adopted in other foreign countries where they had served. Mary was a committed Christian, but Norm was an unbeliever.

Mary used her gift of opulent entertaining in the most unique way I had ever witnessed. On our day off, she invited us to her home for an elegant multi-course dinner. She also invited one or two couples who were not Christians. When we arrived, Norm, with whom we had developed a jovial relationship, usually called out, "Here come the sky pilots—lead us to heaven!" or, "Here come those over-paid, under-worked missionaries!" Instead of the cocktails he served to the others, he always had a supply of Dr. Pepper for us—a treat we couldn't get on the local economy.

When dinner was served, we were ushered to the table beautifully set with the lovely things they had acquired in their journeys around the world. The dignified maid, in her crisply starched uniform, had been flawlessly coached by Mary. As soon as the entree was served, Mary would ask Tom a question, like "What do you think about the second coming of Christ?" This was the door for Tom to share biblical truth, usually generating some interesting discussions. Several of those couples eventually came to know the Lord and to fellowship at the home. Norm, on the contrary, did not.

However, after leaving Clark they were assigned to Monrovia, Liberia, in Africa, where Mary used the same evangelistic tool with missionaries there. Norm eventually made a commitment to Christ. Shortly after, he contracted hepatitis and died within seven days. Mary returned to the States and eventually remarried. She and her husband, Sam Vause, continue to use this unique method of evangelism. They are dear friends and supporters to this day.

Chapter 22

IMPACTED LIVES

In 1965 the OCSC Mission Council met in Okinawa, where Tark and Alma Tarkington had opened a new ministry. Tom and I took the opportunity to sneak away from the Philippines for a short time. What joy to see how miraculously the Lord provided for establishing the Kadena Christian Center and later the Hansen Christian Center. (Another book!)

During that time Udell Meyers, a young marine lieutenant, dropped in at the center. (Udell's testimony appeared in the Fall 1989 issue of OCSC's magazine, FOCUS. Some of it is incorporated in the following account.) He was a believer, but his faith was wavering in the face of separations, temptations, and now deployment to Vietnam. A few nights before while on liberty with his buddies, he had seen the sign for the Kadena Christian Center. Although he knew nothing about it, he sensed this might be a way of escape promised in I Corinthians 10:13.

Our hearts were drawn to him right away as he shared his testimony of how God had worked in his life. We spent hours at the piano, his glorious tenor voice filling the room with songs of joy to the Lord. At the end of the week, bidding him farewell, we invited him to our home in the Philippines if he ever came into Clark. "No, I won't ever get to that place," he replied, "unless it's on a stretcher."

Months later we received a call. "This is Udell. I'm at the hospital." Tom and about ten of the guys rushed over to find Udell on a cot, still in his blood-stained fatigues, fresh from the battlefield in Vietnam. He shared his story.

> We were on the sixth day of a reconnaissance patrol when we encountered a Viet Cong unit with an automatic weapon. Several of my men were wounded. Then a bullet from an AK-47 assault rifle tore off my right thumb and destroyed the receiver on my rifle. Four rounds pierced my right arm; another struck a grenade attached to my ammo belt, missing the firing pin. Another hit a 16-mm reconnaissance camera in my right breast pocket.
>
> In spite of our wounds, we managed to take the ridge and quiet the enemy. We called for the helicopters. When they arrived, the trees were too thick for them to land. So they gave support while an Air Force rescue helicopter under sniper fire lowered a cable and lifted the injured men to safety.

After brief emergency care at a field hospital, Udell was med-evacuated to Clark. By the time he arrived, his arm was seriously infected and not responding to antibiotics. When Tom and the men arrived, they knew immediately he was in intense pain. The men circled Udell's bed, singing, thanking the Lord for his protection, and praying for a complete recovery. Reluctantly, they left him for the night.

What they did not know was that Udell had just been told he was scheduled to have his arm amputated the next morning unless a large number of casualties came in during the night. Were that to happen, he would be sent with them to Tripler Army Hospital in Hawaii, where he would receive special treatment in an isolation ward and be administered a new medication that might save his arm. He didn't share this with Tom and the men as he didn't want the joyous fellowship to turn into a pity party.

After the men left, Udell drifted into a deep sleep and was awakened at 3 a.m. and taken along with several others from his ward to the airfield where they were loaded aboard a C-141 med-evac flight. Most of the wounded already aboard were members of an army cavalry unit that sustained heavy casualties in a fierce battle during the night.

Within hours he was being treated in Hawaii. The new antibiotics were effective and his arm was spared. His recovery was long but complete. Udell and his family later became missionaries with OCSC.

Years later Udell shared his testimony at the annual OCSC Bible and Missionary Conference at Horn Creek, Colorado. During his presentation he noticed a tall black man standing at the back of the room, wearing a big smile and a look that seemed to say, *I know something you don't.*

When they met together, Udell found out his name was Bob White and that he was serving as an Army Chaplain at Fort Carson, Colorado. Then, with a smile, Bob said, "I was one of those ten airmen who visited you in that hospital ward at Clark Air Force Base. There was a spiritual dynamic to that experience that night which played a significant role in my call to the ministry of the chaplaincy."

Dick Lewis, an Air Force officer, recalls his war experience.

As the conflict in Vietnam escalated into an ugly war, I was on the vanguard of the C-130 cargo planes. Two of our squadrons were sent to Vietnam to see if the C-130 could hack the mission. They weren't sure if the turboprop engines and vulnerable fuel-tank wings would take gunfire. We spent time trying to fly at the exact height of the clouds, which meant we were constantly going from one extreme to another in flight altitudes.

Most of the time we stayed at the beach hotel at NhaTrang. If I got in early enough, I went to the Baptist church to teach English to the Christians there, using the Bible as a textbook. If I was fortunate enough to be there on a Sunday, I accompanied the pastor and another fine Christian gentleman, Mr. Thanh, to one of the Baptist churches inland. Mr. Thanh had lost his wife and seven children to the Viet Cong in North Vietnam where he had lived. He managed to escape to NhaTrang, working where he could. He did the preaching; I enjoyed just being there, realizing I was a witness to history in the making. I was told I was taking great risks going inland because of the possibility of being kidnaped or shot, but I prayed and went anyway. When we moved to Saigon the possibilities for getting shot rose about 500%! But I met many more missionaries and saw the church in action.

I really learned to put all of my beliefs into perspective over there. I tried to maintain a quiet time, but it was difficult—I just couldn't find a good place. Then I noticed that immediately after a mission, which usually ended between 4 p.m. and 6 p.m., everyone headed to the showers. So, I stayed behind, spending those few minutes with the Lord. It was a mainstay for my life at that time.

After the three months, we went back to Virginia. Forty-five days later on Thanksgiving Day, I returned to the Philippines for a fifteen-month tour of duty. I was stationed in Mactan in the southern Philippines but made many trips to Clark where I found fellowship at the servicemen's home. The Friday night meetings were especially helpful, as I met and heard missionaries speak. What a privilege to be part of that time in our history!

Fifteen years later I attended a Fourth of July celebration in Ruston, Alabama. At one point in the program, the leader asked all those who had participated in WW II and the Korean War to stand up for recognition. Then they asked those who participated in any way in the Vietnam War to stand. The master of ceremonies said, "Very few of us have had the opportunity to thank you who took part in that war—one that was maligned, bitterly resisted and resented—but still required you to fight and die for us. Thank you, one and all!" There was tremendous applause and a standing ovation. That gesture touched me more than anything had in many a year. I wished it was happening all over America, especially to the wounded, the maimed, and the families of those who did not return.

Jim Thomas recalls his time at Clark:

When I arrived at Clark Air Base at 4 a.m. in August 1965, I felt like asking God what I had done to be exiled there. I was physically tired, 8,000 miles from my loved ones, repulsed by the odor in the air, and sweating from the heat and humidity.

I met Tom and Dotty Hash at the base chapel. They invited me to the Christian Servicemen's Home. I went, but took my attitude of exile along. All I expected was a good meal away from the mess hall. To my surprise, I found a couple with children the age of mine, who loved music, teaching the Bible, and GIs. I'm so thankful they extended Christ-like love to me, for at that time I sure wasn't very lovable. But that love soon melted away the lonely hurt feelings and replaced them with real joy.

I had accepted Christ eighteen years before and had become a good church member. I taught Sunday school, sang in the choir, gave money, and served on boards of various churches.

I had only been at Clark a few weeks when Tom invited several of the men to go with him to Blue Beach for a week-end retreat. It was an outreach, so we had to invite an unsaved friend to go along. Through the Bible teaching and fun times, the man who went with me accepted Christ, and I grew more than I ever expected.

When my family arrived, the first place I took them was to the home. They were made to feel welcome and it became our home away from home. My job required frequent TDYs (temporary duty) to Vietnam. Leaving the family was much easier knowing the people from the home were there for them.

We learned how to witness, experiencing the joy of telling someone about Christ and seeing a life change. Now, years later I have had the privilege of taking many short-term missionary journeys overseas and seeing a host of people come to know Christ as their Savior.

Bill Needham remembers:

Jean and I were at Clark from 1965 to mid-1967. I arrived ten months before Jean could join me.

Victory Hour on Friday nights was a time of fellowship, food, fun, and preaching. The food was provided by the home with the help of various families. The single guys would crowd around the table piled with food the likes off which they'd never seen at the mess hall. Afterward there were ping-pong games, volleyball games, and times of browsing through the bookstore. The home was such a refuge for those separated from family or who had no family.

Solid Bible teaching by Tom, missionary speakers and others brought me into serious Bible study. Milt and Marge Haack were missionaries with Christian Missions in Many Lands who lived near the home. Milt's Bible messages always touched my heart.

A half-dozen of us would pile into the van on a Saturday and go to DZAS, the Christian radio station, to record four or five broadcasts of "The Servicemen's Challenge." I had the privilege of writing several scripts and selecting the music from the station music collection. Tom interviewed servicemen and gave a brief message, and we interspersed recorded and live singing.

One of our favorite but more strenuous trips was to Pagsanjan Falls. We left at 7 a.m. on a rented bus with hard wood seats and open windows and went bumping wildly over rough roads. At one gas stop, young boys and girls rushed up to sell cigarettes, candy, bananas, and, of course, *balut*, (incubated, cooked, nearly-ready-to-hatch duck eggs), a bit strong for our Western stomachs.

Upon arrival at Pagsanjan, we were rowed up the river in *bancas* (dugout canoes) in scenery reminiscent of a jungle river in Africa or South America. The falls were magnificent, but even more impressive was the small refreshment stand set up on a sandbar. Some enterprising Filipino had hauled all of the soft drinks and candy up the river to catch us crazy tourists!

Starting back, we had to shoot the rapids, plunging down through the rocks, skidding around bends, bouncing and jouncing our way to calmer water. "Do you lose many canoes during the season," I asked one of the drivers.

"No, this has been a good season. We only lost six *bancas*," was his sobering reply.

On one of those trips to Pagsanjan Falls we were having a wonderful time swimming around in the pond beneath the falls when one of the men who couldn't swim well was suddenly pulled away by the under-tow. He panicked and grabbed desperately onto our son, David. One of the guys heard the shout for help, jumped in, and pulled them to safety. We thanked the Lord for his guardian angels and for that young airman whom he used to spare us a terrible tragedy.

Bob and Elaine Heavner's lives were completely changed during their tour of duty at Clark. Elaine recalls:

> My husband, Bob, received orders to Vietnam in the spring of 1966. We were stationed at Hill Air Force Base in Utah at the time. Bob was flying the RB-57; I was teaching third grade at the base school. We had dated since high school but were finding by this time, our second year of marriage, that living "happily ever after" was not easy. Our lives were not centered around anything religious, though we did attend church once a week. We referred to it as "punching our card."
>
> Bob had been a Christian since age eleven when he had accepted Christ at a church camp, but had grown little. Mandatory chapel attendance at the Air Force Academy and a civilian minister who preached against electing a Roman Catholic president (John Kennedy) in 1960 fostered in Bob a cynical attitude toward church and Christianity.
>
> I had grown up in a morally good family. We dutifully attended church every Sunday morning, there was no alcohol or smoking in our home, and I seldom heard profanity until I started college. During our high school dating years I would sometimes attend Bob's church with him, not to listen to what the preacher said, but to have

time with my boyfriend. I felt I was such a good person that God would not reject me.

Bob had never learned about being unequally yoked so in 1964, a month after I graduated from college, we were married. On our wedding night Bob asked me to kneel with him beside our marriage bed while he asked God to bless our marriage.

In the summer of 1964, after settling me in our hometown of Akron, Ohio, Bob left for a year in Saigon flying the RB-57 (we thought!). But God had other plans, for upon arriving in Saigon, Bob received orders to a B-57 squadron at Clark Air Base, Philippines. His squadron alternated between combat duty from bases in Vietnam and training at Clark. Each rotation lasted two months. As soon as I found out that families were allowed at Clark, I packed up and joined him there.

Bob found the war challenging but troubling. It wasn't "making the world safe for democracy," as he had hoped. Friends were killed; wives widowed. Technology and education, which appealed to a humanistic part of his mind, seemed to be irrelevant in solving the real human problems and didn't seem to be leading to a better world. The black and white of democracy versus communism, good versus evil, appeared gray.

One member of his squadron asked Bob to join a Bible study at Clark. Bob agreed, and we found ourselves at an Officers' Christian Union (now Officers' Christian Fellowship or OCF) Bible study. Tom Hash was the teacher.

I listened quietly as the various members used words like "saved" and "born again," but soon became indignant. "Why can't you use words everyone can understand instead of religious jargon!" I demanded. At the end of the meeting Tom closed in prayer, quietly asking the Lord to show me what these words meant. It was the first time I had heard someone pray out loud for me personally. A small opening in my wall of pride and morally righteous facade began to break; a tiny flame of spiritual interest was sparked in my heart.

We were invited several times to attend Friday night Victory Hour at the servicemen's home but always declined. We had seen the sign for the home from the base road and envisioned several little old ladies dressed in hand-me-down dresses, and wearing frameless glasses, handing out Bibles to the GIs. But finally, on one particularly boring Friday evening, we went. To our surprise we actually had a good time.

Bob continued going to Vietnam for two months at a time. During the next six months I became a frequent visitor at the home. I gradually became aware that these folks had something I didn't—a peace, a joy, and a special bond. I also began bombarding the Hashes with questions. I listened to Tom and Dotty and to visiting speakers talk about our being sinners who needed to accept Christ personally. I thought they meant the other people there—not someone who had tried to be so morally upright as I was.

In April of 1967, Bob returned to another two-month tour in Vietnam, and I went for what I thought would be another enjoyable but passive evening at the home. I don't remember anything being particularly different that evening. But at the end of the message, Tom asked us to bow our heads. "If you are ready to receive Christ into your life, raise your hand," he invited. Suddenly, I realized that my good works and upbringing were not enough. It was time to do something about Christ. I raised my hand.

Dotty took me aside to pray. It was a quiet few moments, but I knew that my life would never be the same. Before I left the home, Dotty had me do two things that were significant: she had me tell Tom what I had done, and she gave me a set of four verses to memorize. I remember singing all the way home that night—every song I could remember from juvenile Sunday school days, especially *Jesus Loves Me.* Thus began my new life in Christ.

In Vietnam, Bob received a call from me the next Sunday afternoon through the Military Affiliated Radio Station (MARS). I told him that when we met in Bangkok for an R & R together soon, I would tell him the most exciting news in the world. He thought to himself, *Oh, we're going to have a baby.* You can imagine his surprise when, in Bangkok, I told him I had turned my life over to Christ.

My conversion brought Bob back to the basics of Christianity and helped him see his need for growth as a Christian. It launched him on a continuing effort to learn and understand more of God and his Word. As he learned, he began to see that Christianity and the Bible put war, human nature, and all of history into focus.

For the next year and a half, the home became our second home; Tom and Dotty became our spiritual parents. We were fed spiritually and urged to grow. We attended Bible studies and learned about trust. Tithing and quiet time were taught and became a part of our lives. The precious fellowship we enjoyed with the other believers was refreshing and necessary.

A couple of years after our return to the States, we were thrilled to have a chance visit with the Hashes again in Denver. As we were leaving, Dotty said, "Elaine, if you were the only one to receive Christ during our time at Clark, it would have been worth it." I remembered all they had given up in order to minister to us there: their privacy, a normal family life, having to send their children away to school. Was I really worth all that? Then I remembered that Christ thought I was, so much so that he gave his life for me.

The night Bob returned from Vietnam after Elaine came to Christ, their home was burglarized. The thieves entered the house, taking their stereo, TV, and everything else of value. They loaded it all into the Heavners' Volkswagen Kharman Ghia and drove it out of the guarded compound, even stopping to drink the milk in their refrigerator.

When the Heavners awoke, Bob was shocked and angry. Elaine seemed far less upset however. "The Lord is in control. We'll be okay," she assured him quietly.

"How can you say that?," he demanded.

"I told you, Bob, I've invited Christ into my life. He has given me peace."

God did see the Heavners through that ordeal, and they grew spiritually through the teaching and fellowship at the home.

Just before the Heavners were due to rotate to the U.S., they advertised their refrigerator for sale in the local base paper. Some Filipino nationals came to look at it and decided to purchase the item. But before the transaction was completed, they asked Bob to falsify the price on the paperwork so they could avoid paying Philippine customs duty. When he refused, they became angry. Concerned, Bob visited the base legal officer who said the Filipinos might sue him for reneging on a verbal contract. The lawyer advised Bob to leave the Philippines immediately. His commander and first sergeant expedited Bob's departure processing.

Elaine called, telling us they were leaving immediately. We rushed to their home, packed their suitcases, and rushed them back onto the base. That night, as we watched tearfully, they flew to the U.S. In the following days, folks from the home supervised the packing of their household goods, closed out the house, and saw that all was sent.

Thirty years later, recalling these incidents, Elaine wrote, "It scares me to think how our marriage or our daughters would have turned out if I had not become a Christian and if Bob had not begun to mature as one."

Any sacrifices we made during those years were far exceeded by the changes in lives such as the Heavners'. For years I have jokingly said, *I don't think there will be any rewards in heaven for us. We have had them all already.* Poor theology, but straight from the heart!

Ron Dice, now Controller of OCSC/Cadence, recalls his time at Clark:

> Through the persistent, loving encouragement of Captain Jim Stewart, a fellow officer at the Accounting and Finance Office, I agreed to go to a Victory Hour at the Clark Servicemen's Home. Inwardly I felt I didn't need any more "religion"—my works-oriented faith seemed to be enough. After all, I wasn't carousing and sinning deeply like some of my fellow officers. However my presence at the Officers' Club was more frequent, especially on Friday after work. I was beginning to drink for the first time and wasn't losing in those inevitable dice games to determine who bought the next round of drinks.
>
> When I arrived at the home, I sensed an immediate feeling of welcome. The warm and caring environment kept drawing me back and eventually I became involved in the Bible studies Tom was leading. Through the careful exposition of the Scriptures, I began to realize that my eternal destiny was not as secure as I thought. One evening after the study, Tom further explained the plan of salvation. For the first time I understood that I could

know I was saved and it was forever! Tom showed me Ephesians 2:8-9. "For by grace are ye saved through faith; and that not of yourselves, it is the gift of God—not of works, lest any man should boast." A few days later in my room, I placed my trust in Christ as Savior. My spiritual journey began in February of 1965.

The next fifteen months were filled with one life-changing experience after another. For the first time in my life I saw what a Christian family looked like. Tom and Dotty's modeling convinced me that I wanted my marriage to look like theirs. Because I was engaged at the time to Liz, my high school sweetheart, I knew I would soon have the opportunity to put those principles into practice. Solid and challenging Bible teaching at the Servicemen's Bible Conferences at Baguio helped ground me in my Christian walk. Taking the trip to the Banaue rice terraces and seeing the ministries conducted there exposed me to the greater work of missions.

After awhile Tom even trusted me to assist with some of the home's bookkeeping and financial matters. Little did we know that in God's providence I would become the chief financial officer of OCSC/Cadence in 1982. Part of the joy of working at the headquarters now is hearing similar stories of how young men and women are experiencing the love of Christ through the ministry of hospitality by Cadence's dedicated servants.

Tom was generously endowed with the "gift" of delegation. He seldom did anything he could get the men to do, knowing it would help their spiritual growth. One time the brakes on our car were needing repair. When he shared this, one of the newer guys, not a believer, eagerly offered to do the job. With Tom helping, he jacked up the car and started pulling off a wheel. But it stuck tight. Putting his shoulder firmly against the car, he gave a hard yank. The car crashed down off the jack, pinning the man under the fender. Horrified, adrenaline pumping, Tom lifted the car enough for the man to roll out. "My hand, my hand!" the airman shouted. Tom looked down to see that a finger had been cut off. Wrapping the injured hand in a cloth, Tom helped him to our van and rushed him to the emergency room on the base.

When the doctor saw the stub, he asked, "Did you bring the finger?" Stunned, Tom ran to the van, sped home, crawled under the car, and found the missing appendage. Wrapping it in a wet cloth, he raced back to the hospital. The doctor tried to reattach the finger but was unsuccessful. Later in the hospital room, Tom shared his sadness about the young man losing his finger but then explained that the Lord had given much more so he could have eternal life. Seeing the analogy, the young man placed his trust in Christ. At the next Victory Hour, he gave testimony of how he had lost his finger but found something much better—Jesus Christ. The next Andrew dinner he brought two unsaved friends who received Christ also.

Twice each year all three of the OCSC ministries in the Philippines worked together to hold a servicemen's Bible conference in the resort city of Baguio. Missionary speakers like Cyril Brooks, Ed Spahr, Ray Frame, Bill Arvin, and Norm MacIntosh opened the Word of God in a manner rarely heard today. An OCSC missionary also spoke at each conference. Of course, when Jesse Miller, our mission director came, his messages were a highlight. It seemed whenever he opened the Word of God, a shadowy curtain drew back, giving us a fresh glimpse of Jesus, "my Lord," as Jesse so lovingly called him. At the end of each conference, an opportunity to share was given to those who had made a decision during the week. One Saturday night four men stood to testify that they had received

Tom and Sid Hendry singing at the Servicemen's Bible Conference

Christ as Savior and twenty-six from Clark and a number from other places stood to say they had crowned the Lord Jesus king of their lives and would follow him at any cost. Only eternity will reveal the work the Holy Spirit did in the lives of people at those conferences.

Our last year at Clark was one of the most exciting in our lives. The role of the U.S. Air Force in Vietnam was at its peak. Hearts were open to the Gospel more than ever before. Our adult Sunday School class on base, hosted by Hal and Connie Taylor, rose to about seventy-five in attendance, many responding to the claims of Christ.

Every meeting at the home was at maximum capacity. God gave us men like Obe Hokanson, Bill Sandven, Bill Needham, and Jim Stewart to enhance the work. Both singles and families participated in the ministry as well as teachers, technical representatives, and other Americans working on the base. And we had so much fun! Every night laughter filled the home whether it was during a volleyball game in the yard, at a meal, at the ping-pong table, or during a sing time. The joy of the Lord just filled that place!

In May 1967 Tom went to Denver for a Mission Council meeting. Until that time OCSC was governed by the five men of the council: Jesse Miller, Chairman; C.P. Tarkington (located on Okinawa); Sid Hendry (in Taiwan); and Dick Patty and Tom Hash (in the Philippines). With the mission experiencing significant growth, the men determined it was time to go from an internal governing body to an external board of directors. Jesse Miller was designated Executive Secretary at that meeting. That mission structure continues to this day.

While Tom was gone, the mature men at the home took on strong leadership roles. Obe Hokanson, short in

The joy of music was a highlight at the home. Obe Hokanson leads on his Coke box

stature but tall in spiritual maturity and giftedness, taught the Bible classes. He was also a dynamic song leader. We all retain the vivid memory of Obe perched on wooden Coke boxes, master sergeant stripes covering his whole sleeve, enthusiastically leading the singing at most meetings. When his wife, Mary Ann, and their children arrived, they rented the house next door to the home and became not only our dear friends but also our co-workers. We have always considered it unique that our Danny received Christ personally at a Bible club led by Mary Ann while their daughter Rhoda accepted Christ under Tom's ministry.

During our years at Clark, 1964 to 1968, the Lord sent a host of fine career missionaries to OCSC. As the war in Vietnam escalated, military forces were sent to Japan, Taiwan, and Thailand, as well as to Vietnam. Chaplain Dave Meschke, stationed at Sasebo, Japan, began the work there in 1964, with Erv Meyer being the first official OCSC director. Sid Hendry went to Taiwan to assume the Hospitality House from another organization. Annette Mitchell (Margaret Patty's sister) joined him there and they were married in 1965. (Incidentally, that ministry was already named the "Hospitality House," the title given to many new OCSC ministries after that.) Clyde and Jane Taylor took over "Welcome Inn" at Tai Chung, Taiwan in 1966.

Lem and Marge Morgan opened our first and only ministry in Vietnam, at NhaTrang, in 1966. Their children, Cindy and Paul, stayed in the Philippines attending Faith Academy where our OCSC teacher, Barb France (later Musgrove), and Tom and I were their sponsors. Lou and Linda Harrison came to Asia planning to establish another work in Vietnam. However, after the Tet Offensive in 1968, all military personnel were restricted to the base, so OCSC leadership determined it was too dangerous to attempt. (Another book!)

Because the U.S. military utilized national air bases throughout Thailand to initiate air strikes on Vietnam, vast numbers of airmen were stationed there. Jesse and Nettie Miller laid the groundwork for the opening of ministries to the men at Korat by Darl and Jan Goode in 1967; at Ubon by Bill Kramer (later joined by Jeannette) in 1968; at Nakon Phanom by Paul and Carol Kelley in 1968; and at Utapao (Sattahip) by Lou and Linda Harrison in 1969.

Most of these new missionaries spent a short period of time with us at Clark for orientation, planting within our hearts an embryo of desire to help train new workers. This seed germinated during our next two terms, and came to fruition when Tom became a field director in 1978.

The time for furlough was nearing. Bob and Dorothy Bingham, who had worked both at Subic and at Sangley their previous term, were asked to take our place. One of our projects before leaving was to replace the Greenbriar bus with a new, twenty-five passenger Nissan bus from Japan. The Lord provided the cost of $3620 mostly through the faithful giving of the men at the home. Because the order was placed before we left, the bus was delivered to the Binghams.

For the last two years of our time at Clark, the future of our building hung in the balance. The owner of the compound where it was located gave us notice after notice of dates we must vacate, but then changed his mind. Much effort went into searching for a new location, always ending in discouragement. We figured it would take an eight bedroom house to provide the facilities we had there. Of course, nothing like that was available. The home never did relocate and it was closed in 1981.

The farewell party given by the chapel and home family was a gala affair. We wept as gracious words were spoken about our four-and-a-half years in that community. Plaques were presented by the chaplains and commanding general, who thanked us for our service in the chapel.

For Christmas that year the folks at the home gave us five pieces of beautiful matching Samsonite luggage in anticipation of our furlough. After all these years, those bags are still a joyful reminder of those wonderful years at Clark. With the suitcases packed, dressed in our finest clothes, the Hash family boarded the plane on June 17, 1968 bound for the U.S. As we settled into our seats, I felt like a mother hen sheltering her little brood. I wept for joy, thanking the Lord that my precious children were close by, not to be separated again. But there was also sorrow as we waved goodbye to the dearest bunch of people we had ever known. We still marvel that the Lord counted us worthy to be there at such a significant time in the lives of so many. To this day, many of those folks are our dear friends, faithful supporters, and diligent prayer warriors.

The Hash family in 1968

Part VII

Our Second Furlough

Chapter 23

"I LOVE THEM MORE THAN YOU DO!"

In 1967, Jesse Miller had a severe heart attack. Dick Patty was appointed Executive Secretary of OCSC in 1967 in his place. Then in September 1968, Dick was given the assignment permanently with the new title of Executive Director. Sid Hendry was also designated Director of Financial Affairs around that time. It was with great joy we accepted the invitation to spend our furlough year assisting in the home office of OCSC with these dear friends and co-workers.

Since 1961, the home office had been located in a donated church building which the Millers remodeled into an office upstairs and missionary apartment downstairs. With the significant growth of the mission, more workers had been added to the home staff. Now it was time to construct more offices in the upstairs area. This was Tom's assignment for our year of furlough—he helped with the construction and I did the interior decorating.

Harriet Rehnke lived next door to the office building. It wasn't long before she was volunteering in the mail room, shoveling snow from the sidewalks, and generally taking ownership of the facility. Eventually she was paid a minimal salary and her faithful service to the Lord continues to this day, as she has made the adjustments from hand addressing envelopes, to an Addressograph machine, and to computerized systems.

When Harriet learned we were looking for a home, she pointed us to her son, Robert, who rented us a darling three-bedroom place at a price we could afford. Then, to our amazement, a couple going overseas for a year let us use their furniture, including a lovely spinet piano. The Lord's provision for us was remarkable in our eyes. After living so long in a servicemen's center and having our children away from us, this cozy house was more than we had ever dreamed.

Of course, we spent a portion of that year reporting to our faithful donors and supporting churches. Reunions with alumni from our ministries were also a highlight of our furlough.

Toward the end of the year, Dick Patty asked if we would be willing to return to the Philippines to direct the Subic Service Center. Tom was excited and felt God was leading, but I didn't want to go. I knew about Olongapo, the city outside of Subic Naval Base—a place with crime, corruption, filth, bars, prostitutes—and little else. And the Subic center was located right in the middle of it. *Lord, I protested, You can't ask us to take our 8, 10, and 12 year old children to Olongapo for four years. Not at this impressionable age. You must have cut the wrong orders this time.*

Once again the Lord helped me remember those words, "Trust in the Lord with all your heart..." from Proverbs 3:5. God was again saying, *Don't try to figure it out your own way. Trust me. I love them more than you do. I'll take care of them.* Gradually my fears subsided. We were on our way to Subic.

On our last Sunday at our Berean Fundamental Church in Lakewood, Colorado, we had a Clark reunion of all in the area. During the evening service we re-enacted a Friday night Victory Hour at the servicemen's home. We sang and shared testimonies, and then Tom gave a short message. It was fun and gave the folks at the church a glimpse of what goes on in our ministry.

Bob and Elaine Heavner were there. Because we had led Elaine to the Lord, she had asked Tom to baptize her. He was honored to do so. At the end of the service Elaine solemnly stepped into the baptismal with Bob at her side. She gave a short testimony of her faith in Christ, and then Tom prayed and lowered her into the water. As he lifted her out, his eyes caught a glimpse of something floating on the water. *Oh, no!* he gasped inwardly. *It's a rat!*

Bob and Elaine started up the steps out of the water. Tom gave a sigh of relief. They hadn't spotted it. Then he heard snickering and then laughter. Not knowing what to do, the pastor closed the service with prayer, dismissing the congregation. Hurrying to the back, Tom found Bob and Elaine doubled over with laughter as Elaine held up the "rat"—her detached hairpiece.

Once again we traveled to say our farewells to supporting churches, individuals, and family members. Forever etched in my mind is the memory of my parents, arm in arm, waving good-by in front of their country home in Wisconsin. As we drove out of the yard, tears flowed freely. "I may never see them again!" I sobbed to Tom. Matthew 10:37 took on a new meaning to me that day, "He that loveth father or mother more than me is not worthy of me." It was my last glimpse of my father. He died of heart failure three years later.

Part VIII

Subic Bay

Chapter 24

OLONGAPO CITY

Our trip to the Philippines, with stops in Honolulu, Tokyo, and Hong Kong ended in Manila at 4 a.m. on July ll, 1969. We were dead tired but glad to be on the ground to stay.

After four hours of sleep, we began the hot, bumpy ride north to Subic Bay. Little had changed in the year we had been gone except that we felt hotter and stickier than we could ever remember. As we topped the mountain on the zigzag road and began the descent into Olongapo, the city outside the base, our discomfort gave way to depression and discouragement. The area surrounding the Subic Service Center was filthy! Sin was flagrant and disgusting. Our only joy came in knowing God had brought us—and that was by faith, not by feeling.

The center itself was fabulous. Approximately four times larger than the Clark home, its 8,000 square feet of space had been perfectly planned and built by Dick Patty and Ray Kalbach. It was located just outside the main gate of the base. The men walked across the Olongapo River—the only one I had ever seen that was so dirty burning refuse could float on it—turned right and were at the door. A sign at the corner read, *Don't go wrong—go right—to the Subic Service Center.* It was awesome to pray that God would fill all those rooms with sailors. But he certainly did.

Subic Service Center

When Ben and Connie Cady handed over the keys, we were engulfed by a somber feeling of inadequacy. We knew absolutely nothing about the Navy. We had to learn a new "language"—Navy jargon. At our "change of command" ceremony, they jokingly gave us a *Blue Jacket's Manual* (the official Navy handbook), but I hid in the office for days reading it from cover to cover. I didn't know the difference between a destroyer and an aircraft carrier, the black shoe Navy from the brown shoe Navy. And "gator Navy" sounded like some sort of reptile to me. And the abbreviations! The Air Force didn't come close in that arena! Finally realizing the only way to learn was to admit my ignorance, I'd simply ask as a sailor walked into the center, "What does that mean?" as I pointed to the insignia on his uniform. When he said his ship was a DD, I said, "What's that?" Actually, many took great joy in educating us. We grew to love the vast traditional customs and culture of the Navy. From a practical standpoint, it certainly helped us to better prepare for dinner when we knew whether a CVA with 5,000 men on board or a DD with 200 was in port.

Subic Servicemen's Center from on base, across the Olongapo river

There was a good group of permanent party men stationed at Subic and the adjoining Cubi Naval Air Station who came regularly to the center, most of them having a keen interest in the things of the Lord. After experiencing such an effective work with the airmen at Clark, we endeavored for weeks to use the same format with this group. But just when things looked encouraging, the fleet would arrive, and it all went awry. It took some time for reality to set in—this was not Clark. So when the ships were at sea, Tom gave his energies to the regulars. When the ships came in, they became our key workers to reach out to the fleet.

On August 8 Typhoon Viola hit. It was Sunday morning. We were preparing to leave for the base where Tom taught a Sunday school class at the chapel. The winds were high, the rains just beginning. During one strong gust, we heard a thud. Rushing to a window we saw, to our horror, that a two-story high wall had fallen against the side of the center. The wall was the remains of a gas station that had burned the previous year and had protected the center building from catching fire. The burned station had been removed, leaving the wall beside the large vacant lot. Fortunately it didn't break–it just leaned, crushing a drain trough. But its position was precarious. If it cracked, it would take out the whole side of the downstairs lounge.

Tom rushed onto the base to his waiting class. When he told them what had happened and that he didn't have a clue about what to do about it, one of the men showed interest, excusing himself from the class. Before long several high ranking men from Public Works on the base were standing at the wall, deciding what to do. "It's definitely a hazard to both Americans and Filipinos," one declared, rubbing his chin.

"It's got to come down," agreed another. Within a few hours, several mobile cranes began inching their way out the gate to the vacant lot, which was now cordoned off for safety. Two iron braces from the cranes were fastened lengthwise around the back of the wall. Then they were hooked to a bulldozer which gently pulled until they were taut. By then a large crowd of curious spectators had assembled. Slowly, slowly the bulldozer inched forward. Then a strong tug. The entire wall rose straight upright and then slammed over into the vacant lot, landing with a deafening roar. Dust, debris, and hats went flying. Shouts and whistles went up from the watching crowd. The job was accomplished without a hitch. Funds from the Subic chapel paid the meager charge for the service; then the

Cubi chapel gave us money to build a new wall at a safer height.

The war in Vietnam continued with a vengeance. After the Tet Offensive in 1968, American ground troops were gradually withdrawn, placing the burden of battle into the hands of the Navy. The Seventh Fleet was augmented into a mighty seagoing force. WestPacs (Western Pacific cruises) were extended up to a year or more. Subic Bay was the first port after leaving Hawaii. Young sailors on their first cruise soon learned that Olongapo was a place unlike any other with 600 bars, 3500 "registered" (supposedly free of venereal disease) prostitutes, and where a million dollars a month was spent by men like themselves. Many called it "the armpit of the world"—a place to forget any morals they ever knew and have fun! (One ship's newspaper quipped, "...and the Subic Service Center is the Right Guard!") The old salts regaled the recruits with stories of their exploits in "Po City." Wide eyed, these fresh-faced young men flooded out the gate straight into the arms of Satan himself.

The poem I wrote for our 1969 Christmas newsletter describes it well:

CHRISTMAS IN OLONGAPO

'Twas the night before Christmas and all through the town
The juke boxes blared out a loud, raspy sound;
From out of the racket somewhere down the street
Came *Joy to the World* with a rock and roll beat.

The clubs, dimly lighted, six-hundred or more
Were open—the hostesses stood at the door.
The girls had all fashioned their dresses with care,
Their nails were all polished, they'd fixed every hair.

The men in their uniforms glistening white
Were out for a fling in "Po City" that night,
The money they'd saved many days out at sea
Could buy about anything. (Nothing was free!)

One strolled down the street toward the lights and the noise
And made conversation with two school-age boys;
"Hey, Joe," they said, "we know a place you can meet
The prettiest girls to be seen on this street!"

They pulled on his arm as to show him the way;
He answered, "Naw, just wanna look! Go away!"
They ran down the street and were lost in the throng.
The sailor then noticed his wrist-watch was gone.

"Buy me a drink?" asked a girl with brown skin;
(Once she was pretty, but this life of sin
Had taken its toll.) Then she snuggled in near;
"Okay," he said, "Bring her a glass of cold beer!"

Then out on the street there arose a commotion;
They ran from the bar to the door in one motion,
In time just to see a young sailor emerge
From a doorway—he uttered a filthy curse-word.

He fell then, a bullet wound showed in his head;
His assailant stood staring, then turned 'round and fled.
A trickle of blood, then a pool on the ground;
The crowd was so quiet, no one made a sound.

It seemed that he lay there an awfully long time
Silent and still. Then a high, distant whine
Was heard. It came closer, so slowly it seemed,
As it threaded its way through the street to the scene.

They brought out the stretcher, the Shore Patrol crew,
Then lifted him on it— 'twas all they could do;
Then gently they covered his face with a sheet,
As *Joy to the World* played in rock and roll beat.

The crowd dispersed slowly, back to the clubs,
Back to the liquor, the kisses and hugs,
Back to the hotels (they pay by the hour),
Back to the reefers, the pot, and the mire.

Staggering back to the ships in the bay,
Many just fell in the street on the way;
Others were dragged by a buddy less drunk,
Dumped in their vomit and clothes on their bunk.

Back in Olongapo, back in the town
Juke boxes one by one quieted down;
Away in the distance somewhere down the street
Echoed *Joy to the World* with a rock and roll beat.

Most of the men in white who walked out the gate into Olongapo—our keen, clean shaven young American guys—were not looking for a quiet place to read and write letters and keep away from sin! We were there—right outside the gate, but most couldn't care less! At midnight as they staggered back onto the base, they were utterly pathetic! We wanted desperately to reach out to them.

But some of the Christian men truly yearned to keep from yielding to the sin of that wicked place. Ray Hauser, who has served as a missionary with OCSC/Cadence for many years remembers his first trip out the gate:

It was 1969. I was a nineteen-year-old sailor on board the USS *Samuel Gompers.* It was my first time away from home and we were pulling into Subic Bay in the Philippines. I had met one other Christian, George McIntire, on board the ship of over 600 men. The sailors, especially the old salts, talked in detail about Olongapo, the city outside the base. But George told me about this Christian place—the Subic Service Center.

Being a new Christian of just a few months and having just experienced my first two weeks at sea, I was anxious to find Christian fellowship. So when the ship docked, I headed for the Subic Service Center.

Following the directions I was given, I walked through the main gate and stepped onto a short bridge spanning a small river. It smelled like raw sewage. A number of young Filipino boys were diving from this bridge for coins the sailors threw into the dark brown polluted water. I was in Olongapo. My senses were accosted by the filth, the sweltering heat and humidity, the dirty little children running through the streets picking the pockets of unsuspecting sailors, the cages where the children were confined when caught by heavily armed police, and the music blasting from juke boxes in the hundreds of bars lining the main street. In the first half block, I was propositioned by several prostitutes. I came to the first cross street and turned right. A half block away was the Subic Service Center.

As I walked through the door it was as though I was back home. Behind me was this weird and scary world; in front of me were Tom and Dotty Hash, who welcomed me into the safe, clean haven. If there ever was a time I needed someone it was then, and they were there for me.

Though I was a believer, it was in this center and under the Hashes' ministry that the foundations for my Christian life were laid. I had grown up in the church but I didn't experience regeneration until the night before I entered boot camp. Now the combination of being overseas and away from home opened my heart and mind to the things of the Lord like nothing else ever had. I was ready to benefit from the ministry the Lord had for me in that place. I directly link my being involved in missions and ministry today to walking through the doors of the Subic Service Center.

One evening a sailor dropped in at the center to "check us out" on his first night in Olongapo. Tom played some ping-pong with him, asking about his background. "My dad's a pastor," he replied, "but I've had enough of his preaching. I wanna have some fun!" He headed for the door.

"Where are you going?" Tom asked.

"I just want to see the town," was his hasty reply.

"That's no place for a Christian," Tom warned. "Satan is waiting for you on those streets." Then Tom quickly went through four steps in backsliding so the young man would be warned: 1) I tell you; 2) a friend and I tell you; 3) we take it to the church; 4) we turn you over to Satan. But he headed out the door anyway.

About an hour later he came back. His cocky look was gone, replaced by an ashen, wide-eyed stare. "Well, how was it out there?" Tom asked.

"Man, I don't ever want to go there again. I'm not willing to run *that* far from the Lord!" he responded shaking his head. From then on he came to the center regularly whenever he was in port. We prayed that more men would be frightened like that.

Olongapo was a dangerous place to live. We were careful but knew our safety was in God's hands. Each night before the children went to sleep, we prayed, "Lord, please keep us safe tonight. And please be with Alfonso, our night watchman, as he and our dog walk around the center all night." One morning

"When I walked through the door, I was back home."

The chuck wagon at the Subic center

The sailors took pride in presenting their ship's plaque for display at the center

Sunday night vespers at the Subic Center

just before dawn, we were jolted awake by a loud knock on our door. "Mr. Hash! Mr. Hash! There's been a robber!" It was Alfonso. Our hearts sank.

All five of us jumped out of bed, opening the door to see Fonso standing there, his eyes wide. "There was a robber, but I scared him away!" he stammered. In our jammies, all five of us followed him down the stairs, outside, and around to the back of the building. Sure enough the screen was cut. Someone had tried to get into the office. Alfonso had come around the corner just in time to frighten him away. We stood in awe. Danny's eyes were wide. "Wow—a real live robber!"

Later that day after the children left for school, I walked around to look at the window and again thank the Lord for his protection. There, pinned to the cut screen, was a note scribbled by eight-year-old Danny. *Dear Mr. Robber. I think you should know that* ***GOD*** *lives in this place!* We never had another robber.

Usually there was a handful of Christians who timidly came into the center right after landing in Subic the first time. We could always tell a first timer by the way he looked around as he entered the door. Tom and I were there to welcome him to a safe haven in a very stormy sea. Home cooked meals, chocolate chip cookies, a cozy bunk room that slept fifteen, times of singing around the piano, and good Bible teaching kept them coming back rather than going downtown. Their in-port period was usually only two to three days long; then they left for the Gulf of Tonkin off the coast of Vietnam. There for sixty days they faced the perils of war twenty-four hours a day.

When the ship returned, the Christian group had often doubled in size. The men who had been at the center before eagerly brought out the new believers. We poured our lives into theirs for two or three days; then they were gone again. Immediately a new battle group arrived and we repeated the process. The Christian men were faithful in getting out the word about the center.

By 1971 over 100 men came in most evenings. We planned a sit-down dinner for seventy each night. The dining room held about fifty, so the rest ate in our adjacent living room. The food was placed on a buffet table with two lines. If it looked like it might not stretch, I served the entree onto each person's plate to make sure it went around. It was important that everyone have a first serving, but we didn't worry about seconds. The men were very understanding. The cooks kept a supply of canned pork and beans in the pantry and hot dogs in the freezer, so that if we ran out of food, we could come up with "beanie-wienies" in no time.

To keep family continuity, all five Hashes sat together each evening as did our co-directors. Several fellows could join each unit at their table, so the guys were not isolated from us. We had so much fun! Peals of laughter would be heard at a table over here, or someone would break into a song over there.

Years later when we were on furlough, someone asked Danny, "What are you going to be when you grow up?"

Not missing a beat, he quipped, "I'm going to be a missionary on furlough! You get to go through the supper line first!"

After dinner Tom led a time of testimony and singing. How they loved to sing! The "Jesus People" movement was taking place in America, especially in southern California, ushering in a whole new style of music. These men came directly from there. Tom and I warmly embraced the new form, realizing how much it meant to the men. I learned to play the new songs on the piano. We made our own song sheets (a no-no we learned later), adding pages as we learned new songs. We encouraged those who played the guitar to do so.

Usually Tom allowed only those who had come to Christ since the last in-port to share their testimony or we would have been there all night. Tears flowed unashamed as a sailor told of his new-found faith in Christ. What joy!

After the sing time Tom taught a Bible lesson. Aware that his next opportunity to open God's Word to them would be two months away, he carefully prepared his lessons to meet their immediate needs. During the Bible study, I usually went upstairs to spend time with the children while they prepared for bed. When the study ended, I returned to serve the refreshments.

We had a 16mm movie projector (before the days of videos, of course) and a fair-sized library of Christian films. After the Bible study Tom often started a movie in the air-conditioned lounge for those who wanted to watch. While it ran, he played ping-pong or witnessed to someone, keeping an eye out for the end of the film. Then he went in and gave an

Dotty playing the piano so the men could sing

invitation for men to receive Christ. Usually one or two (or more) responded, so Tom or one of the other faithful men would talk to them, confirming their decision. Later in the evening, I often went to the piano where a bunch of guys gathered around to sing. Sometimes the joyful music went on for hours until my fingers ached and my body dripped with perspiration from being surrounded, unable to get a breath of fresh air. But it was worth it!

We knew the tremendous value of Christian literature in the lives of the men. Our little Christian bookstore was always humming with activity. I spent most evenings there, talking with the guys and pointing them to books I knew would help in their growth in the Lord. The last thing a new believer needed was a thirty-pound "family Bible." Often we encouraged someone with no Christian background to start with a Bible story book along with a Bible.

We didn't utilize the financial profit from book sales to run the center ministry. Instead we returned some of it to Overseas Missionary Fellowship (OMF), the group that imported the books for us in order to keep a good supply coming. We also gave national pastors a big discount on Bibles and study books because one book could cost them a week's wages. We also gave away many books and distributed thousands of tracts as part of the ministry.

The more mature Christians loved stocking up on good books to take back to the ship. They would keep them in their footlockers for a few days at sea until all the junky stuff on the ship had been read. Then they started leaving good books lying around. One guy told us, "I went into the head (bathroom) and found this book, *The Late Great Planet Earth.* I couldn't put it down! It scared the hell out of me! I accepted Christ as my Savior right there in the bathroom." Not all were that dramatic, but God used Christian books.

The bookstore always hummed with activity.
Dotty bantering with a sailor.

The air-conditioned bunk room was a welcome respite from life aboard ship. We ordered new sheets, bedspreads, rugs, and matching towels from the States to make it homey. The sailors signed up for space as soon as they arrived at the center. We also had a number of futons they could use when the beds were full. On special occasions we even let them sleep on the couches in the lounge. We encouraged the permanent party men to use the bunk room only when the ships were out at sea. They were very understanding.

The center closed officially at 11 p.m. If there were many sailors still in the center, Tom loaded them into the twenty-five passenger Nissan bus and drove them back to their ships. As he stopped at the gate where all IDs were checked, someone often called out, *Attitude Check!* The whole bus resounded with *Praise the Lord!* Then they sang chorus after chorus all the way to the carrier dock across the bay. Many times Tom could barely stay awake for the return trip.

Because the center officially opened in the afternoon, I spent most mornings working in the office. With high bookstore sales each night, the shelves needed restocking and inventory records needed to be kept. (No computers or electronic calculators then—only a hand operated adding machine.) Correspondence and Bible study preparation were also done in the morning hours. Tom's days were spent preparing his studies for each evening, meeting chaplains on base, and overseeing the maintenance on the large building. The phone seldom worked, the electricity often failed, and it seemed something always needed repair.

One time we received a new full-length Christian film and announced to the center full of men that it would be shown that evening. Suddenly we were engulfed by an intense electrical storm. One bolt of lightning cracked so hard most of us jumped from our chairs. The whole town was plunged into blackness. The sudden silence of the juke boxes gave an eerie stillness, disturbed only by the raindrops hitting hard on the nearby tin roofs. The ever-present candles were lit and we all sat in the soft glow wondering what to do next. We had a small generator for such emergencies which Tom tried in vain to start. Then suddenly the city lights came back on—but not ours. Assessing the situation, Tom determined the transformer beside our building had been hit by the lightning bolt. He dispatched Alfonso, our night watchman, downtown to get someone to repair the damage. Soon two city employees arrived in a rickety jeep. "Oh, sir," they said, "it needs a new fuse."

"Well, please go get one," Tom replied. "We have a meeting going on here."

"Oh, sir, we don't have any. *You'll* have to buy one at the hardware store downtown." Tom got the necessary pesos and they set off for the purchase.

Soon they were back. *Now we really have a problem, Tom mused. That transformer is at the top of a twenty-five foot pole and they don't have a ladder.* Then he watched in amazement as they began to assemble pieces of bamboo pole, binding them together with pieces of cut-up inner tube. On the end they placed a bent coat hangar. *They can't even see up there!* Tom reasoned. No problem! One man held the pole while the other pulled off a headlight from the jeep. It was attached by long wires just for that purpose. He held the light so it shone on the transformer, the other man removed and replaced the fuse, and they returned the light into the socket of the jeep. Instantly the center lights blazed on. Tom's "thank yous" trailed off as the men drove away. Standing there in the rain Tom reflected admiringly, *I wonder if it was the Filipinos who invented the phrase "necessity—the mother of invention."*

The vile, flagrant sin in Olongapo was disgusting. But we knew in the bowels of those bars and places of prostitution were some innocent, young Filipino girls who came from the provinces because they could earn money. Some were sent by their parents to help feed the family. But before long they were immersed in the cesspool of sexual slavery, possessions of the club owners. The ultimate goal for a bar girl was to marry a "rich" American and go to the States. The steps in that process were to meet a sailor or marine who would "keep" her when he was out at sea, sending money for rent, food, and clothing and assuming she would be available when he came back into port. For security, if she was lucky, she might have one or two more men "keeping" her. Of course, she could also ply her trade when her "men" were out at sea. It was a roulette game with the chance that both of her men might come in at the same time. Violence often erupted as a result with one or more of the trio being killed.

If all went well for the girl, the sailor went through the paperwork and procedures for an official marriage. Then she received an American passport and ID card so she could shop on the base. The lucrative black market was the result of many of these wives who bought in the commissary or exchange and sold the valuable items for a profit to merchants who then sold them in shops throughout the country.

Marriages performed in Olongapo were not considered legal by the authorities on base. One day a frustrated marine came into the center. "I got married to a girl last night," he groaned, "but I was so drunk I didn't find out her last name or where she lives." I don't recall if we were able to assist him in any way or not, but the sad incident remained in our memories.

Occasionally out of curiosity a young sailor wandered into the center with a bar girl in tow. The moment she walked in our door and saw me—an American woman—she felt ill-at-ease. As the young man played ping-pong or got a Coke at the chuck wagon, she sat as near the door as possible or pulled on his arm saying, "Let's go!" Often I or a woman co-worker sat down beside the girls to tell them of Christ. They always left with a tract explaining the way of salvation and the name of the church down the street where they could seek counsel.

The greatest heartache was to see the small children (mostly Amerasian) on the streets. The boys quickly learned to snatch a sailor's watch or wallet while his buddy distracted him or to lead a sailor to his "sister" who paid him to do so. But the little girls selling cigarettes, gum, and candy broke our hearts the most. We knew they would soon graduate to a more lucrative business.

The mail situation at Subic was even more troublesome than it had been at Clark. We had our own mail box at the post office in downtown Olongapo, but that didn't seem to help. One time Tom and I went inside to speak to the postmaster about our lack of mail. Waving to our box, he said, "Find it yourself." So we looked around the area. Mail was everywhere.

We crawled under some desks, looking through the piles. We found several pieces addressed to us, some with money inside. It was very discouraging.

When Tom's Aunt Ida died (she had been his "mother" during his teen years and was "grandma" to our children), Tom's sister sent a telegram. It was received in Manila that same day but then put into a regular envelope and mailed to us. It arrived three weeks later. Missionary Dad Brooks in Manila read about her death in an OCSC publication before we even knew. This was very painful. We called Tom's sister as soon as we heard explaining the situation but were never sure the family fully understood why we had not acknowledged the sad event.

Two years later when my father died, my mother notified us through the Red Cross on the base. I called immediately, but it was just one hour before the funeral. When Tom's father became ill later that year, Tom did make a very quick trip to Kentucky, for his father was not a believer. Just before Tom arrived, a nearby preacher led his father to Christ. Tom had the great joy of hearing his father acknowledge that decision. He died two days after Tom returned to the Philippines. It was difficult to have three parents die during that term and not be able to attend their funerals. Maybe that's what the Bible means when it says we leave father and mother to follow Christ.

Learning of our great distress with the postal system, the chaplain was able to get permission for us to receive letters (no packages) through the U.S. mail system on the base. So for the last two years at Subic, that stress was relieved.

Chapter 25

FAITHFUL SERVANTS

As more and more sailors found refuge at the Subic Service Center, the task of keeping the ministry operating became monumental. Ten wonderful Christian Filipinos worked to keep the building spotless and the meals prepared. Because automatic washers or dryers were impractical under those circumstances, all thirty sheets, pillowcases and towels were hung on the line each day. Alfonso watched over us all night. We became a fine-tuned team. Even though we were their employers, we all knew the ministry could not happen without them. They worked twelve-hour days, six days a week, usually with a smile. When we first arrived, we told them, "When there is money, we all eat; when there is no money, nobody eats." They ate two or three meals at our place each day. We provided the funds for them to buy rice, fish, and vegetables which they cooked in the laundry room. (They didn't particularly like American food.) We laughed together. We cried together. We prayed together. Their needs such as doctor, dental, or family problems became ours to share. We dearly loved them.

Faithful servants: Florentina Salang, Nita Labasan, Paz Falloran

One of Tom's most humbling experiences happened early in our time at Subic. It was the day he didn't have enough money to pay all they had earned. Assuring them it would be available soon, he gave them what he had. A short time later, one by one, several of those precious Christians came into the office, placing some of their meager salary on his desk. We wept. Within a day or so the funds came in. Their pay envelopes contained all back pay and a little extra besides.

Our helpers didn't have to ask for pay raises. As the center funds increased and they had to work harder, longer hours, we compensated them. We were careful to keep their salary levels equal to or a little higher than they could have earned on the base. If we hired a new worker who was not a believer, the others were faithful in their witness and soon won them to the Lord. We held a Bible study for them weekly with Tom or one of our co-workers teaching. Those times of discussion gave insightful glimpses into their hearts and lives.

In my first year at Clark I had the silly notion that I could share my kitchen with our cook, Rosie. After that year of utter frustration for both of us, I determined either she or I had to go. I went! Having learned that lesson well, I surrendered the kitchen in our Subic apartment to the house girls. They used it for all the center cooking. There was another apartment in the facility where our co-workers lived. We wanted to keep that kitchen private for them. The arrangement worked well.

Since the cook was the highest skilled worker among the women, she usually was the overseer for the others. I planned the menus each week, providing recipes she would need. I gave her a petty cash fund to use for the purchase of fresh fruits and vegetables and locally baked bread. She kept accurate records of money spent. She felt I trusted her, which I did, and she saved me hours of work.

One morning the cook came to me with a puzzled look on her face. "Excuse me, ma'am," she said shyly, showing me the menu I had written out. "What is pluppy Jell-O?" Filipinos have difficulty pronouncing p's and f's, usually reversing the sounds. I had written "fluffy" Jell-O, which meant Jell-O mixed with whipped cream. She called it "pluppy." Of course we got a kick out of "prench pries" and "coppee fot" and they called Dick Patty "Mr. Fatty." I'm sure they were often equally amused by our foreign ways.

One day I was in the market buying some material for a dress. The clerk asked how long I had lived in the Philippines. When I replied, "Nine years," she responded, "Don't you speak Tagalog?"

A little ashamed, I excused myself by saying, "You Filipinos speak English so well, I haven't needed to learn Tagalog."

"But don't you learn Tagalog in elementary schools in America?" was her surprised remark. All Filipinos begin learning English in the early grades.

Art Lubasan was a middle-aged Filipino man, skilled in carpentry, whom we hired for special building projects. A godly man, he brought a special presence to the center. I loved talking with him as he sawed wood or painted. One day he announced, "I believe God is calling me to become a pastor. I am going to Bible school to prepare." I was astonished because he was the father of five growing children and I knew they had no money for such an undertaking. But he assured me that God would provide. The Bible school was located near Clark Air Base, a three to four hour bus ride away. He came home on weekends and worked odd jobs in his spare time.

His wife, Nita, became a dear friend to me. A fairly good seamstress, she took what jobs she could find sewing for Americans. I tried to give her as much work as possible and even taught her to make lined window drapes, an item in high demand by Americans.

Art completed his studies and took a pastorate in a town several hours north of Subic. But in 1985 he became ill from leukemia and the Lord took him home. Nita, committed to the education of her children, took a higher paying domestic job in Hong Kong, sending the money back to the children, who were cared for by relatives. We corresponded occasionally during that time.

Many years later, after we returned to America, we received a letter saying Nita's employer had brought her to the States and she was living in Maryland. In the letter was a check for our ministry. Tears fell as we sat in humble disbelief, wondering what to do with such a hallowed gift. We did put it into our account, but you can believe we were very careful how that money was spent. She was deeply loved by her employer who even paid her way to Colorado to visit us. Then she retired, moving back to the Philippines to be with her grown children and grandchildren. All of her children are college graduates, strong believers and servants of the Lord. I anticipate with great joy the day Art and Nita receive their reward in heaven. Mine will pale in comparison. I count my friendship with the Lubasans as one of my most cherished memories.

Art and Nita Lubason with their children in 1978.

On Mondays the center was closed. So every third Monday Tom and I set out for Manila to get supplies. The night before, Tom took the American dollars which the sailors had so generously donated from the safe, counted them carefully, and put them in a brown paper sack. Always taking one or two of our biggest sailors along, he walked the block to the money exchanger's hut on the corner. There were lots of vendors who would gladly exchange our coveted dollars, but only two of them were authorized by the Philippine government. Standing at the window, watching cautiously from the corner of his eye, Tom waited impatiently as the lady carefully counted the money. Then she put the exchange equivalent in the bag and handed it back to Tom. He returned home quickly, counting the pesos upon arrival. One night he was amazed to discover she had overpaid him by 100 pesos. He hurriedly retraced his steps, placing the bag of extra pesos on the counter at the window. When he explained the situation, the vendor was shocked. Stammering, she thanked Tom profusely. After that night, she had him go to the back side of the hut, tell her the amount, and leave immediately without anyone counting money. They trusted each other. And it was much safer for Tom.

As the ministry increased and the volume of purchases in Manila mounted, I was fearful as we left Olongapo with a briefcase full of pesos. Surely there were people who knew what we were doing. I imagine our guardian angels worked overtime during those trips. When a supermarket finally opened in Manila, we were able to charge our purchases, then pay by check the next time we came. The amount of cash we carried was thus reduced and my fears declined significantly.

Leaving before dawn to reach Manila, we bounced over the zigzag mountain, dodged carabaos and ox-carts, and cautiously slowed at each police checkpoint. Hot, sweaty, and dusty, we arrived in the city about the time the stores opened. We rushed from store to store, bought case upon case of groceries, boxes and boxes of Christian books, and several coolers of frozen meat. By evening we were exhausted. If items were still on the list, we stopped at the home of Ken and Elaine Brooks, missionaries with Christian Missions in Many Lands (CMML), who purchased them for us and shipped them on a local bus the following day. On our way out of town, we often stopped at a local steak house treating ourselves to an elegant dinner—at about $2.00 each.

Our van was filled wall to wall and floor to ceiling when we started the grueling trip home. A prime target for hijackers, we prayed for safety. The heavy loads and deep chuck holes were a dangerous combination. Many times we found ourselves beside the road where Tom unloaded the cases of stuff to retrieve the spare tire. When the center gate closed behind us, twenty hours after leaving that morning, we collapsed exhausted into bed, thanking the Lord for his protection.

On November 18, 1970, Typhoon Patsy careened into Manila, her 200 kilometer-an-hour winds virtually destroying Faith Academy, the school for missionary children. As soon as we heard the news, we headed for the city. Entering the outskirts, we saw wreckage everywhere. The electricity was off and the flooded streets caused endless detours. Eventually we climbed the hill up to the school. As we entered the campus, Tom stopped the car. We couldn't fathom the devastation. We just sat there and wept.

Dennis and Betty Ortman, missionaries with OCSC, were dorm parents of elementary girls. Betty had just given birth by C-section to their first baby girl. The typhoon rolled the sheet metal right off the roof of their house, dumping it in the front yard. The ceilings were saturated with water. One bathroom was completely exposed. By the time we arrived, the children had been picked up by their parents, but their clothes, books, and beds lay everywhere, soaking wet. What a mess! We stayed a day or two, putting mattresses and clothes out in the sun to dry. A deep heaviness engulfed the hearts of everyone at Faith. How would they ever rebuild?

The word got out and God's people responded. Money poured in. When the chaplains at Subic and on the ships heard, their response was immediate. They loaded up a helicopter with building supplies and men. Since they had no idea how to locate Faith from the air, they asked Tom to go along as "spotter." Landing in the athletic field, they soon unloaded the aircraft and went to work. School resumed before long, and when the reconstruction was complete, God had supplied funds and labor to make the facility even better than before. We were glad to be a part of that miracle.

Chapter 26

"I HAVE CALLED THIS CHILD"

The situation in which we and most other OCSC missionaries found ourselves was conflicting—neither fish nor foul. The missionary community, in which we actually fit best, did not consider us "missionaries" because we worked with and lived like Americans. We were not military, of course, so did not have access to all of the services and goods on the base. In most places, however, through the generosity of the chaplains, we were granted as much liberty as was legally possible. Sometimes this included the use of the medical services at a nominal cost—a precious commodity to us. We always held these privileges with open hands, being careful not to abuse them, aware they were privileges, not rights. The parameters under which we lived were determined by the Status of Forces Agreements (SOFA) between the United States and the host country. If the military had their way, we would have received full privileges. But in countries like the Philippines where there was an active black market, there had to be laws regarding goods taken from the bases.

Sometimes our own military folks who loved and cared for us became irate that we did not have more privileges. We carefully explained why, being careful not to join in their "pity party."

The children were able to attend school on the base during those four years at Subic, the costly tuition paid for by a host of dear friends. While it was wonderful to have them at home rather than in boarding school, it presented some unique problems too. They were about the only children in the school system to whom the exchange and commissary were not available. They didn't have base passes or I.D. cards. (Ours came from the chaplain.) They were given assignments to be done at the base library but were not permitted to enter without I.D. cards. When the classes had parties, we were asked to send items we could not obtain. So at the beginning of each school year, I sent a note to each teacher explaining the situation. *I'll send anything home-baked for the parties,* I assured them. Several of the teachers went the second mile, offering to purchase "American" notebooks and pencils for the children. I usually declined because it was technically illegal.

There was a prevalent prejudice of the American children against the Filipinos. It was not that the parents necessarily promoted the idea—it was just there, probably due to the wide gap between the national and the "rich American." The Filipinos often called Americans "Joes" from the term GI Joe. They always greeted us with "Hi, Joe!," not necessarily a derogatory term. But the prejudiced Americans would turn it around with contempt, calling them "Joes." The children in school soon learned that we lived on the economy. Of course, the thing to do was to exchange items from their lunch boxes. Danny was crushed when children in his class refused to exchange their "American" foods and sneered, "We don't eat *JOE* food!" So Tom and I scoured the up-scale stores in Manila (inexpensive for us) to find unique items for the children's lunches. Before long the kids were standing in line to see what Danny had brought, hoping for a trade. I know more than once he laughed, "But I thought you didn't like *JOE* food." Definitely the "old nature" coming out!

Tom and I have done numerous mental autopsies on the school situation. Now with 20/20 hindsight, we realize we sacrificed their education somewhat to have them at home, especially Danny. His first year at Subic was third grade. That year they initiated the innovative open classroom concept. Each time I visited I came away with the distinct feeling they were doing everything possible to keep a child from learning. With Danny's highly active body and short attention span, it was disastrous. Then too, many (not all, of course) of the young teachers took a "hardship" assignment to the Philippines in order to qualify for an attractive one in Europe. Therefore their hearts weren't always in sync with their place of residence. With all of that said, we would still probably choose to have the children at home.

Danny may not have gained academic excellence at Subic, but his entrepreneurial skills soared. With his allowance he purchased a few packs of bubble gum in a store downtown. At recess, he sold them for the "going rate" on base, at a considerable profit. That night he purchased more and sold more. Soon he was buying it by the box. One day I received a note from his teacher asking for a conference. "We don't want to squelch his budding business," she said, smiling, "but we have had complaints that the children are spending their lunch money on his bubble gum. Parents are not happy." That venture ended but his appetite was whetted.

Not wanting to deny David and Danny the joy that every American kid has in opening a "shop," we gave in to their pleading one day and let them set up a lemonade stand in front of the center. It was an instant success! We looked outside to see people lined up clear down the street to get some of their American drink in *clean* paper cups. Then we noticed several other vendors right outside our gate (where everyone drank from the same cup) glaring at the boys. They were not happy! Not wanting a riot on our hands for upsetting the economic balance of the community, we put the kibosh on the lemonade stand. But for a day or so, coins jingled in the boys' pockets. The venture, though short-lived, was a definite success.

Toward the end of that school year, Danny's class spent a day at the beach. Running at full speed (normal for him), he failed to duck under a foot bridge—the blow put a gash in the top of his head; blood gushed everywhere. He was rushed to the base hospital, but they couldn't stitch him up without our permission. Because our telephone worked only about half the time, their calls never connected. Finally a shore patrolman arrived at our door with the grave news. Running to the gate, we called, gave permission, and then proceeded to the emergency room. We were met by a little boy with a big bandage and a sheepish grin.

We loved all three of our children, being careful to be impartial. Most of the time we were optimistic about what they were becoming. Each one gave testimony to knowing Christ as Savior and spiritual growth was evident. They had lots of friends on the base and were doing okay in school. It was our practice (and still is) to pray *every* day for our children. But it was Danny who really kept us on our knees. It wasn't that he was really naughty. He was just so active and into everything. Early in our marriage Tom and I were rather naive about children. Often we agreed, *Boy, our kids will never do* ***that!*** when we observed a rascally child. And we did pretty well with Lori and David. But when Danny came along, it all went awry. Books *did* get torn, scribbling *did* appear on the wall, teachers *did* want conferences.

Each evening at Subic I spent time with the children in our apartment while they prepared for bed. Then when they were settled, I cherished a few minutes of quiet in my room until they were asleep before returning to the activities in the center downstairs. One night Danny was especially difficult. I knew if he would just be still in bed for a few moments he would drop off to sleep. But he was all over the place. I disciplined, cajoled, and threatened before he finally gave up. Exhausted, I slumped into the chair. *Lord, I just don't know how to handle him! I get so mad at him! How can I possibly cope, let alone teach and train him effectively? What will happen to this child?* I wailed inwardly.

As I poured out my frustration, a still small voice whispered to my heart. *Don't be afraid. I have called this child. Danny will serve me.* Stunned, I sat in silence. *Thank You, Lord,* I murmured. As the truth of that promise took root in my heart, a deep peace settled over me. As the days went by my attitude toward Danny changed. God had given me hope for his future, and I believed God.

But Danny was still Danny. His insatiable love for animals was blooming to full flower. One day I saw him standing on a tall box reaching over the fence which had broken glass imbedded into the concrete on top to discourage intruders, bartering his allowance with a Filipino boy for some mice. I caught that one in time to abort the transaction.

But the day we took a bus load of men to the nearby New Tribes mission station for a baptism service, I wasn't as quick. Everyone was back on the bus. Tom turned the key. "Where's Danny?" someone called. We glanced around. I jumped out onto the roadside, and there he was, bartering with all of his heart and allowance for the tiny half-dead puppy in the hand of a Filipino boy. I was too late. The deed was done. Danny climbed on the bus grinning, the pathetic little animal clutched lovingly in his hands. The Filipino boy was smiling too—he *knew* he had won. The dog would be dead by nightfall. He just didn't know Danny.

You know how it works! Danny slept soundly while Tom and I spent most of the night trying to pacify the poor little creature. But with Danny's love and our hard work, we nursed that wretched little pup to health. Chocky (short for Chocolate Drop) became a pretty good watchdog, and gave the children their first experience of watching a birth when she had puppies. We were all saddened a few years later and feared Danny's heart would break when Chocky died delivering her second litter.

But the cat was the biggie! That one cost Danny two allowances—maybe because it was almost grown. Its first night in our apartment, as Tom was trying to get it settled, the cat turned on him, yowling and scratching. Horrified, we watched the blood ooze from Tom's arm. The cat died. The veterinarian on base sent its body away to test for rabies, but in the meantime Tom had to take the anti-rabies shots in his stomach each day. After five treatments when the report came back negative, the rest of the series was canceled. To this day Daddy has more than one scar on his body from Danny's episodes with animals.

By the time David was twelve, his height and weight were about normal for his age. He still became ill quite often and usually had high fevers, but the doctors didn't seem concerned. So when he came down with mumps and wasn't as sick as usual, we treated it somewhat casually. He recovered quickly.

One morning at breakfast I asked David to pass the butter. He was looking away from me and obviously didn't hear me. Tom looked at me quizzically. Later that week we received a note from David's teacher. "I think you should have David's hearing checked. He is not responding well," she wrote.

Danny and David in Little League football

The doctor at Cubi examined him. "David definitely has a hearing problem," he said with some concern. "You will need to take him over to Clark Air Force Base where they have a good sound chamber and equipment for further testing."

After spending a day at the Clark hospital, the doctor met with us and reported, "David is totally and irreversibly deaf in his left ear. It was probably caused by the mumps."

"Isn't there anything we can do?" we asked incredulously.

"No, we have no treatment for this kind of deafness. Just try to protect his good ear."

We left the hospital and drove back to Subic, all three of us in deep reflection as the truth of the diagnosis sank in. In our wildest dreams we could not have imagined how difficult that caution would become as rock and roll music became a big part of David's teen-age life. Or how many times I was to warn, "David! Turn that stereo down or you'll be deaf as a doornail by the time you're thirty!" And who would have dreamed he would become a professional in the sound industry by his mid-thirties!

Both David and Danny were permitted to join the Little League teams on the base. Because most of the games were played in the evening—the time when the center was the busiest—Tom and I took turns cheering in the bleachers. They both played baseball and David had the unforgettable joy of being on a winning team.

Danny especially loved football, probably because it provided an outlet for the excessive energy we tried so hard to keep under control. But he had a difficult problem: he was at the maximum age of twelve but fell short of the minimum weight of fifty-six pounds. After some games the coaches allowed the smaller boys to play a "fifth quarter." Danny excelled—the rows of stars on his helmet giving candid evidence. "Danny sure is a hard player," his coach remarked one day. "I wish I had more like him."

The final game of the season was played on Thanksgiving weekend. With many of the players away on vacation, the coach had difficulty assembling a team. Danny just knew this was his grand opportunity. Before weigh-in, he stuffed his pockets with some rocks which would bring him up to the required weight. But thankfully his conscience kicked in and he changed his mind.

Seizing the opportunity, Danny rushed to his coach, "Oh, please, *pul-ee-se* let me play!" he begged. "I promise I won't get hurt!" The coach looked at his pleading eyes, sighed, and said, "Well, Danny, if your parents will give permission and not hold me responsible for injuries, I'll let you play."

Danny dashed over to us, jumping up and down as he pleaded for that opportunity of a lifetime. What could we say? "Go ahead," we responded, my response being much more reluctant than Tom's. He dashed off.

As the two teams lined up on the field, our hearts sank. On the other team was a boy who had to be at least 120 pounds, the weight maximum. He was *big!* They made several plays and then the coach called Danny over and said sadly, "I'm sorry. I just can't risk it. That kid could kill you!" Thus ended Danny's football career.

Chapter 27

POVERTY, WEALTH, AND WATER

While we were busy rearing three school-age children, the ministry continued to grow. Ralph and Wilma Porter with their two children came from Okinawa to help. One of Ralph's first jobs was to take over "camel duty." Most of our time at Subic we had to transport all of our water from the base. Not only was the city water unsafe, but it was rarely available. We hooked up our "camel," a homemade tank trailer, to the van, drove on base to a fire hydrant (we had permission from the base authorities), filled it, and came back. The contents were emptied into our underground reservoir then delivered up to the kitchens and bathrooms by electric pump. It held 1,000 gallons—four camel trips. Just the toilets in the six bathrooms could use that much water on busy days. And if one valve stuck open, it was gone in a few hours. When the electricity was off (often!) we carried the water up by bucket. We were greatly relieved when Ralph took over the camel duty. Later, the base public works department ran a line directly to our center. It was safe and plentiful, but we had to be alert to people illegally tapping into it.

Wilma Porter and I proved to be as different as two women could be. Wilma was a pragmatic farm girl, easy going, steady and practical, a matter-of-fact no-nonsense wife and mother. While I was...well, if you've read this far you know. Ralph called me a "la-dee-dah," his term for someone who loved candles, crystal glasses, ruffles and fluff.

Wilma and I took turns teaching our women's Bible class at the center. Her practical, down-to-earth Bible lessons met the women's needs in a special way.

Tom and Ralph were opposites also. Ralph was eager and aggressive, while Tom was calm and passive. We made quite a team!

Even when David and Danny antagonized their Rebecca and Daniel to the point of tears, the four of us were able to work through it and remain amiable. They are still dear friends and co-workers.

Firmly believing in the biblical principle "Freely ye have received, freely give," we provided everything at the center without cost to the men (except the books in the bookstore, of course). The Coca-Cola truck came several times a week, depositing cases and cases of drinks in our pantry. The cost to us was about two-and-a-half cents a bottle, about the least expensive drink available. The guys would come in hot and thirsty, walk to the chuck wagon in the game area, fill a glass with ice from the ice bucket, and sometimes down several Cokes. We also had coffee available, but it was usually only the old salts (Navy chiefs whose bodies ran on the stuff) who wanted it.

Fresh baked cookies were always on the counter. Our cook baked three double batches every day. Sometimes she put them all together in a big Tupperware container on the counter. I'd watch the guys dig through them until all of the chocolate chip cookies were gone and then eat the others.

Chocolate chips were not available on the local market—we either had them sent from the U.S. or were given them by people on the base. They were a controlled item in the commissary, so families were limited in how much they could buy, but our dear folks were always generous.

During our entire time in the Philippines, I struggled inwardly over the deep poverty surrounding us. I didn't enjoy having children paw at me, asking for money, but I often felt guilty for having so much in comparison. At Subic we lived in a lovely, huge building, while all around us people slept on the streets, sometimes in our entryway.

One morning I happened to look out the window of our apartment, watching the people in the field below. They were squatters, living in cardboard boxes covered with tattered pieces of plastic. Here and there were patches of concrete where others had previously built more permanent dwellings, only to be torn down by the authorities. One day I noticed a little girl about two years old sitting on one of those concrete slabs. (Little girls wore only dresses while little boys wore only shorts.) As I watched, a puddle appeared under her. She moved over, and soon another one appeared. She had diarrhea. Before long she was playing in the puddle, and soon had it in her hair. Seeing the mess, her father came over and picked her up. He found a plastic dish pan, filled it with water (illegally tapped from our water line), took off her dress and began to clean her up. But he had no soap.

My heart ached as I realized I had all this "wealth" in our huge building, including a whole *case* of soap. I went to the supply closet, took out a new bar of soap, walked downstairs and around to the back. Not able to speak the language, I handed the father the bar of soap, indicating he could use it to wash the baby. His eyes got large, and he looked around wondering if I was an angel from heaven. "I live up there," I said, pointing to the window above. He smiled and bowed in appreciation. I went back inside.

But I couldn't resist the temptation to see what he would do. He scrubbed that little girl from head to toe until she was pink, then digging through a box of stuff, found a wrinkled but clean dress for her. Then it seemed from nowhere came several other children who received the same treatment. When all were clean and dressed, he threw the water out in the dirt, and then carefully wrapped the bar of soap in a scrap of plastic.

The contrast of the abject poverty of those dear people who lived right beside Americans who must have seemed wealthy beyond belief left an indelible mark on my heart. Not being sure how to respond in a Christ-like manner, we developed a policy that when people came to our door asking for help, we always offered them food—a small bag of rice and a tin of meat. We kept those supplies in the pantry at all times. If they refused the food and wanted money, we kindly sent them on their way. We always gave them a Christian tract which encouraged them to go to the nearby evangelical church on our street. With so many of "them" and so few of "us" we were amazed that the number coming to our door was never more than we could handle. The Lord graciously kept the situation under control.

We also yearned for our children to learn to give from their "wealth" and from their hearts. Several years, usually after Christmas when they had new toys, we had each child select three toys they were willing to give away. On the way to Manila they were to watch for a child they could share with, and then call out for Tom to stop the car. Then they took the toy to the child.

Danny vividly recalls the time he decided to give away his game of Twister. "The game had a large plastic mat with circles painted all over it. I found just the right little boy in front of a *sari-sari* store, hollered for Dad to stop and joyously handed the game to him. He was surprised beyond words, and obviously thrilled. But later that day when we came back through that town, I was deeply disappointed to see the brightly colored plastic sheet spread over the roof of the little shop. Evidently the boy's father felt the game would better serve to keep the rain off the roof than as a toy. I was angry at first, but Mom and Dad explained why a father might do that and I began to understand. Those were such valuable lessons about 'Kingdom values.'"

One rainy season it looked as through we should go into the ark-building business. It rained continually for thirty-nine days and thirty-nine nights. Since the only way into Olongapo was over the zigzag mountain, the road closed completely due to landslides. The entire city was cut off from the supply of any materials. The surrounding areas were under several feet of water, stranding many Filipinos in their homes. We were so proud of our Americans on base. They set up a volunteer assembly line in one of the mess halls and made "nutri-buns," a 500-calorie, high-nutrition bread. These were sealed in plastic and dropped by helicopter to the farms and villages in the flooded area. Tons of used clothing were gathered and distributed to people in need.

From that crisis and others during our nine years in the Philippines, we witnessed a beneficent spirit among our countrymen. Most were generous to the point of sacrifice when a special need arose. But steal from them, and they would become negative, prejudiced, and maybe downright hateful.

We had made a run to Manila just before the rains began so our pantry was full. Instead of serving meals at the center we all ate at one of the restaurants on base. We opened our pantry to our house help, their families and friends, allowing them to purchase the food at the price we paid—less than the cost in Olongapo. We made some new friends through that outreach and enriched our relationship with many.

The Lutheran Servicemen's Center at the other end of the bar strip, was located near a stream. We were good friends with the director, often encouraging him to reach the men who missed us, got through the town, and ended up at his place. When the stream overflowed, the first floor of the center was almost half full of water. A group of our folks helped shovel out the silt and muck that remained when the waters subsided. It was an awful mess.

There are two seasons in the tropical climate of the Philippines: wet (rainy) or dry. Both tend to be extreme. When it's wet, it's very wet; when it's dry, it's ground-cracking dry. One rainy season I took Danny over to Clark for some tests at the medical facility. It was raining hard as we began the journey home in our car. Before long we came upon a flooded area on the road. A group of entrepreneurial Filipino boys were milling around at each end. As I slowed the car to a crawl, they rushed to my window shouting, "Push, ma'am?" They wanted to push the car to the other side of the flooded area. By putting the transmission into neutral and turning off the engine of the car I could prevent the fan from throwing water onto the engine causing a stall. It was a deal I couldn't resist. I switched off the engine and the swarm of boys gradually eased us to the other side. I gave the leader a handful of centavos and we were off. Of course, the next time I applied the brakes they didn't work. This incident was repeated about five times in the three-hour trip and after the last "portage" the brakes stopped functioning entirely.

Now I had the awesome task of navigating the zigzag mountain. As I topped the last hairpin curve and started the

Flooded roads were always a challenge

Interesting sign just before starting the descent on the zig-zag mountain descent, I tried the emergency brake to see if it would provide some help. It did slow the car a bit. Shifting into the lowest gear, I steered and Danny prayed. Most of the trucks were moving slowly also, which helped, but it was a white-knuckle trip all the way down into town. When we entered our driveway at last, I almost hit the garage door trying to stop. I slumped down into the car seat and we bowed in a prayer of thankfulness. Tom was sympathetic to my story but thought I was exaggerating a little until he took the car for repair the next day. "The brakes are completely gone!" he remarked with astonishment. *Right!* was my silent reply.

Chapter 28

IN NEED OF A MIRACLE

One day an American visitor from town was talking with Tom at the chuck wagon. During their conversation, a young sailor came in, helping himself to the soft drinks—first one, then two, then three. "Uh, Tom, did you see that fellow? He's had three drinks and didn't pay for any of them," the visitor remarked.

"Oh, that's okay, " Tom replied, "they're free."

The sailor ambled into the bookstore which was also my office. Tom and the visitor continued talking. Before long the young sailor left. I went to Tom to share some good news. "See," Tom said to the visitor, "we can't afford to charge for the drinks. That young man just gave us $100!"

It was not our policy to have an offering box or to pass an offering plate. Money was rarely a subject of conversation. However, when a sailor had been the recipient of our hospitality a time or two, he became curious about where the money came from. Our usual reply was, "We, as missionaries, receive our salary from churches and individuals in the States who have a love for servicemen. The center is supported by the men who come. You can't pay for the meal you ate tonight—

someone has already provided that for you. But if you want to help so the next person can enjoy the center, you may do so." Then we told him how to give and always gave a receipt.

Tom (the people-person-to-the-max) developed his delegating skills to their fullest at Subic while I (the perfectionist-detail-oriented-paper-work-person) watched horrified at times. My philosophy was, *If you want a job done well, do it yourself,* while his was, *Never do yourself what you can get someone else to do.* His theory was far superior to mine in getting people involved in the ministry and growing in their walk with the Lord and love for service. Mine was safer and lots less messy!

As we got to know mature, faithful men from the ships, Tom often sent them off to a quiet place with a young unbeliever who had shown an interest in the Lord. They returned to share their new faith in Christ. At times when we needed to be away, Tom asked trustworthy men to take charge of the center. Sometimes there were special young single men who showed good leadership ability. Tom was quick to give them responsibility. But the one thing he didn't let them do was to drive our vehicles. It was far too dangerous—not just because the driving defied American logic and experience, but if they had an accident the complications were legion. But then Jack McCullough came. He was a quiet young believer from a farm in Minnesota—a joy to have around. His sweet spirit, servant attitude, and responsible maturity soon won our hearts. He became our resident chauffeur, driving the guys and sometimes our kids where they needed to go. After discharge from the Navy, Jack prepared for the ministry, became a pastor, and is presently serving as Chairman of the Board of Cadence (OCSC). I'm glad we treated him well, since he's now our boss!

It was a special joy to see some of our former Clark guys come into Subic. Kent Abendroth, one of our regular guys during the Clark days surprised us one time, arriving on a ship. And Art Burnett, who had been with us briefly at Clark, came in on a Coast Guard ship. Jim and Freda Stewart, back for a second tour of duty at Clark, came to visit us now and then. I recall there was a shortage of paper products on the economy and we were unable to get colored toilet paper for our bathrooms. "Oh dear," I cried to anyone who would listen. "We're just going to have to shut down the center because I can't buy blue tissue." Freda came to my rescue, bringing over a package of the rare item. She saved the center from sure disaster. No wonder Ralph Porter called me a "la-dee-dah."

Trips were usually memorable. The sailors enjoyed getting away from "Navy town" out into the provinces. We delighted in taking them. One weekend Bob Bingham invited us to bring our gang over to Clark for Victory Hour. Tom was ahead, driving the eight-passenger van full of guys. I came behind in our car with five sailors in it. We had just come off the zigzag mountain onto the plains when a Filipino man bolted out in front of Tom. Tom slammed on the brakes, swerving in vain to miss him. As the man tumbled in the road, we watched horrified as the van skidded, then tipped onto two wheels, starting to roll. The man had fallen and would be crushed! Miraculously the vehicle bounced back upright and stopped. The man jumped up and ran away. We sat there shaken.

Soon we were surrounded by people. Then to our surprise, a policeman emerged from a nearby *sari-sari* store. After listening to accounts of the incident from everyone, he said to Tom, "Come with me to the police station." He rode along with Tom, leading us to the nearby town. I followed closely behind, terrified. We had heard the horror stories of what can happen when a rich American harms a poor Filipino on the highway. My imagination ran rampant! Tom followed the policeman into the station. We waited. Soon our vehicles were swarming with people, mostly children. In the stifling heat, we couldn't possibly close the windows, yet we recoiled as hands reached inside to touch us. Would it become a mob scene? What was happening to Tom inside? We prayed silently for a miracle!

After what seemed like an eternity, Tom emerged. Since he had refused to pay on the spot, they had taken his driver's license so he would return for a hearing. Relieved we continued our journey.

The next day while talking with our maid, Florentina, I told her of the incident and how frightened we were. "Where did this happen?" she asked. When I told her, her eyes widened.

"Oh, ma'am, may I have the day off? My husband is from that town and his father is the Chief of Police there! I will go and intercede for Mr. Hash."

Hours later she returned. "My father-in-law will help you," she told Tom. "But you must be there by nine o'clock tomorrow morning."

Accompanied by Flor's husband, Tom returned to the station. When they arrived, Tom was made to sit for a long time while the arresting policeman, the chief, and his son discussed the case in Tagalog. Evidently the injured (or uninjured?) man had gone to Manila for x-rays and had not yet returned. Tom listened as their voices grew louder and angrier. Finally the chief shouted, "This man is a friend of my family," pointing at Tom. "I will take responsibility for him!" Tom paid a small sum for the cost of the x-rays, was given his license, and released. We learned later that this dear Christian police chief had paid the highest honor to Tom—placing him with his family, above his job. God had given us our miracle!

The 25-passenger Nissan bus provided a way to take more men on trips

After about a year at Subic, we were able to purchase a new twenty-five passenger Nissan bus, just like the one we had ordered for the Clark servicemen's home. When it arrived we were overjoyed. Now we could take even more men on trips.

Heading for Manila one day with the bus full and another full car behind it, I was last, driving our car full of sailors. Trying to stay with the caravan, I accidentally passed a car in front of a policeman. Rushing out into the road, his shrill whistle screaming, he frantically motioned me to the side. The other two vehicles went merrily on their way. Motioning for two of the sailors to come with me, we climbed up into the little police shack. "You passed in a no-passing zone," the policeman shouted in broken English.

"I'm sorry," I murmured, afraid he would hear my knees knocking.

"You must pay the fine!" he roared.

"How much is it?

" Eighty pesos."

"Eighty pesos!" I cried. "That's too much!"

"It says so right here," he shot back, waving the "rule book" at me. "Read it for yourself!" Sure enough, the fine for passing in a no-passing zone (even if it was unmarked) was eighty pesos.

"I don't have any money," I replied honestly. He didn't believe me.

"How much do you want to pay?" he asked. I proceeded to explain that my husband was in a vehicle ahead of me and would be here as soon as he discovered I was gone. He had some money. That concept was not easily translated into Tagalog in his mind. He interpreted my response as meaning I would not pay the fine.

"Give me your license, and you can come back next week for a hearing at the courthouse," he said, holding out his hand. Knowing from experience that such a decision would cost double or triple the asking price as well as require a return trip, I tried again to assure him my husband would be there any minute. My prayers were getting more urgent as I silently pleaded with the Lord to help Tom notice my absence.

After what seemed an interminable time, Tom drove up. No one ever looked so good! He quietly assured the policeman that everything was okay. They bartered about the amount of the fine, and Tom paid it. Pocketing the receipt, we were on our way.

Later when examining the receipt, I noticed the absence of an official stamp—the money went into the policeman's pocket. We were always careful about bribes, but this one slipped by unnoticed. Also, we knew that these public servants were paid very low salaries, assuming they would be subsidized by "tips." When stopped by a policeman, most foreigners produced a license with a twenty peso bill behind it. But for missionaries with high moral standards...well, it was always a dilemma.

One of our favorite trips from both Clark and Subic was to the island of Corregidor out in Manila Bay. We drove an hour or so down to the tip of Bataan peninsula where Jesse Miller had faced defeat in 1942. There we hired *banca* boats and their drivers (always eager to earn a few pesos) to take us across the bay. Only two or three of us could ride in a boat, so we often needed ten to fifteen of the dugout canoes with outriggers. The drivers coaxed their ancient outboard motors to life and off we went into the often choppy waters. The ride was always eventful, either from motor failure (requiring a tow by another boat or paddling to shore), or from sudden squalls that stirred up the bay, rocking the boat and necessitating vigorous bailing. Amazingly, we never lost anyone, but a few came close.

Banca boats—canoes with outriggers—a common form of water transportation

After the hour-long boat trip, we landed on the beach. From there we toured the historic remains of Corregidor, where American soldiers bravely made their last stand at the beginning of World War II when the Philippines fell to the Japanese.

Atop the big rock covering most of the island we saw the large gun emplacements designed to repulse any sea-going invasion force bound for Manila. (The Japanese came from a totally different direction, so the guns were never fired during that war.)

The rock was honeycombed with tunnels that served as barracks, military headquarters, hospital and mess hall to the troops. Day after day the skeleton force huddled in the bowels of that impenetrable rock as the enemy bombarded it from the air. From that place, General Douglas MacArthur was spirited away to Australia where he promised, “I shall return!” Defeat was inevitable.

The process was repeated at the end of the war when General MacArthur kept his promise and recaptured the Philippines. Years later, Corregidor became a developed tourist attraction for both American and Japanese visitors.

Chapter 29

TIME WARP

Vacations were rare and precious. We always went to Baguio where it was cool, staying at Doane Rest, vacation homes provided by the Association of Baptists for World Evangelism (ABWE). Preparing to go meant getting umpteen people to carry out our daily tasks at the center—so complex that many times I wanted to abort the plan. But when we eventually got everything packed and were in the car, I was glad. The children loved those times. Snuggled around the fireplace on rainy afternoons, we read volumes of books aloud. We were a family all by ourselves, only five of us sat at the table for meals, and mom did the cooking.

I tried to think of special foods to prepare on vacation, so one day while shopping in Manila, I spotted a box of Chef Boyardee Pizza Mix. *The children will love this,* I thought to myself. It was imported and expensive but worth it. The day we were to enjoy the treat I announced it to the family, knowing anticipation is half of the enjoyment. With a flair, I tore open the box. Whew! The foul odor of buggy flour assaulted our nostrils; then the little creatures came running out with abandon. The whole thing ended up in the trash. So much for good intentions.

Tom had made many trips from Baguio up into the jungles of northern Luzon usually taking one of the boys with him. But Lori and I had not had that experience. So during one vacation, Tom made arrangements for us to fly by MAF aircraft to visit national missionaries with New Tribes Mission in the Ilongot tribal area. After a short flight over the jungle, the pilot said, "Look, there's the landing strip." All I could see was a postage stamp size spot among the trees. Coming in low over the treetops, we dropped to the grass and came to a quick stop. Cautiously we climbed out of the plane. Having been notified by radio that we were coming, the entire population of the village was there to greet us. Dressed in their colorful, matching native dresses, the women smiled and chatted. The men in their g-strings and spears looked foreboding. The national missionary was a Filipino lowlander who spoke English, but his wife was from the tribes and only spoke her dialect. The men were shouting. "They want you to hurry," the missionary said to Tom. "They are going to hunt wild pig today and waited for you to arrive so you and the boys could accompany them. Your wife and daughter can stay in the village with my wife and the other women." In moments they were gone.

The missionary's wife smiled, motioning for Lori and me to come to her house. We entered the thatch-roofed hut. It was clean and orderly, one fairly large room with a table and chairs in one corner and a partial wall separating the sleeping area. At her invitation we sat down at the table. Since we couldn't converse, we just sat there, smiling at each other.

Then she motioned for us to follow and led us on a tour of the village, saying the dialect name of goats, children, and foods. We repeated them until she nodded indicating we had said it right. The women were cooking *camote* (a bland potato-like vegetable) over an open fire. Responding to our curiosity, they gave us some. We ate it, smiling our approval. A little salt would have made quite a difference.

We noticed a basketball court in the center of the village. On closer inspection, to our great joy, we recognized the hoops that had been donated through Operation Handclasp and channeled to the missionaries via our center. It made us feel that hauling all of that stuff to the missionaries was well worth the effort. Basketball (with unique rules) was *the* village entertainment.

When we arrived back at the missionary's home, she prepared lunch. Lori and I sat at the table while she served us. It was set with real china dishes—chipped and mismatched, but china nonetheless. We knew we were being highly honored. She served a rice dish and *calamansie* juice (like lime juice) in jelly glasses. We ate with tablespoons. Later as Lori and I walked about again, we noticed the only *calamansie* tree in the village. It had no fruit on it—she had given us her last one.

After lunch we saw an old guitar hanging on the wall, missing two strings. I indicated I wanted to play it; she smiled with approval. Lori and I walked to the church building next door—an open area covered by a thatched roof on poles. The "pews" were logs arranged in rows on the mud floor. Children were cautiously standing around. I strummed the old guitar and Lori and I began singing songs like *Jesus Loves Me* and other choruses. The children smiled and drew closer. Soon women joined the group. To our surprise and joy, they began to sing with us in their dialect. Then we encouraged them to sing some of their songs to us. We spent the entire afternoon singing and smiling and stopped only when the men returned with their prize pig suspended from a pole.

The hunt proved to be quite an experience for David and Danny. After wading through several streams, they spent much of their day pulling leaches off their bodies. "I was right there when the boar rushed us," Danny recounted breathlessly. "I was hiding behind the man's legs and he lifted his bow and shot the pig. You should have seen his smile as the boar fell down dead!"

Dinner was served around the open fire with everyone dipping into the same pot. We didn't ask what we were eating. Wooden bowls replaced the china we had enjoyed at lunch. We learned that those who lived in the village were all believers. Others of that tribal group lived individually in the jungle, but these believers had come together to worship and be taught by the missionary.

In the evening we all gathered together on the floor in the missionary's home. There wasn't room in the house for everyone so many stood or sat in the open windows looking in. Various Ilongots took turns giving their testimonies, interpreted by the missionary. They told of their life before Christ when they had been headhunters—full of fear and murder—and how the Lord had changed them. They even reenacted the war dance they did before going on killing raids, emphasizing clearly that Christ had changed their hearts and they no longer did them.

At bedtime we were given the hosts' bed on the floor. It was a "real" mattress, though not what we were used to. We were deeply humbled and honored. The children were on mats on the bamboo floor. We slept in our clothes, since the people showed considerable curiosity as they watched our bedtime preparations through the open windows.

The next morning the plane came to take us back to Baguio. Everyone walked to the landing strip to see us off. We waved goodbye. A lump formed in our throats. Even though our language and culture were worlds apart, the love of Christ had knit our hearts together during those few hours.

Chapter 30

WAR WITH A VENGEANCE

Sunday night vespers at the center was a highlight of the week. At 5 p.m. the chairs were set in rows in the lounge, then filled with sailors, families and children. Frequently we invited a missionary from Manila to come for the weekend to speak to the group. The missionaries loved it because it provided them a unique opportunity to fellowship with other Americans and to preach in English. We loved it too, for often they were excellent speakers and deep men of God. After much singing, sometimes a funny skit or a stirring testimony, the missionary opened the Word of God, ministering to our hearts. The chaplains didn't have services at the chapels in the evening so joined their groups with ours.

One night Bob Hilts from Overseas Crusades (now OC International) presented a musical program of vocal and trumpet music. During his stirring rendition of "Onward Christian Soldiers," a rat came running across the floor. Some in the crowd became fidgety, some giggled, some squealed. Seizing the awkward moment without missing a note, Bob chased the poor creature, blowing his trumpet at him, even following him up the back curtains, until he escaped and the song was finished. It took some time for all of us to settle down after that.

After vespers we served dinner from the chuck wagon. Often the married women brought food to supplement what we made. Then followed hours of games: ping-pong, maybe a Christian film, and just lots of fun. Wilma Porter, Lillian Davis, and Faith Nagle (now Brown), led some mean games of "Speedy Scrabble." The young guys were determined to beat the "old" chiefs (and Tom) at the ping-pong tables, but seldom did. They kept coming back to try, though.

Our children enjoyed those times too, for often friends their age came with their parents. We didn't encourage teen age girls to come to the center without their parents. The mix between them and young sailors was...well, you can guess. But sometimes Lori's teen-age friends came after school to play ping-pong or just hang out with her. Of course, Tom and I were always there at those times.

As Lori became a teenager, the Lord marvelously provided a vibrant Christian group she could be a part of. Dave Touchton and George Middleton, two Christian permanent party sailors, somehow managed to corral a bunch of kids and mold them into a fine youth group in the chapel at Cubi. We have contact with several of those kids today, many of whom have matured in the Lord. After leaving the Navy, Dave developed his strong gift of giving, supporting ministries around the world, including the Hashes. George, following counsel from Tom, attended Moody Bible Institute and has been a pastor for many years.

All OCSC missionaries who rear their daughters in center ministry are apprehensive of the teen years. But Lori spared us any moments of concern. Even though many of the sailors were still in their teens and thought Lori was a doll, she was a master at keeping them under control. She, along with some of her girlfriends, were great buddies with the guys, going on base for ice cream or to White Beach for snorkeling—always for fun, never pairing off.

One evening I was in the office and Lori was at the door talking to me. A cocky sailor sidled up to her with a hint of a leer in his eye. He put his arm behind her and leaned on the door casing. Lori simply stepped aside and gave him a sweet look that said, *Don't* ***ever*** *do that again.* He got the message.

The men of the U.S. armed forces have been and always will be our deepest love. During our nine years in the Philippines we watched those young men faithfully serve our country for the cause of freedom. As the war in Vietnam became a hotbed of controversy in the U.S., the men were being bombarded by the media, causing many to seriously wonder about the integrity of their mission. Marines who had witnessed the slaughter of human lives sometimes used the quietness of the center to sort out the questions plaguing their hearts and minds. Often we served as sounding board and counselors as we listened to their stories and sought to comfort and encourage them from the Scriptures.

We saw sailors overwhelmed by the war in Vietnam sitting in a quiet corner, not wanting to move, basking in relief from the steel bulkheads that were their home month after month. Submariners, faces pale from lack of exposure to the sunlight, loved the open, airy atmosphere of the center.

Many of the men experienced an ethereal joy when we took them to the New Tribes Mission training camp, where missionaries Fred and Virginia Pennoyer welcomed them warmly. The men enjoyed breathing the fresh air, helping cut grass and trees in the jungle, eating tropical fruit plucked from the trees, or simply sitting on a rock listening to the trickle of the stream.

Though we were somewhat detached from the unrest in the U.S., we did read about it in the *Stars and Stripes* newspaper. But the intensity of hatred on both sides of the faction regarding the war in Vietnam didn't really touch our lives. That is, not until Jane Fonda showed up in our little town of Olongapo! She and her cohorts led demonstrations in the marketplace in the center of town. She planted lawyers there to teach the sailors how to rebel against the government. She even went to North Vietnam to consort with the enemy. I know of no situation that riled my ire like that one. For months after she left, sailors came into the center asking where the lawyers were. "We're not communists here! And I don't know where they are!" I replied, not very sweetly. Fortunately I didn't know. The Lord did several "attitude checks" on my heart in those turbulent days.

Our relationship with the chaplains was one of the most rewarding elements of our time at Subic. Every chaplain stationed at Subic or Cubi was supportive of us and our ministry. Every Thursday morning Tom was invited to attend the chaplains' meeting on the base. Besides the resident chaplains, those from the ships in port also attended. Tom and the director of the Lutheran center were given an opportunity to explain our ministries, encouraging the chaplains to avail themselves and their men of our services. As a result of those meetings, many, many chaplains made arrangements for Tom to plan trips or retreats for the men on their ships.

An unseen and unexpected result of those meetings was the ministry Tom was able to have in the lives of so many chaplains. Like the other military men, they were overseas, far from their families, fearful of the war, and bombarded with temptations. Because Tom was "neutral" and not military, he was able to come alongside a vast number of those men, encouraging them in their walk with the Lord.

Our philosophy of working within the chapel program was one of cooperation without compromise. We found that the more liberal the chaplain, the more we were needed in the chapel. If we had an evangelical chaplain who faithfully taught God's Word, we could enhance his ministry. Often we thought back to our traumatic days in Panama when we failed to work with chaplains. How different that time could have been.

Both kinds of chaplains discovered quickly that we were not a threat to them. They knew when we invited a single serviceman to our home after the service, in a short time he would be back ushering, singing in the choir, or teaching a Sunday school class. Even chaplains who did not appreciate our evangelical stance were content to let us help increase attendance and participation. It did much to enhance their efficiency reports. And we were content to serve.

Instead of sitting in the chapel finding fault with the chaplain, we encouraged the people from the home or center to spend time praying for him. We saw some remarkable changes in chaplains' lives and messages. We know it was through love and prayer.

A highlight of our time was when Chaplain Stan Beach and his wife, Ellen, arrived at Cubi chapel. (Cubi was the naval air station adjacent to Subic Navy Base.) Stan was a graduate of Taylor University, like I was, and was commissioned to the chaplaincy by the General Association of Regular Baptists (GARB). While they waited to find housing in town (on the list for eventual base housing), they lived with us for about a month. Their daughter Laurie was our Lori's age, and Randy was David and Danny's age. It was Stan's first duty assignment after being twice wounded in Vietnam while he served with the Marines.

Stan recounted his amazing story:

I was a young lieutenant on Operation Prairie and spent most of my time with Kilo Company until I was wounded. For several days we battled to take Hill 400, which was protecting Communist infiltration routes. The North Vietnamese were waging a fierce counterattack with automatic rifles, mortars, machine guns, claymore mines, booby traps, and grenades. We assaulted the hill four times but were driven back each time. On the fifth try we succeeded because three marines slithered on their bellies to lead the successful attack.

Before this operation (we had been there for Operation Hastings), a premonition seemed to overtake us. Instead of the usual, "If I get hit do this...," it became, "When I get hit...." I, too, succumbed to the pessimism. I left my personal items with Father Ondo to send to my family. But, in God's providence, this pall became God's instrument to draw several to him.

I wasn't allowed to carry a weapon— all I had was my trusty "sword" of God's Word. My pulpit was often ammo or C-ration boxes. In combat I stayed with and assisted the corpsmen. I had completed field medical school at Camp Pendleton and Camp Lejeune.

I deliberately stayed in the field with the men, many of whom sought me out to talk about spiritual matters. I think about twenty men came to Christ in that short time. There's nothing more wonderful than 100 stinking, smelling, unshaven Marines standing around, singing a hymn.

Just the night before we launched our operation, I crawled from hole to hole with Captain Carrol, the company commander, to pray with the perimeter guards. I used Psalm 140:7 and shared about God's "helmet liner," Jesus Christ. A Jewish man trusted Christ, then a Catholic man.

I finished my rounds to find Bruce Williams, a hospital corpsman, waiting to talk to me. He came from a Christian family and sensed his need of repentance and faith. We prayed and he trusted Christ. My only follow-up was to give him my pocket Bible.

We had no water or food for three days. The enemy flanked us several times. We couldn't evacuate the dead or wounded. Bodies were beginning to decompose and smell. During lulls in the firefights, I would run the 200 meters to the rear command post to check on the wounded and scrounge up some water for the wounded up front. On September 28 I heard they had gotten some water dropped on the command post. I returned and filled my canteens, ready to move up again. But I learned another company was going to replace Kilo and wanted me with them. I claimed a "spider hole" and used the time to read and pray.

The next thing I recall was a strange smell, absolute silence, and an overwhelming sense of peace. Then men began to scream 'INCOMING!' I tried to get to my hole but realized I wasn't making any progress. Then I saw my leg—the boot heel was near my belt line. My arms and stomach were covered with blood.

When the choppers finally arrived to evacuate those of us who were wounded, I was placed into a mesh wire basket and carried to the evacuation zone. I recall feeling great sorrow because I had let the men down. I handed my cross to a corpsman, asking him to carry on in my absence. Just then a heavy mortar attack came in and the chopper had to pull away. Bruce Williams saw me and rushed over. He removed his flak jacket and placed it over my body, then shielded my head with his own body. He was seriously wounded by mortar fragments; he saved my life!

> I was med-evacuated to the Navy hospital ship, USS *Repose*, which was positioned off the coast of Vietnam. The orthopedic surgeons on duty when I was brought aboard were becoming terribly discouraged, for day after day they had to amputate limbs from the young men. *We were trained to heal men—to make them well—not to maim them for life,* they agonized.
>
> The surgeons had developed a new procedure they felt would be effective in saving some of the limbs. When they saw my injury, they were quite sure I qualified for the new procedure. So instead of amputating my shattered leg they repaired it.
>
> I spent many months recovering from my wounds and then in rehabilitation to recover the use of my leg. Even though it would not bend at the knee, I was deeply grateful to have it at all.

Accounts of Chaplain Beach's heroism spread quickly across the Far East and the United States. *Newsweek* Magazine (October 10, 1966) carried a detailed account and NBC Television interviewed Stan. The United States government awarded him the Bronze Star Medal for saving the lives of several marines during the fighting, and the government of Vietnam presented him the Vietnamese Cross of Gallantry with Palm, the highest military decoration given by that country.

Many years later, Stan was able to locate Corpsman Bruce Williams and recommend him for the Bronze Star Medal also. It was presented to Bruce thirty-one years after saving Stan's life. Stan recalled, "This man, risking his life for me, was the common attitude among Marines. But his act humbled me in the realization of Christ's sacrifice for me while I was still a sinner."

Stan's strong goal was to stay in the Navy as a chaplain—an enormous challenge, for it meant waiving all disability and proving he could function effectively. His biggest challenge was maneuvering rapidly up and down the ladders (stairwells). He qualified and soon received orders to Cubi Point Naval Air Station in the Philippines. That is where we met.

Chaplains Dave Meschke and Stan Beach visit in the center bookstore

Chapter 31

THAILAND SAGA

Our last three years in the Philippines, Tom was given the role of Southeast Asia Director with Thailand and Vietnam falling under his leadership. OCSC had four ministries in Thailand and one in Vietnam. The missionaries in Thailand asked Tom to come to speak at their Bible conference. We asked Graham and Gwen Nattress, a missionary couple from the New Tribes Mission station nearby, to come to stay with the children. Faithful people at the center would assist with the ministry. But the week before our planned departure Danny developed a hernia and was admitted to the hospital for surgery. He recovered well and came home the day before we were to leave. Weighing the pros and cons of going and staying, we opted to go, knowing the children were well cared for. But it was a tough decision.

Those two weeks in Thailand resulted in some of our most vivid memories. The Bible conference at Pattaya Beach was so powerful. Besides speaking, Tom had the privilege of assisting in the baptism of several men in the Gulf of Thailand.

Following the conference, we planned to visit all four of our ministries in the country. We stayed with Lou and Linda Harrison in Sattahip and then Lou took us to the bus station for the four-hour trip from Bangkok to Korat to visit Darl and Jan Goode. "I really didn't want you to ride on this line," Lou said, shaking his head as he came back with the tickets. "The Hino line is much safer, but there was no room." A strange foreboding crept over me.

Settling into our seats, Tom leaned back to enjoy the trip. I sat bolt upright as the bus pulled out of the terminal. *It's just my usual uneasiness on the highways,* I thought, trying to assure myself.

"Relax, honey. You always imagine the worst and it never happens," Tom, the eternal optimist, said cheerily.

We twisted through the narrow streets of the bustling city and then into the country, where the rice fields faded into a blur as the driver shifted through the gears.

I studied this man. He was young—late twenties perhaps—decked in a neat gray uniform, complete with braid-trimmed hat and spotless white gloves. He sat erect in his seat like an enthroned monarch, the huge windshield extending to the floor in front of him.

Bodies lurched in unison as he pulled on the steering wheel, swerving to avoid pedestrians, animals and slow-moving vehicles. With each open space, our speed increased. I reached over, taking Tom's hand. He patted mine, smiled, and leaned his head back, his eyes closed. But fear, like a gathering storm, was stirring inside me.

We had been told by other missionaries that a faithful Buddhist will not allow himself to show fear. (Perhaps this accounted for the high incidence of head-on collisions in the country. If a driver drew back, it revealed he was afraid.) Not only did this driver evidence no fear, but he also seemed to be playing a game, actually enjoying it.

Suddenly he slammed on the brakes, yanking the wheel to the left, gravel flying. A fruit vendor jerked her cart out of the way, mangoes and papaya tumbling to the ground. We slid to a stop.

I couldn't believe it! He deliberately tried to run into her, turning abruptly at the last moment! Was there a hint of a smile on his face? I was angry! I glanced around at the other passengers hoping someone would react. No one even seemed to notice. Dust billowed in as the door opened to allow a passenger to board.

Reluctantly I slid back in my seat as we raced off, the fear mounting again. Closing my eyes, I prayed, confessing my anger, asking God to deliver me from the churning within. But the inevitable crash kept flashing across my mind's eye.

Entering a small village, we pulled into a station. I noticed several other buses—one a Hino bus with a sign "Korat." Hope sprang alive! Maybe we could transfer! No, I knew it was impossible, first, because Tom would think it silly, and second, how would we make anyone understand our intention?

Back on the highway, I tried desperately to gain composure. Words from Scripture came unbidden: *God has not given us the spirit of fear....* That's it!

Father, I prayed, *I know this fear isn't from you. Surely you can give me victory. Please give me that 'peace that passes understanding' promised in your Word.*

Looking up, I saw that we were gaining on the bus in front of us, the distance between us evaporating. I glanced at the speedometer—one hundred ten kilometers—almost seventy miles an hour! Now our bumpers were just inches apart. Tom shifted toward the edge of his seat, a trace of fear in his eyes.

We pulled out to pass. The other driver speeded up. We were racing side by side. Horrified, I saw a truck coming straight toward us.

I stormed heaven. *Is this it, Father? After serving you as missionaries all our lives, forsaking all to come to Asia in obedience to your will, must it end like this? Our three children will be orphans in a foreign land!*

My hands flew up automatically to protect my face. I gasped as the oncoming truck careened onto the shoulder, gravel flying—we sped by with only inches to spare. My heart beat wildly, pounding in my ears. I glanced around to see if others had noticed the close call, then slumped sheepishly into my seat.

Then the Lord spoke softly to my heart. *My child, you've spent all of this time and effort praying for yourself. Why don't you pray for the driver? Don't you think I can deal with him?*

Doubt swept through my mind, but haltingly I began, *Okay...Lord..I don't understand this...but please, do anything to slow him down—anything!*

Within moments we heard a loud crack. A rock from between the tires of a passing truck hit our windshield, shattering the safety glass. Amazingly the window remained intact. Braking to a stop, the driver and his assistant surveyed the damage, speaking excitedly in Thai, obviously shaken.

When they eventually decided to go on, the assistant held a cloth over the grinding glass to steady it as we pulled cautiously onto the highway. We didn't exceed twenty miles an hour the rest of the way into Korat!

Reflecting on the incident, I realized God wanted me to learn trust in a new dimension. From experience I knew he could comfort me, could calm my inner spirit. I was praying on familiar ground.

But he wanted me to see that the scope of his care went far beyond my inner struggle; that even though my situation seemed totally out of control, he was in full command. He, who spoke to the waves and said *Peace! Be still!* allowed a rock to fly and commanded, *Slow down! My child is afraid!* I realized anew how much he dearly loved me.

The next trip, much to my relief, was an overnight ride on the sleeper train from Korat to Ubon to see Bill Kramer and his new bride, Jeannette. The Denver Zephyr it was not, but we slept a few winks on the lumpy mattress in our compartment.

The bus ride still fresh in my mind, I was overjoyed to learn we would fly from Ubon to Nakom Phanom (NKP) on the Mekong river. The only Caucasians on the domestic airline non-stop flight, we were delighted when the attendant handed us an English newspaper. Then the headlines caught my eye: ***American Hijacks Plane to North Vietnam***. To our dismay, we discovered that the exact flight we were on had been hijacked the day before, landing on a beach in North Vietnam. My sense of security vanished in a flash.

It wasn't long before the plane was circling to land. "Guess we're there," Tom said, remembering it was a non-stop flight. We knew that the Thai military, the U.S. military, and the domestic airlines all shared the same runway on the military base at NKP. So when the plane came to a stop in the middle of a rice field, we felt uncertain as we slipped out of our seats toward the exit. From the stairway we could see only one building—a small shed in the middle of the field. A dilapidated taxi waited nearby.

Tom asked the attendant for our luggage. It had been stuffed behind the pilot's seat, so he jostled it loose. "Nakhon Phanom?" I questioned hesitantly, glad I knew that Thai word. He shook his head and named the place. With red faces but inner relief, we got back on the plane. We learned later that the plane only stopped there once a week, and this happened to be the day. Thus it was a non-stop flight—usually. What if.... A short time later, as the plane once again circled for a landing, we were relieved to see the flight line with American and Thai planes parked all along the runway and our missionaries, Paul and Carol Kelley, waiting to meet us.

Tom and I learned to embrace the concept *The darker the night, the brighter the light.* It was true in Olongapo City, a very dark place where the Subic Service Center shown bright in contrast, as well as in Thailand where our missionaries lived under great hardships to be a light to the hosts of American military men sent there to protect the cause of freedom. We left the country thanking the Lord for his faithful servants willing to serve in such a dark place at great personal cost. At the end of the two-week trip, the Philippines looked mighty good as we jostled along on the Victory Liner toward Subic Bay.

Chapter 32

IN THE BAY

The holidays were especially meaningful in our centers overseas. The incredible loneliness felt by the men far from their loved ones and families provided prepared soil for the Word of God to penetrate. We did our very best to make those times memorably happy.

The tropical climate certainly didn't remind us of Christmas at home, but we did have poinsettias in full bloom on our back fence. We decorated the center rooms elegantly (one year we had five trees!), made lots of goodies, and played Christmas carols over the sound system. On Christmas Eve after attending the service at the chapel, we had refreshments by candlelight, sang carols and then all gathered around the tree in the lounge. Tom invited those who were experiencing their first Christian Christmas to share their testimony. Lots of tears glistened in the reflection of the shimmering tree lights. "I have sung Christmas carols all my life," one shared, "but never knew what they meant until now."

Then our family read the story of *God's Trees*, each one taking the part of a tree. The first tree wanted to become a baby's bed, but ended up as the manger in Bethlehem. The second tree dreamed of being a stately ship, but became a lowly fishing boat from which Jesus addressed the crowds. The third tree only wanted to stay in the forest and point to God, but to his deep sorrow was hewn into a rough cross for the murder of Christ. As each tree realized how much better God's plan was than their own, they discovered they were part of a miracle. "This tree, all bedecked with ornaments and lights," Tom shared, drawing our attention to the beautiful tree, "is a picture of that tree adorned with the Son of God. His gift to you is eternal life." Then he shared the plan of salvation, inviting anyone to receive Christ that night.

We encouraged the guys to not open their gifts from home on their foot lockers in the barracks or ships, but to bring them out to put under our tree. The children had the privilege of distributing them. Each year we carefully selected a meaningful gift we could purchase in quantity for the men. Those who came to the center for the first time that night couldn't believe there was a gift with their name on it under the tree. It was fun. Some of those men still have those gifts.

Every available bed or couch in the center was occupied by a lonely sailor on Christmas eve. We provided a buffet breakfast the next morning and then the singles went to the couples' homes for Christmas dinner. That allowed the house help to have the day off and us to have private family time when we opened our own gifts. Then, at the invitation of one of the fleet sailors, our family had the special joy of eating dinner on board one of the ships—a gourmet delight! In the evening the center was open for games, a movie, singing, or whatever brought joy to the men.

Danny Wilson spent one Christmas with us. He later became a missionary to Haiti. Writing from there he recalls:

> I will always remember your Christmas story about the three trees. That was the best Christmas I ever spent

away from home. You made my day. I recall fondly a lonesome sailor who found a home for awhile. Won't it be great when we all get to heaven and see Jesus face to face? The reunion will be the best.

One Christmas the chaplain at Subic arranged a unique caroling experience for us. The group from the center and some from the chapel boarded a Navy MIKE boat. Since many ships were usually in port for the holidays to help the morale of the men, we rode from ship to ship singing Christmas carols. As we chugged alongside a ship, the music wafting over the bay, we could hear the call on the 1-MC (public address system): "Now hear this! Carolers approaching on the starboard side." The men rushed to the deck several stories above us, listened as we sang and then waved as we made our way to the next ship. At the last one, we were invited into the galley where we were served cookies and ice cream.

Grande Island is located in Subic Bay, a half-hour ride by launch from the Navy base. During the Vietnam days, with so many men coming for R & R (rest and recreation), this tiny island was placed off-limits to all but military personnel. The chaplains took possession of two houses on the island to be used for religious retreats. Ralph Porter, our co-director, mobilized the men to renovate the structures and before long a nice retreat center was in operation. Since the island was strictly for R & R, there were facilities for volleyball, swimming, and other recreation. The heavy jungle vegetation was a peaceful respite from life aboard the ships. A Christian Filipino man was hired to maintain the facilities and guard against thievery.

Before a ship arrived in port, arrangements were made with the chaplain on board to encourage his men to attend a retreat. Tom and Ralph usually arranged for the meetings with the food being brought from the ships. Often they did the teaching and speaking, but if a missionary from another organization was in the area, he was invited to share. There was no routine schedule for these retreats. They could be on weekdays or weekends—whenever a ship was in port. The concept was so innovative that the Navy made a big "to-do" about it at the time of the dedication and *Stars and Stripes* carried a full article. We were thrilled to have another means of effective ministry in the lives of the men.

The Retreat House on Grande Island

With so many new believers coming and going, Tom had the privilege of baptizing a number of men at various times. A favorite place for such a service was at one of the beaches on the base. One particular baptism stands out. Twelve sailors had given their testimony to Tom and were ready to be baptized. A large group from the center was present as we sang songs of salvation, and one by one the men were led into the bay. Each gave a short testimony of his faith in Christ and was lowered into the water. As the last one came up, another sailor stepped forward. "I have been listening to the testimonies of these men and have just received Christ as my Savior. May I also be baptized?" Remembering the story of the Ethiopian eunuch in the Bible, Tom agreed.

Other times we loaded the vehicles and drove a half-hour up the zigzag where we parked and walked along the river to the New Tribes Mission training center for Filipino missionaries. With the right placement of some large rocks, the small river formed a pond—the perfect setting for a baptism. Many men from both Subic and Clark remember that place where they gave witness of their faith in Christ in the rite of baptism.

Doug Kurtz wrote to thank us for one of his times at Subic:

> 1 April 1972 At sea—Vietnam
> Dear Tom and Dotty,
>
> I am writing to you in the name of our Lord to thank you from all of us here on the USS *Tripoli* for all that you have done for us. Thank you for having the Bible conference where the things of God were revealed in the messages you shared. They made me look at myself to see that I wasn't being the kind of Christian that I should be—that I must put all my trust in Christ. God has really moved on this ship and is making people realize that Christ is the only answer.
>
> I especially want to thank you for the baptismal service where I testified that I had been made alive in Christ....

Chapter 33

THE PRODIGAL

The Subic Service Center was there to serve the American military personnel. Since there were all kinds of people in Olongapo who would gladly have availed themselves of our facilities, we were careful to keep our primary goal in sight. But one day Don came in the door. He was quite a sight: balding gray hair, teeth missing, no shoes (just slippers), ragged shorts and T-shirt, and the skinniest body I had ever seen, covered with tattoos. He wanted to read the American newspaper, *Stars and Stripes.* He was also hungry, we discovered, and relished our home cooked meals. After several visits, we learned he had come to Asia as a mercenary (soldier of fortune) but ended up in Olongapo when his job fell through. His visa and passport had long ago expired, he couldn't work because Philippine law prohibited it, and he had no money to return to the U.S. We learned he had been married in the States and had some children, but had long ago lost contact with any of them. He lived on the streets of Olongapo or with one of the street girls who would take him in. We didn't particularly enjoy having him around the center or around our children, but he had a monkey that Danny came to adore. And we did have compassion on this destitute man.

He was involved with a Mafia group that hijacked ships plying the coastline of the Philippines. His life was in constant danger. He drank heavily, stole what he could, and was in an advanced stage of asthma. One day when he came to the center he could barely walk—ugly purple bruises were all over his body.

"What happened to you?" I exclaimed. "You look almost dead!"

"I thought I was," he replied softly. "A bunch of thugs beat me up. This is the first time I've even been able to walk. They almost killed me!"

He lived with a woman in a little grass hut on the beach. One morning he awoke hungry, but there was nothing to eat. The woman was gone. He knew his grim life was about over. Barely able to crawl from the plywood board he slept on, he dragged his wretched body to an opening in the hut. Despair engulfing his soul, he looked outside. There he saw some pigs under the next hut foraging for food in the mud. *If I could only get over there, I'd get that stuff,* he groaned to himself.

Suddenly he recalled a story he had read once in a Bible he had stolen from the Lutheran Servicemen's Center. Mustering all his strength, he reached on a dirty shelf for the "hippie Bible," as he called it, *Good News for Modern Man.* He remembered seeing stick figures depicting the parable of the prodigal son. *That's me!* he cried when he found the picture. He read how the father had come running to his wayward son. *Oh God, I need you as my Father, he sobbed. I am such a sinner. Please save me!* The Father heard him, welcoming him home.

Immediately he was changed. It was Sunday morning. He wanted to go to church. Somehow he managed to get to the road where a man came by and offered him a ride.

Arriving in town, Don saw a Seventh-Day Adventist church, the denomination he had known as a child. "Stop here!" he shouted. As he left, the driver handed him a few centavos.

The service had just begun. He sat in a wooden pew at the back, listened to the singing and preaching and was overwhelmed with the peace in his heart. When the offering plate was passed, he put the centavos in. Now he knew something incredible had happened to him.

His woman, Lourdes, also came to know Christ, and they were married. Together they made journeys to the Negritos, aborigines who lived in the jungles, and dispensed medicines and the Gospel to them. One time Don went alone. When he failed to return on the appointed day, Lourdes came to see me. "Oh, ma'am, I'm so afraid something has happened. And I don't have any money for food," she wept. Putting some pesos in her hand, I wrapped my arms around her tiny shoulders and we prayed together for Don's safe return. Later in the day he came home.

One day I asked Don, "Now that you are a believer, have you had any contact with your family back home? Don't you think you should at least let your mother know you're alive. I'll bet she has shed many tears over you."

He did write and soon received a letter from his mother. She was overjoyed to know he was alive after a twenty-year silence. She wrote, "Your father died several years ago. He left a trust fund for you in his will." They continued writing, and eventually she sent money for plane tickets and the necessary paperwork to permit him to leave the Philippines. The day came when Don and Lourdes boarded a plane bound for America.

To their surprise, the trust fund was sizeable—enough for them to live on and continue missionary work in the U.S. When they came to visit us in Denver, Don was driving a new Jeep station wagon. They used the cassette tape player in it to listen to Christian tapes. When I happened to go downstairs for something the next morning, Don and Lourdes were having devotions together in the family room.

We went to a restaurant for breakfast, but when it came time to pay the bill, Lourdes snatched it out of Tom's hand. When we protested she replied, "Oh, no! Don't you remember the day when I came to you for help. You hugged me, gave me money, and prayed with me! Now it's my turn to thank you." I didn't remember but was humbly pleased to let her pay.

The Prodigal

I've thought many times of Don living a pauper's life in a faraway land, not knowing the treasure his father had prepared for him. How often I live in poverty of soul when my heavenly Father has provided in abundance for my every need. Sad, isn't it?

Our co-worker, Ralph Porter's greatest love was street evangelism. He trained some of the sailors and took them out into town with him. On one of those nights they met Roger and witnessed to him about his need for Christ. When he showed interest, they invited him to come to the center where he accepted the Lord as his Savior. He then poured out his sordid story.

He had taken his discharge from the Navy some time ago, determined to make a fortune with the gambling syndicate in Olongapo. He learned too late that Satan is a hard taskmaster. As his debts mounted, so did his worthlessness to the underworld. But they wanted their money. He was desperate to escape their clutches, but had no money or way to get out. He stayed with us for several days.

With great joy he attended the Bible studies, eagerly soaking up the truths of God's Word. When I learned his story, though I was happy for his changed life, a deep fear overwhelmed me. I could just imagine those gangsters storming our place with guns blazing to get this guy. I couldn't sleep at night. During the day I kept an eye on the door, expecting them to charge in at any moment. I was paralyzed with fear for us and for him.

One day Roger told Ralph, "I want to right some of the wrongs I have done. I am willing to go to the authorities on base to reveal the identities of the leaders of the syndicate." Cautiously Ralph contacted the Office of Naval Intelligence (ONI). They were very interested. Before long an officer was at our door to gain the information. The agreement was that in exchange for the right information, the Navy would see that Roger got out of the country. Now all panic broke loose in my mind.

The next day, at the agreed upon time, Tom and Ralph put Roger into the van, covered him with a rug, drove to the base, and delivered him to the authorities. I just knew an ambush was waiting for them in the two blocks between our driveway and the main gate. Wilma and I stayed on our knees pleading with the Lord for safety as they ran the gauntlet. Before long Tom and Ralph returned unharmed. The episode was over. I slept that night for the first time in days. Whether my fears were real or imagined doesn't matter. God answered my prayer.

Ralph recalls some of the frustration he felt during his days at Subic:

> At night our young, virgin, single men poured into the city in their clean white uniforms. But by the end of the night many came running for the gate to escape being beaten and robbed. They were drunk, dirty, and penniless. I was deeply angered with the Filipinos for destroying our men.
>
> I was driving the van down the street one day when in my anger I mumbled, "If one Filipino gets in my way, I'll run over him!"
>
> But then my Heavenly Father spoke to my heart.
>
> *What's the difference between you and these Filipinos?*
>
> *I have Christ Jesus in my heart, and they don't!*
>
> *What are you doing to win them to me, Ralph?*
>
> *I'm trying to run over them!*
>
> *Did I send you as a missionary 9,000 miles from home, to kill Filipinos with your vehicle?*
>
> I got the point! Right there I repented of my sinfulness and renewed my commitment to win both "my people" and the Filipinos to the Lord.

Chapter 34

ANARCHY

The political situation in the Philippines in the early 1970s deteriorated to the point of tyranny. President Ferdinand Marcos was losing control of the country. Most Filipino men carried guns in their belts. At the doors of the bars downtown signs read, *Turn in your guns at the door.* It was like an old wild-west movie. A person only needed to stand at our gate for a few moments to see a crime committed—a pocket picked, a watch stolen, a fistfight break out, or a person murdered. Of course, Olongapo had always been dangerous. Dick and Margaret Patty remember the time a bullet came flying into the kitchen of the Subic Service Center. The hole in the cabinet was mute evidence of long-term violence in that place. But now it was totally out of control.

Frequently, threats were made against the U.S. military bases, so then the gates were closed. Armed American military men were poised on the roofs of the houses near the gate in case a demonstration got out of hand. Military families who lived off base were told to have a bag packed for emergency evacuation in case of a revolution. We inquired with the U. S. Embassy and were told we would be evacuated from the base.

So we placed our important papers and American money in a brief case and locked it in our safe. We read in the newspapers and heard on TV reports of riots and murders in Manila.

Late one night when Ralph was driving home from Manila with a van-load of sailors, he came to an unfamiliar checkpoint. Men in black uniforms rushed out brandishing guns. He panicked, thinking they were revolutionaries, and sped off. They started shooting but he didn't know the rounds went into the air. "Ralph, stop! They'll kill us!" the sailors shouted, hitting the deck of the van. Ralph screeched to a stop.

The guards rushed up shouting, "What do you think you're doing? Why didn't you stop?"

"This isn't where the regular checkpoint is located. I thought you were rebels!" Ralph responded, obviously shaken. They were the regular police and soon let him go. It was a scary time for Americans as well as Filipinos.

We had just finished our usual shopping trip in Manila, being careful to listen to the radio to avoid the areas where demonstrations were being held. With the van loaded to the roof as usual, we began our late night drive home. We suspected something was wrong when we drove into Olongapo—the streets were empty. The bars (which at midnight were just getting started) were quiet and deserted. An eerie stillness lay over the whole town. As Alfonso quickly closed the gate behind us, he motioned us inside.

"Haven't you heard?" he asked breathlessly, his eyes wide. "The President has declared martial law. Everyone must be inside by 10 p.m." As reality set in, we silently thanked the Lord for his protection. We could have been sitting in a town jail somewhere.

The impact on the country was instant. People who normally had little regard for the laws of the land suddenly became fearful to jaywalk or even toss a piece of paper on the street. It was rumored a person could be arrested for absolutely no reason at all and held without charge for any length of time. In the larger cities, amnesty was granted to those who turned in their guns by a certain date. The cache was huge.

President Marcos told the people his move had come within hours of a revolutionary coup. He removed all government leaders, threw out the constitution, and declared himself dictator. His long-range plan was to restructure the entire government. There was much speculation as to whether he did actually save the country or not. But the situation changed drastically in a few hours. After the initial fear wore off, life did return to some normalcy. We were quite unaware of the political ramifications taking place during those years, but Mr. Marcos appeared to us to be a benevolent dictator who stabilized a country in chaos. He ran the country quite well in the immediate future. Sadly, it all ran amok. When he was deposed, snatched away to Hawaii by our armed forces and later died, there was a sense of sadness in my heart for him.

Chapter 35

"IT'S YOUR BABY!"

The old Dodge van was showing its age, but we still used it for trips when the Nissan was full and for shopping trips to Manila. One day Tom was driving a group from the USS *Coral Sea* to visit the historical World War II site on Corregidor. The van hit a deep hole in the road. The men bounced up, hitting their heads on the roof, and then came crashing down onto the hard, broken seats. "You sure do need a new vehicle," remarked Chaplain Dave Meschke, who was riding beside Tom. "Hey, guys, don't you think we should start a fund for a new van?" Soon after the ship returned to sea, we received a check for $1,000 to start the van fund.

We posted a little thermometer on the bulletin board showing the progress of the fund. Not wanting to be outdone by the *Coral Sea*, the guys from the *Kitty Hawk* started a collection when they got back out to sea. We received this letter from the ship's skipper:

> Your Service Center has been providing outstanding service to the officers and men of the USS *Kitty Hawk* and embarked Air Wing. In appreciation, the Protestant

congregation met and by a unanimous vote decided to donate $1,000 to your center for the purchase of a van. Our best wishes for continued success in your fine work.

Signed: M.W. Townsend, Captain,
U.S. Navy, Commanding Officer.

In only six gifts, the fund was complete and we ordered a new 1972 Ford van. Dave Meschke arranged for it to be sent to Subic on a Navy ship.

Tom's excitement was at its peak the day the ship arrived. He rushed onto the base only to discover the ship was anchored out in the bay. "No problem," the project officer assured him. "We'll get it. Come on!" They boarded a small landing craft, which soon pulled up into the larger ship's bay. There on the lower deck was the shiny blue van.

The crew unhitched the chains that held it secure during the voyage and placed two planks over the gap between the two ships. The larger ship was higher than the small one, so the planks made a steep decline. "Okay," the chief yelled waving at Tom, "drive it off!"

"Uh, I've never done anything like this before," Tom replied haltingly.

"It's your baby. If it goes in the drink, it's your problem!" the old salt snorted.

Hands trembling, Tom climbed into the driver's seat and turned the key. The engine gave a smooth start. Easing it into the lowest gear, he edged the vehicle forward. The chief stood in front guiding him onto the planks. Slowly, he inched onto the makeshift ramp, eyeing the water below. "Easy does it!" the chief yelled. Then the bus lurched down the grade coming to rest on the deck of the smaller vessel. With a sigh of relief, Tom pulled the emergency brake tight.

Soon the boat was chugging to shore where the back ramp was dropped into the water on the beach. The whole procedure had to be repeated. Tom eased the van toward the ramp and then jammed his foot on the gas, plunging the van off the ship into the wet, soft sand. The wheels bogged down but then gradually gripped hold and inched slowly onto the beach. Tom's shoulders sagged in relief. Later he learned that the tie-down chains had broken the rear brake lines! A spontaneous prayer of thankfulness was dispatched heavenward.

"It's your baby!"

Within a short time customs was cleared and the Ford van took up its home in our driveway.

Chapter 36

HELP

After Ralph and Wilma Porter left for furlough, we ran the center alone for several months. With so many sailors coming, it took all of our efforts to keep the ministry going. Faithful families and singles stationed on the base assisted ably when the fleet came in, which was almost constant in those war years. Chief George and Lillian Davis were always available, as were Joe and Norma Raines, Fred DuPont, Lt. Chuck Dunham, Ed and Melba Waggoner, Dave Hancock and a host of others. But they had full-time jobs on the base. We needed another missionary couple.

The Lord was sending new missionaries to OCSC and they needed some training before going on to their own ministry. The work at Subic was flourishing and the facility was ideal for two couples, so Executive Director Dick Patty asked if we would be willing to have a couple serve with us for about six months.

Abe and Ellen Teeny were the first assigned to come. We were *so* excited! We needed help so badly. We cleaned and painted their apartment until it shone, counting the days to their arrival. I thought it would never come, but it finally did.

Taking one last glance through their apartment, confident it was perfect, we set out for Manila to meet their plane.

En route we stopped at Ken and Elaine Brooks' home. It wasn't Monday so they were surprised to see us. "Oh, we're on the way to the airport to meet the Teenys," we said joyously, glancing at our watches.

"Oh, no!" Ken exclaimed. "Didn't you get the word? They aren't coming for several months!"

I burst into tears. I just couldn't believe it! I was devastated. Even Tom was greatly disappointed. Again our mail system had failed, our phone was useless, and I experienced one of the deepest disappointments of my life.

During our four years at Subic, we ran the ministry by ourselves one-fourth of the time. I knew my weariness was out of control when we arrived at a missionary friend's home on one of our Manila trips and I saw a half-finished puzzle in their living room. Envy overwhelmed me. (I love puzzles!) To have time to work a puzzle seemed like the ultimate luxury. I went into their bathroom and had a good cry.

A few months later the Teenys did arrive, and we were greatly blessed by their presence and help during the next seven months. They were older than we were, and had much wisdom—a definite asset to us and to the ministry.

I had written to Ellen saying we couldn't get "convenience" foods in the Philippines. On one of their days off, Ellen decided to prepare a meal for Abe. She stood in the pantry, searching the shelves, and then came to me and exclaimed, "How in the world do you fix a meal from what's in there?" What the average American woman interpreted as "making it from scratch" was totally different from our "scratch." For example, instead of having canned vegetables, we bought them in the market, cleaned them, cooked them, then prepared the casserole. This was part of the adjustment to a different culture.

When the Teenys moved on to their own work, John and Joan Hobson came for six months. Their daughter, Judy, was such a joy. But she was nearly the undoing of Danny. He was four years older, but she was taller and could read circles around him—not real affirming to his young ego! But she couldn't out-talk him! Nor could she ignore Danny and David's harassment. Somehow we got along, and Judy turned out just fine, but the process was a challenge to both sets of parents.

Joan was a special friend to me. Not only did we work well together, but she had the courage to point out some of my blind spots. I was putting together a long shopping list for our trip to Manila the following day. "What can I get for you?" I asked Joan.

"Oh, please get a jar of raspberry jam," she replied.

"Uh....Joan, that would be an imported item and very expensive," I cautioned. Our grocery fund was joint so this request impacted the whole. I rarely allowed myself to purchase such luxuries.

"That's okay, please get it anyway. John loves raspberry jam," was her quiet reply.

"Uh....

"It's okay," she repeated. "You spend lots of money on candles for the dinners. I would like raspberry jam for my husband." I thought about this for awhile and then saw clearly what Joan had observed. I was willing to spend any amount of money for the "guys" but was stingy when it came to personal things. It opened my eyes to become more balanced.

Another time we were preparing the dessert after Bible study. Lori was helping in the chuck wagon. Evidently I, her perfectionist mother, repeatedly corrected her for the way she put on the whipped cream. After Lori went upstairs, Joan spoke gently: "If I had been Lori I'd have thrown it in your face! What difference did it make?" She was right, I was wrong. I ran upstairs to apologize to Lori. I have always been thankful to Joan. She and John are faithful servants of the Lord to this day.

In training new couples for servicemen's center ministry, we had an interesting experience. About the third Sunday after their arrival, we found the wife unwilling to attend chapel. "I just can't go there," she would wail. "I feel like I'm compromising!" Tom and I were sympathetic, recalling our experience in Panama, but we tried to put things into perspective for them.

"Did you come to the mission field to serve or to be served?" we asked. "If you came to be served, then you probably need to return to your church where they serve you." We also explained that a chapel is not a local church. It does not have elders and deacons and the chaplain who preaches there has his own beliefs and denomination, but the chapel does not become that faith group. And our purpose in being there was to serve, not to be served.

"But my child's Sunday school teacher isn't even a believer!" she wailed.

"Then you should volunteer to be a teacher," was our response. "If you are depending on a Sunday school teacher to provide all of your children's religious instruction, you're making a terrible mistake. If you are training them well, one hour at the chapel will not counteract faithful teaching."

Eventually all of them learned to function within the pluralistic structure of the chapel and found it to be a great outreach and blessing; but the adjustment was difficult for some.

On Mondays, the only day the center was closed, we tried faithfully to observe our one day of rest. It was also the day off for most of the house help. After the children left for school,

Tom and I often spent a few hours at the air-conditioned library on base or took a picnic to the beach where we swam and read books. After school we picked up the children and either returned to the beach or went to an early dinner at the officers' club. Then we returned to our apartment where we played games or Tom roughhoused on the floor with the children. Those were great times.

It was Danny's tenth birthday. For days he had tried to get us to reveal our plans for the special event. But we were determined to surprise him—not an easy task. Over and over he coaxed, "Oh, I know....!" Then he would play out a scenario he thought would be great. The day before the event he was positive he had it all figured out.

After school on the exciting day, we all got dressed in our finest clothes and drove onto the base. With each turn Danny told us where we were going. "Nope!" was our only response. When we arrived at the Cubi Officers' Club, we were ushered to a "reserved" table. "Cool!" Danny remarked. (We had been there earlier in the day to make arrangements.) We had a nice dinner. "I know—now we're going home to open presents," he announced confidently.

Just then the band, which had just assembled, struck up the familiar strains of *Happy Birthday to you...dear Danny.* Then they sang it again, the room filled with Navy pilots resounding in song. Speechless at last, Danny just sat there grinning. Then the spotlight swung around to his place as a host of waiters paraded in carrying a big cake, candles blazing, and a pile of gifts. We had succeeded! We got him!

One Monday afternoon while at the beach, we were shocked to see smoke rising across the bay. "That's Olongapo!" I shouted to Tom. Jumping in our van, we raced toward home. When we reached the base gate, fire engines were screaming toward town. Relieved that the fire was not near the center, we rushed in to find Ralph Porter pacing on the roof of the two-story building. "I didn't know if we should start packing to evacuate!" he shouted. Tom and he assessed the situation and decided to hang loose and see which way the wind blew the flames. Fortunately for us, the firemen soon got the blaze under control and we were safe. But the entire central market was destroyed.

One night we almost did burn the center down. The power was off when the children went up to our apartment to go to bed. As usual, I lit a candle and put it on the edge of the bathtub. They went to sleep and I returned downstairs. Soon the power came on. Three hours later when we opened the door to our apartment, we saw strings of black stuff hanging from the ceiling and walls. Stunned, we rushed into the children's rooms and found them sound asleep, the air-conditioners humming. But covering the intake grates were the same black strings. We soon discovered that the candle had burned down, causing the acrylic holder to melt into black residue. The tile above the bathtub was blackened, but the flames had failed to catch the wallboard above. The entire apartment was draped with the black goo. We cleaned for a couple of hours, then dropped exhausted into bed, thanking the Lord for his protection.

After the hot, busy evenings in the center, we relished a cool shower before going to bed. The benefit of the air-conditioners in our bedrooms was two-fold: they kept us cool at night, allowing the windows to be closed, and their loud hum drowned out the sound of the juke boxes—that is all except for the "oom-pa-pa" of the bass guitars. Nothing could silence them.

I loved crawling into the cool sheets at night. In fact, sometimes they were downright cold to our tropically acclimated bodies, so I suggested we send to the States for an electric blanket. Wrong! "What! Cool and heat the bed at the same time with electricity? That's ridiculous!" was Tom's swift, not too gentle response. Oh well, I tried!

An event indelibly etched in our minds and hearts was the day the first POWs arrived at Clark Air Base from Hanoi, North Vietnam. We took a group of our Subic folks over but were not prepared for what we experienced. Standing on the scorching tarmac of the flight line in the blazing hot afternoon sun, we saw journalists and television cameramen from every nation in the world, including all of the major networks in America. We had constructed some signs welcoming the men home, pictures of which were later emblazoned on the front pages of newspapers around the globe.

When the first plane arrived and the back of the plane dropped down, we knew we were part of a significant historical event. One by one the former prisoners stepped from the plane squinting at the bright sunlight coming to a snappy salute as their names were read over the loud speaker. It was their first glimpse of freedom! They wept and we wept and so did you if you watched that monumental event on your TV.

Early in 1973 Jerry and Irene Bates came to serve with us and eventually be our replacements when we went on furlough that summer. One day Tom was writing a check to send to another servicemen's center in northern Japan for the purchase of their new van. Wanting Jerry to understand our philosophy of *freely you have received, freely give,* Tom called him, showing him the check for $1,000. "We have some extra money this month and they have a special need," Tom explained.

"Tom, I just don't think you should do that," Jerry responded. "You're leaving and I'm going to have to pay the bills. I know you have extra money, but I'm not sure I will."

"Jerry, the same God is going to supply for you as he has for me," Tom responded, putting the check into the envelope and sealing it.

A few days later the phone rang. It was the base chaplain. "Tom, the Navy Chief of Chaplains is here from Washington. He's heard about the center and wants to see it. We'll be there in a little while."

We turned to, quickly spiffying up the place and waited...and waited...and waited. Tom was pacing, looking at his watch. He knew our vespers service was to begin at 5:00 p.m. and it was now 4:30. Just then, in came the admiral with his entourage.

We gave him a quick tour of the facility. He couldn't help but see the sailors and marines everywhere; families were arriving, bringing food for dinner. At 4:50, the guys began the process of converting the lounge into a meeting room—folding chairs came out of the closet and the piano was rolled into place. Sensing he might get caught in the service, the chaplain turned to his aide and whispered, "Do you have the check?"

"Yes, sir," responded the aide, placing it into his hand.

"We value what you are doing for our men, "the admiral said kindly. "Here is a small token of our appreciation." Tom took the check, thanking him graciously, and slipped it into his shirt pocket. The chaplains left and the meeting began.

Later that evening, Tom went to his office and looked at the check. "Hey, Jerry, come here!" he called. "Remember that verse I was explaining to you the other day....*Freely you have received, freely give or is it freely give and freely you will receive?* Look at this check." Jerry stared at the zeros. Exactly one thousand dollars! That incident was a boost to Jerry's faith as he and Irene assumed the leadership of the Subic Service Center. They served there faithfully for the next six years.

One day, shortly before we were due to leave for furlough, I discovered a lump in my breast. The doctor at the base clinic confirmed that it could be a problem, but said the pathologist was in the States so there was no point in removing it before our departure. That night, while sitting in the van on the base waiting for Lori to finish Bible study with the youth, I faced the reality that at age 41 I might have cancer. Any woman who has had this experience can relate to the gamut of emotions it brings. As I sobbed before the Lord, I finally had peace as I cried out to him, "Lord, I have given you my life. If you choose to take it from me this soon, it's okay. I submit to your will. But no matter how long I live, I will continue to serve you as faithfully as I am able." Three days after our arrival in the States, our dear friend Dr. Roland Icke removed the lump. It was benign.

As a farewell gift to our household staff, we planned an all-day trip to Manila for them. To our surprise, several had never even been to the capital. Wanting it to be especially memorable, we asked each one what they would like to see there. They wanted to visit the Rizal memorial and other famous historical sites, just like we would want to visit significant places in Washington D.C.

That Monday morning, they and their spouses arrived dressed in their finest. We boarded the Nissan bus—almost every seat was filled. We had never seen all of them together in one place before! Arriving in Manila at noon, we stopped at a restaurant we knew they would enjoy. The manager knew Tom from the many stops he had made with the sailors. Soon we were all seated at a long table. Tom ordered the dinner for all, and soon steaming plates of fried chicken and rice were served. "Let's give thanks to the Lord," Tom announced, taking the hand of those on each side. Everyone followed his example, and we bowed our heads and hearts before the Lord. As they ate and chatted happily, Tom and I made a startling discovery. For four years we had been the sole support for this host of people as well as all of their children—a total of about 65 people! It was an unforgettable moment in our lives. Fourteen years earlier we were having difficulty raising the $100 a year rent on the servicemen's home in Panama. Now this! We silently thanked the Lord for his amazing provision.

Knowing we were returning to the U.S., many of the naval officers offered to take a box of our things when their ship returned home. When the opportunity came, Tom and I quickly packed one that could be easily carried and stored in a stateroom. Eventually thirty-six boxes were sent with thirty-six different men on thirty-six different ships. (It was ethical because it was at no expense to the government.) We sometimes say it took the whole Seventh Fleet to get us back to the U.S. We did wonder if we would ever see the stuff again, but amazingly each box eventually arrived safe and sound.

The Christian community at Subic gave us a wonderful farewell. The beauty of the sun setting over Subic Bay as we ate dinner atop the Subic Officers' Club is indelibly planted in our hearts and minds. Dressed in our matching outfits (Lori was sixteen, David fourteen, Danny twelve), we sang several songs as a family. Many gracious words of appreciation were spoken; then the chaplain presented us with a check for $1,000 as a going away gift. We were thrilled and humbled at this outpouring of love, but the pain of saying goodbye to those dear friends almost spoiled the evening.

On May 21, 1973, the Hash family was packed, eagerly ready to begin the journey to the "land of the big BX (base exchange)." Except for Danny. As we pulled away in the van, he was on his knees, peering out the back window, sobbing... "Why do we have to leave. Why can't we stay here? Why do I

Our family at the farewell given by the people at Subic and Cubi

have to leave all my friends?" Who were these friends? The sailors, Filipinos, families with their children, all waving good-bye, dabbing away their tears.

You thought I cut the wrong orders when I sent you here, didn't you? the Lord reminded me. I promised I would care for the children—that I loved them more than you do." A collage of memories flooded over me: the children hearing the exciting testimonies of the men, sharing the joyous times of singing, watching them grow in the Lord, and becoming best of friends with so many. We wondered how being around all of those young sailors would impact Lori as a teen, but she became best of friends with the finest Christian young men America was producing ... and right in her own home. They took her to the base for ice cream; they went on group snorkeling trips; they brought her trinkets from Hong Kong and Singapore. They were her dear friends! David and Danny felt they had oodles of big brothers who took them shopping, played games with them, and entered their worlds. They were wonderful years for us and our children. *Yes, Lord, these four years far exceeded our fondest dreams for our children and for us. Thank you!* Later that day we boarded the plane bound for America.

Note: In 1991 Mt. Pinatubo erupted. The volcano was located about forty miles west of Clark Air Force Base. The first day of its eruption, the ash blew directly at Clark and nearby Angeles City. The destruction was so thorough that the base was evacuated and never reopened. Angeles City was devastated.

The following day a typhoon blew in, the winds changed direction, and the eruption blew wet ash over to Subic/Cubi Navy bases and Olongapo City, about forty miles south, heavily damaging the base and most of the city.

Shortly after that negotiations over the base agreements between the U.S. and Philippine governments broke down, resulting in the withdrawal of all U.S. military personnel from the country. OCSC turned the Subic Service Center building (which had minimal damage) over to a missionary serving local Filipinos.

Could God simply have had enough of the sin of those two places (like Sodom and Gomorrah) to bury them in volcanic ash? A thought to ponder.

Part IX

Travis Hospitality House

Chapter 37

STARTING OVER

Until 1973 all ministries of OCSC were located overseas. After closing the center in Vietnam, Lem and Marge Morgan went to Germany in 1972 and opened the Hospitality House in the Kaiserslautern area. Europe was to become OCSC's largest field from the end of the Vietnam War until the end of the "cold war" in 1989. Dick Patty served as Director of Europe Ministries from 1978 to 1991.

In 1973 OCSC was asked to assume two existing ministries to the military: Fellowship Ranch near Fort Leonard Wood in Missouri and Travis International Hospitality Inc. (TIHI) near Fairfield, California. TIHI was an outreach to Asian military personnel sent to the U.S. for training, but as the Vietnam War wound down so did the influx of those men. Founders Jesse and Edith Johnson wanted to see the work continue in the OCSC format. Tom and I were asked to direct the Travis work; Lou and Linda Harrison went to Fellowship Ranch. Even though it meant no time of rest for us, we agreed, sensing the Lord's direction.

Our arrival at San Francisco from Manila was memorable. As we deplaned into the terminal, a host of people swarmed about us—mostly former sailors and their wives—hugging, shouting, laughing. Even my mother was there. Steve and Jessie Ciupek, dear friends from Subic, had welcomed her when she arrived from Wisconsin and brought her for this grand reunion. After gathering our baggage, we discovered that everyone wanted to take us to Travis, a trip of over an hour. So the Hash family arrived at the Travis Hospitality House in four different cars. Roland Kincher, the temporary OCSC director, welcomed us all warmly. We were at our new home. But we had no concept of the vast changes that were about to come into our lives.

The following day the new Ford van arrived, purchased with generous gifts from the men at Subic. It was even the same color and style as the new one we left there. For the next two months we drove thousands of miles, visiting friends, speaking in churches, singing as a family, touching base with our supporters, and seeing our wonderful land of America. It was a new world for our children. The first time we went to Penneys, Lori waited at the door. "I can't go in there," she said. "I don't have an I.D. card." At age sixteen she had never bought a ready-made garment. In the Philippines you went to the market, selected fabric, found a picture of a garment, took it to the dressmaker, and had it made. But it didn't take her long to figure it all out—she soon became an astute shopper.

Toward the end of August we arrived back at Fairfield. The Travis Hospitality House was beautiful. Located just two miles from Travis Air Force Base, the building was set on four-and-a-half acres of land. A large horse stable and small creek gave it a lovely pastoral setting. The house was only six years old. A Spanish style two story, it had four bedrooms and two baths upstairs. A large guest area enhanced the first floor as well as a two-car garage that the Johnsons had finished for a meeting room.

Travis Hospitality House

And the kitchen! After surrendering my kitchen to the house help for the past nine years, the "miles" of counters and cabinets caused my suppressed homemaking instincts to spring alive. I couldn't wait to make that spacious area my own. The entire house needed furniture and refurbishing but that was just our cup of tea.

However, there was a serious problem: the substantial ministry funds we had at Subic remained there. Our missionary salary couldn't begin to meet the needs nor could it pay the monthly rent of $350. Without a significant ministry in operation, resources were minimal.

The purpose for OCSC establishing a ministry at Travis was loosely defined—it could have developed in any of several directions. We knew that most military personnel going to or coming from the Far East funneled through that base, so there was potential for making contact with alumni returning from our ministries in Asia to the U.S. and possibly contacting and providing direction for some going out.

We also knew that an OCSC family located on the West Coast could represent the mission as well as assist OCSC staff passing through. Then, of course, there was no other existing ministry in the community other than the Navigators specifically targeting the thousands of single airmen assigned to the base, so a traditional servicemen's home was a strong possibility.

Tom and I had not pioneered a ministry since our Panama days and those were painful memories. The needs of our teen-age children were very important to us. After initial adjustments to America, we settled into a comfortable family routine. But the ministry remained evasive.

The installation chaplain on the base was unfamiliar with OCSC, so denied our request for a base pass. This caused the hassle of stopping at the gate each time to request a guest pass—a time-consuming process. Making contact with singles was difficult. One young airman did come to the house occasionally, but just at meal time. After a few times he admitted that the only reason he came was to save money toward his upcoming marriage. We felt it best for him and for us that he not return.

Our egos took a real hit about that time. After such a flourishing ministry at Subic, there we sat ready to serve and no one was interested. We did some real soul-searching. We had a perfect house, but no one to "fill our rooms." We didn't feel justified living in such an expensive house without using it for ministry. In fact, we couldn't even pay the rent—it had to be subsidized by the home office—another blow to our self-esteem. Then to have to ask the only single man coming out to stay away seemed like the bottom rung.

Many times we wept, asking the Lord when he would allow us back into ministry We were unaware that God was causing us to rest after four exhausting years at Subic, giving us precious time as a family, preparing our children of twelve, fourteen, and sixteen for the years to come. Had we started with a strong ministry, which we desperately wanted, we would have burned out in a short time and possibly negatively impacted our children. How gracious he was to protect us from our own desires.

Roland Kincher, who had been the director of the ministry for eight months, continued to live with us for quite some time. He was a bright spot in our lives, bringing encouragement and joy.

When we arrived at Travis, Hal and Connie Taylor, who had been our adult Sunday school class leaders at Clark, were there. Endowed with the gift of hospitality, they soon opened their home for a Monday night Bible study which Tom taught. They also invited us to their church and soon the children were well established with the youth group. When they started school they already had a few friends.

Within a few months, Mel and Judy Anderson and their three children arrived from Clark where they had been very active at the servicemen's home with Bob and Dorothy Bingham. Even though Mel's base was a half hour away from us and their living quarters another half-hour beyond that, they still spent many hours helping with the ministry.

Then a few months later, Cliff and Edith Woods, whom we had known at Clark, received orders to Travis. Our inner circle was definitely growing as all of us reached out to others, inviting them to the Bible study and special activities.

Maintaining that large home and the surrounding acreage was quite a chore. Neither Tom nor I had done much manual labor in the past four years, so this was a welcome change. We painted most of the interior, adding new wallpaper and draperies and a few pieces of new furniture as we could afford them. Mowing acres of grass, planting flowers, putting up a new sign and white fencing added much to the appearance.

In each place of ministry, Tom established an advisory committee to assist him. At places where the military people stayed for a year or more, he had two groups: the advisory committee which was made up of mature Christians who counseled Tom on all areas of the work—similar to an elders' board in a church. He also had work committees which helped plan and carry out the activities of the house.

On more than one occasion, the advisory committee proved to be a "shield" for Tom, caring for sensitive or disciplinary matters. This often enabled Tom to continue to have a ministry in the lives of those who were affected.

Chapter 38

PEOPLE, PEOPLE EVERYWHERE

Then the influx began. It seemed like everyone we knew in the Philippines or on the West Coast arrived to "fill our rooms." They came during the day and in the middle of the night. They all had special needs and we were the ones the Lord chose to help meet them. Trips to the base air terminal and San Francisco airport became almost daily activities. We barely got the guest room linens changed before the next bunch arrived. Rarely did we eat a meal alone. There was no time to feel sorry for ourselves now. This was God's work for us at this time and hospitality was our special love.

Retired Army chaplain Herman (Gus) Gustafson had been teaching a Sunday morning Bible class at the base terminal for many years. He asked Tom to take it over. Travelers listened with interest when they heard the announcement over the loud speaker: *Terminal Bible study to begin in the lounge in ten minutes!* Four of the regular men who attended that Bible study were involved with the Navigator ministry in the area. Interestingly, Tom had baptized two of those men in Thailand several years previously.

A ladies' Bible study was started at the house; the evening study at Taylors' home continued to grow. Norm and Joanna Jewell arrived from Clark where they had been active at the home and stayed with us while seeking housing and became a great help.

On August 23rd, a year after our arrival, we began the Friday Fellowship with twenty-five people present. That day the temperature was 108 degrees, the septic tank overflowed into the downstairs bathroom, Satan was on the prowl attacking us all day, a lady came for counseling, and Tom picked up Jack McCullough in San Francisco at midnight and returned him at 5:30 a.m. the next morning. But the meeting went well.

Three days later Tom was away on a trip. I was scheduled to leave at 4:15 a.m. to pick up some OCSC missionaries at the San Francisco airport. But I had no money and no gas. I awoke at 3:45 to pray. At 4:15 Tom drove in. He had $8.00. I jumped in the car, praising the Lord.

During the month of August 1974, we served 559 meals and had 157 stay overnight, not including the Hashes. We cooked and washed linens day and night and the Lord sent us a host of hurting people for counseling.

About this time a terrible accident occurred at the Kadena Christian Center on Okinawa where Obe and MaryAnn Hokanson were the directors. The neighbor children had come onto the center property to play and a volleyball net stanchion fell, killing the little girl. The ensuing lawsuit brought by the parents was devastating to the Hokansons and to the mission. Due to technical entanglements, mission leadership thought it best for the Hokansons to return to the U.S. We were asked to take their place.

Tom and I agonized with the Lord concerning that proposal. Our children were well settled into school, church, and a close circle of Christian friends. While we knew the

Dotty bringing home the groceries

ministry on Okinawa would be fruitful and very rewarding, we were unsure if it would be best for the children. It was a déjà vu of 1969 before going to Subic. Tom, the eternal optimist, was more enthusiastic than I. Wanting to be obedient to the Lord and to Tom's leadership but with less than great excitement, I agreed.

On July 25th Tom called together the advisory committee of the house to discuss the proposal as well as the future of the Travis ministry. After much discussion and prayer, a letter was drafted to the home office, requesting not only to keep the house open but to increase the ministry, with the Woods and Andersons volunteering to fill the gap we would leave.

On August 5th the Hokansons arrived from Okinawa. They stayed with us, making contact with Dick Patty and others in the home office concerning their future. During this time we received an anonymous letter offering a gift of $4,000 for the purchase of the Travis building. We were pleased and deeply grateful but the timing of it muddied the waters a bit.

Early in September it was determined that Dick Patty, Executive Director of OCSC, would come out to discuss the future of the ministry. Tom and I made a covenant with the Lord that if he wanted the hospitality house to continue, he would send in enough money to pay the rent and phone bill by the time the decision was made. Our financial support that month amounted to $472 with no funds for the ministry.

The night before Dick arrived Tom and I had a restless night. About midnight we heard scratching in the closet. Assuming it was a field mouse—the house was located in an open area—Tom got up without turning on the light, reached in the closet, and banged on the floor. "Oh, no!" he groaned. He flashed on the light only to discover he had killed Missy, Danny's pet hamster which had gotten out of its cage. We sat on the bed holding the precious pet, wondering how in the world we would tell Danny. Of course, in the morning he was heartbroken, as were we. He prepared a meaningful burial but his heart ached for days and ours ached for him.

On September 12, 1974 Dick Patty came and met with the advisory committee of the hospitality house. At the beginning of the meeting the sixteen men had a long time of prayer, seeking God's direction for the future of the ministry. They discussed all the pros and cons of continuing the work at Travis and whether Tom and I should stay or go to Okinawa, but were unable to come to a decision. After a short break for refreshments, they again sought the Lord in prayer. When the discussion resumed, there was a unanimous decision that the ministry continue and that the Hashes stay there to direct the work. This turn of events came as a surprise to everyone. At the end of the meeting one of the committee members, not knowing about our covenant with the Lord, gave us a gift of $350. That gift, along with several other smaller ones more than paid the rent and phone bills.

Tom and I sensed the decision was from the Lord and agreed to stay. Later it was learned that Roy and Bettie Jordan were available to lead the Okinawa work. Before Dick left we told him we would no longer accept financial assistance from the home office but would trust the Lord to bring in all the funds; and in agreement with the committee, we would proceed toward the purchase of the property.

The ministry among couples and families was beginning to take hold, but we eagerly desired to reach out to the vast single airman population on the base. We prayed earnestly for the Lord to send us one keen Christian single who would be the catalyst to reach out to others.

One day a young airman came to the door. He was tall, average looking, dressed in bibbed overalls—definitely not what most twenty-year-olds wore in that day. "Hi, my name is Duane Kinney. I'm a Christian and I love to work for the Lord. Do you have anything I can do to help?" We were a little stunned, but Tom invited him to join him at work in the garden. We learned that Duane had recently arrived at Travis and was assigned to maintain the fire equipment on the base. He worked regular hours so had much time off.

Soon he was coming to the house during all of his free time. We enjoyed his easy-going manner and sweet spirit but never dreamed that he was the one we had been asking the Lord for. Soon we realized that each time he came, he brought someone along. His loving, caring manner; genuine smile; and servant heart were used by God to touch the lives of many. Several of those men and women came to a personal relationship with Christ.

David and Danny were becoming fast friends with Mel and Judy Anderson's son, Terry. They were quite a dangerous trio, but sure had fun. Danny was spending a weekend at their home when we received a call from Judy. "Danny is having some kind of episode!" she said, her voice quavering. "First he couldn't see, then parts of his body went numb, and now he has a terrible headache and is vomiting. What shall I do?" We advised her to bring him home as soon as possible.

He came home, the headache subsided, and on Monday we took him to the doctor. A brain scan (the forerunner of the MRI and CT scan) was ordered. With fear and trembling we went for the report. "We did a complete examination of Danny's brain," the doctor said soberly, "but we couldn't find a thing." We haven't let Danny forget that report! Actually, the episode was a migraine headache—the first of many that would significantly affect Danny's life well into adulthood.

We first met Dave when he arrived at Subic as a young sailor and came out to the center. He was a believer and longed for Christian fellowship. When we celebrated his eighteenth birthday with a special cake, tears welled in his eyes. "I've always wanted a birthday cake. This is my first one." he murmured. We learned that Dave and his brother had been placed into an orphanage when their dysfunctional parents could not care for them. He told us of a sad, abusive childhood, but he was determined to make something of his life. He came to the center whenever he had liberty and soon grew very close to our family. He was a bright, gifted young man. He loved to sing and often sang solos at chapel and the center.

Shortly after our arrival at Travis, Dave showed up at our door. "I got the assignment I asked for so I could be near you. I am stationed in Oakland now," he announced with his big smile. We welcomed him warmly and he made the hour-long drive whenever he was free. Again he became a close part of our family. At times we invited him to sing with us when our family provided special music for events in the area. He responded to the Bible studies and was growing in the Lord.

When he received his discharge from the Navy, he found a job in the area and moved into our home. He was helpful around the house and gave freely of his money toward the purchase of groceries or anything he felt we needed. We were the only family he had ever known.

One day he rushed in, waving a paper. "I've been accepted as a student at Christian Heritage College in San Diego," he announced with a big smile. We were overjoyed and sent him off to college with our blessing. After a couple of years we stopped hearing from him, he didn't come home for the holidays, and we discovered he had dropped out of school. Then we learned he had joined the gay community. We were heartbroken.

Years later, after we moved to Denver, he showed up at our door again. "I am making a new start," he said. "I've come back to the Lord and am in a recovery group in a church downtown." We were pleased and saw him a few times. Then he disappeared again.

Several years later he called. He was crying. "I just attended the funeral of my 'companion.' He died of AIDS this week. Can I see you?" We met him at a restaurant and he poured out his heart. He wanted so desperately to be freed from his lifestyle.

"Dave," I asked him frankly, "are you a candidate for AIDS?"

"NO!" he almost shouted, "I could never get AIDS!"

Then he disappeared again. From an occasional Christmas card or letter we learned that he had gone to Michigan to care for his mother and then to Philadelphia. He said nothing about his lifestyle so we assumed he was still a practicing homosexual. He did admit that he had tested positive for HIV but did not have AIDS.

Then in the next letter he said he had full-blown AIDS. In spring of 1997 he called. We could hardly hear as he faintly announced, "I am moving to Denver soon. I have been accepted into a hospice there." We said we would welcome him. We knew he wanted to be with us when he died. We were leaving for a trip, but assured him we would call the hospice when we returned. But when we got home, he had left a faint message on our recorder: "I can't come. I can't walk, I can't sit up...." Then silence. We tried desperately to locate him but the people at the number we called didn't know him. I still weep inside to think he died alone, calling for us. Dave isn't one of our "success stories," but he was a young man into whom we poured much of our lives.

Chapter 39

GIANT STEPS

We invited the director of Young Life, a ministry to teens, to use our house for their weekly meetings. They were a lively bunch—reaching out to unchurched youth—but each week several young people committed their lives to Christ.

Mary Schaefer brought her teen daughters to the meetings. Often she sat in our family room and visited with Tom or me. One night she told us this story:

"My husband, Bob, died recently after a long illness. Because of this, his estate is tremendously depleted and his real estate and building businesses are floundering. In fact, the estate debts are about half a million dollars and the assets are nowhere near that. I am a homemaker. I know nothing about business. If it survives under my leadership, it will be only because of God's grace. Under the circumstances this doesn't make any sense, but the Lord has told me to tell you I'll give you $6,000. I have been a tither since childhood and have learned to obey the inner voice."

Tom and I didn't know what to say, except to murmur a humble "thank you" and a sincere promise to join her in praying for the success of her business endeavors.

One night she came in waving a check. "Here's the first thousand I promised. I want you to have it toward the purchase of your building. Please don't tell anyone, though, since it isn't a particularly good business practice to give away your first thousand dollars of profit. But I promised the Lord the first-fruits and here it is."

We were overwhelmed by the gift, first by Mary's remarkable giant step of faith and obedience, and then that God led her to give it to us. But that gift was another confirmation from the Lord that we should proceed with the purchase of the house. The Lord honored Mary's faithfulness and caused the business to prosper. Six more times in the next three years she gave us checks of a thousand dollars each.

When Jesse and Edith Johnson leased the house from Mrs. Elaine Rogers, an option to buy the property was included. Donors had given them $6,000 toward the purchase which they generously gave to us. Mrs. Rogers had agreed to OCSC subleasing, but whether we could utilize the option to buy was questionable.

After much prayer and consultation, we arranged a meeting with Mrs. Rogers and explained our desire to purchase the building for the agreed-upon price of $55,000. We had $15,000 available as a down payment. We asked Mrs. Rogers if she would carry a second mortgage of $18,000 which we would agree to pay in $6,000 increments over the next three years. We would assume her loan at the bank for $356 a month with thirteen years remaining. "I will take this up with my financial counselor," she responded, with a friendly smile. Several days later she called: "My finance man doesn't think it's a great idea, but we know Someone he doesn't. I have decided to take your offer."

On April 4, 1975, Sid Hendry arrived from the home office for the eventful signing of the papers. Tom and I agreed to remain at Travis until the second mortgage was paid. With much prayer and some trepidation the transaction was made. We knew we had done the right thing, but had no idea where the first $6,000 would come from during the next year. The Lord would have to provide in a very special way.

When we returned to the house we found Bill Walters, one of the airmen who came regularly, sitting on the couch practically in tears. "I'm so sorry I didn't get here in time," he quavered. "I sold my car today and it took longer than I planned. But here is my gift for the purchase of the house." The check in his hand was for the amount of $1,044.50. Selling his car was a great sacrifice, but he willingly did so. Instantly the Lord whispered to our hearts, *See, I am already providing for the first payment.*

"Oh, Bill," we said, hugging his sagging shoulders, "Your gift means far more to us now than it would have a few hours ago." Our tears of rejoicing blended with his as together we thanked the Lord for his faithfulness. Bill's love for OCSC's ministry continued for many years and he served several short term assignments at Fellowship Ranch in Missouri.

When we registered OCSC as a tax-exempt organization in the state of California, we were surprised to receive a generous tax refund. Then when the mortgage at the bank was changed to OCSC's name, the monthly payment was reduced to $250 retroactive to the date we moved in, resulting in another refund. God was blessing in ways we had not even imagined.

The following January the first $6,000 payment was available, so we called Mrs. Rogers and made an appointment to see her. She seemed a little aloof when we arrived. Then we explained: "Because you were so generous to us, we want you to know that we have the money for you now even though it isn't due until April. The Lord has provided in abundance." Instantly her demeanor changed. "Oh, my," she said with a shy smile, "I thought you were going to tell me you couldn't make the payment. I'm so pleased. No, you keep the money until April. I don't need it now."

The other two payments came in also, and in 1978 we held a mortgage burning celebration in testimony of God's faithfulness. OCSC received a clear title on the property in 1988.

Mel and Judy Anderson and their three children lived a one-hour drive away from the hospitality house and Mel worked thirty minutes away. They were so involved in the ministry that they made the drive many times a week. In vain they looked for affordable housing in our area. Gradually the Lord moved us in the direction of purchasing a home for them. Tom and I had seven thousand dollars in a savings account earmarked for the children's education and our retirement. We had always assured the Lord that his name appeared first on our bank account and that he could have the money at any time. Now it seemed he would put our commitment to the test.

We learned of a small, newly constructed home for sale. It even had a government rebate incentive offer to the purchaser. After the first visit Tom and I and the Andersons were confident we should buy it for them to live in. They would make the monthly payments from their military housing allowance, but to keep the payments low enough, we would need to put all of our money down. On that awesome day when we withdrew our life savings and bought that house—our first time in the housing market—we sat in our car in front of that little house on Marcia Lane and prayed, "Lord, all we have is truly yours. You know this is all of the money we have, so please, please take good care of it." (How's that for ambivalence?) Three years later when we left California and sold the house, the housing market had taken such an upward spiral that our money had doubled. Had we left the money in a savings account, it would not have been enough for a down payment on a house in Denver. *Freely you have received, freely give or is it freely you have given, freely receive?* Once again God showed his special provision for us.

Faithfulness in observing our day off was always elusive for us. If we stayed at the house, the phone rang all day or someone usually came to the door. Yet where could we go for the day? One day Tom came up with an idea. "Let's get some camping gear and start camping," he said enthusiastically.

"No way!" was my immediate response. "The only way I'll go camping is if I have running water and wall-to-wall carpeting." Roughing-it was never my forte.

A few weeks later he came home very excited. "I bought a little camper trailer for us," he announced with a big grin.

"Oh, no..." I began, but he interrupted.

"It's okay, honey. I stopped on the way home and Dick Lunoe put in your wall-to-wall carpeting. You'll love it. Come and see!"

Reluctantly I walked outside and there it was! An *old* silver and white non-impressive fifteen-foot trailer. I stepped inside and sure enough, there was the postage-stamp-size carpeting and a sink with a faucet. No bathroom, of course.

A few days later we set out to spend our day off on the coast. What a disaster! We learned a lot of dos and don'ts about camping and amazingly I was willing to try it again.

Many of our days off we simply pulled the trailer to the nearby city park where we read books, studied, and rested. When the children arrived from school we had a nice picnic there in the park, then pulled the trailer home. Since this was before the days of remote and cell phones, we didn't have to answer the phone one time the whole day. It was pure joy. I loved it!

We also found that the little trailer was a great ministry tool. On several weekends we planned camping retreats to Yosemite National Park. We used the tiny kitchen in the trailer like a chuck wagon (and I didn't have to sleep in a tent!).

Many times in the winter we pulled it up to the mountains for a day of tubing or sledding. After a few runs down the hill, the guys and gals loved coming into the warm, cozy trailer for a cup of chili or hot chocolate.

Tom and I both grew to love that little trailer. It was God's provision for rest for us during that period of intense ministry. I'm so glad Tom gently taught me to appreciate camping.

Chapter 40

MUSIC, BOOKS, AND MOPS

Our children became involved at the Fairfield Baptist Conference Church, later to become Parkway Community Church. Pastor John Hanson and his wife Sharon welcomed us warmly and became dear friends. Tom and I attended the base chapel on Sunday morning and the church on Sunday evenings. The church had a large number of teens attending, including ours, but no youth pastor. In that era, Christian musicals were the "in" thing, so Sharon and I organized the youth group into a choir—I led and she played the piano.

Before leaving the Philippines we had purchased a bass guitar for David, but neither he nor I knew how to tune or play it. We needed a bass accompaniment for the musical, so one night I tuned it like a ukelele (which I did know) and I played through the entire musical on the piano, calling out the bass notes for David to play. The second time through David played every note on his own, confirming my hunch that he was musically gifted.

Our first presentation was a smashing success, but the greatest benefit came from the work the Lord did in the hearts of the teens. The group learned and performed three different musicals in the next three years. David eventually learned to tune the guitar properly and went on to become a professional bassist and presently has his own business providing sound, lights, and video services for various national Christian organizations. It was a humble beginning for him.

Pastor Hanson had the unique ability to be non-possessive of the people in his congregation. This enabled us to have a healthy working relationship for all of the five years we were at Travis and continued with our successors. He served faithfully on our advisory committee. When John's brother, Rich Hanson, came to the church as youth pastor, he had a profound impact on the lives of our three children, especially Danny. The Hansons continue to be faithful servants.

Lori was one of the soloists in all three of the musicals we performed. She was an excellent student, a growing Christian, maintained an ordered lifestyle (like her Dad), and brought great joy to our hearts. She was active in the youth group at church, but had a healthy relationship with the guys and gals at the house too. Many nights after the evening activities were over we found a bunch of them, with Lori in the middle, all sitting on the long kitchen counters, laughing and having a great time.

We vividly recall the day she came to us in awe. "Dad, Mom, there's a new guy here and he's younger than I am!" She had always looked up to the men as old and mature. Now she was unsure how to respond.

By her own choice she did not date the servicemen. She loved doing things in groups, but never encouraged any of the young men toward dating. We were very thankful for her attitude. And when she chose to enter Moody Bible Institute, we were, of course, very pleased. She met Terry Einfalt in her last year of college and they were soon married. They served with OCSC for ten years.

On one of Tom's trips to Denver, Don Baker, logistics coordinator in our home office, was fretting over an old Chevrolet station wagon that was giving him fits. "If someone offered me fifty dollars for this thing, I'd take it in a minute!" he sputtered. "Sold!" Tom responded. He drove the car back to California, walked into the house, and handed Danny the keys. "Here's a car for you. You owe me $50!" Tom announced. Sixteen-year-old Danny was ecstatic. From then on he filled it full of kids and took them to the youth meetings and church. It was at this time that we saw the Lord answer our prayers and turn Danny's love for animals into a love for people. Years later Danny served in youth ministry with OCSC/Malachi for six years in Germany. At the time of this writing, he and his wife Laura and little Jacob, are missionaries in Poland, training pastors in youth ministry. Who would have thought....!

After many years of seeing the value of good Christian literature in the lives of believers, we sensed a burden from the Lord to open a book store in the Fairfield community. The horse stable on our property could be converted into a suitable facility. With Cliff Woods serving as general contractor and Mel Anderson his assistant, the construction began. There were no available funds at the start, but soon a large donation came in. Then the naval unit where Mel worked on Skaggs Island had suspended ceiling parts to give away and the Woolworth store downtown was closing so donated shelving and display cases. Someone gave enough money to purchase all of the dry wall at $1.05 a sheet. It seemed whenever there was a need either the money or the materials were available.

The men worked for months in their off-duty hours. On the frequent Saturday work days we provided a big breakfast and lunch for everyone. One day Judy Anderson and I were preparing chili for about twenty-five people. We had two big pots on the stove—one contained the chili the other chocolate pudding. We were chatting and I was busily opening pudding boxes. "Oh, no!" I cried. "I put the pudding in the chili! What'll we do?" The thought of throwing the chili down the disposal was out of the question so with a chuckle and a flourish, we stirred the pudding in. It was the best chili we ever made.

The Book Nook was dedicated and opened for operation on February 7, 1976. The building also provided an office for Tom and one for the book store. I managed the store for almost a year but when the demand on my time became overwhelming, Norma Bassett took it over. For several years it was the only Christian book outlet in the greater Travis area. Several years later, when another store was opened in town, the Book Nook was closed.

Dedication of the Bible Book Nook

The ministry continued to grow. A singles' dinner and Bible study were started on Wednesdays. New people came, got excited about God's Word, studied hard, and matured in their faith.

The group coming for Friday Fellowship soon grew to about one hundred—absolute capacity for the meeting area. After a planned pot-luck dinner which the married women helped provide, we held an informal service with lots of singing, skits, sometimes a Christian film, a concert by a singing group passing through, or a speaker. A Bible class for the children was held during the meetings.

With so much continual activity, keeping the house clean was always a challenge. Tom and I have always had high standards for order and cleanliness. My mother described Tom as "fastidious;" I call him "the original Mr. Clean." For me, cleaning is the means to an end—something to be endured in order to have a clean house; but for Tom it is doubly satisfying, for the process as well as the outcome bring him joy. (Eat your hearts out, gals!)

For two years Tom and I did most of the cleaning. Because Monday was our day off and we couldn't bear to relax in a dirty house, we found ourselves spending most of the day cleaning. One Monday afternoon I was vacuuming the stairs having a severe "pity party." With tears dripping onto the carpet I complained to the Lord, "We work so hard all week and on our only day off end up cleaning all day! It just isn't fair!"

That summer our family went on a five-week deputation trip while Mel and Judy Anderson ran the house ministry. When we returned the "angels" came on duty. Judy enlisted Edith Woods, Marlene Paulson, and others to come every Saturday and Monday morning to help clean. Those dear ladies dusted, mopped, and scrubbed toilets with the joy and dedication of saints. They arrived at eight and by eleven we

Friday Fellowship at the house

were sitting in a spotless house with our feet up, sipping tea and giggling. Is it any wonder they remain some of our dearest friends to this day? As we look back, we marvel at how the hospitality house/servicemen's center had the unique facilitating ministry of providing a platform for others to serve.

After a year of securing visitors' passes each time we went on the base for chapel, the installation chaplain rotated out and we were given our own passes. This made life much easier. Tom taught an adult Sunday school class and I became organist at one of the chapels. Most of the singles from our ministry attended chapel with us while the families went to local churches in town.

Chaplain Charles Hudson led the service where we attended chapel. The building was one of the oldest historic sites on the base and was often referred to as "the country church." The Hudson family was African/American so the majority of the congregation was also black. We had two choirs which sang on alternate Sundays: the chancel choir (a mixed group) and the gospel choir. I played for the chancel choir. The organ was located in the balcony and usually the services were so well attended that when I left the organ to play for the choir, I had to put a note on the organ bench: "Reserved for the Organist!" Chaplain Hudson handled the Word of God with wisdom and grace, ministering well to the hearts of his congregation.

Mike, who was also black, sang in the gospel choir and came to the hospitality house regularly. On more than one Sunday he took great joy in causing a stir. At the end of the service, while everyone was waiting in the aisle to exit the chapel, he stood in the front and called to me in the balcony, "Hi, Mom!"

"Hi, Sonny!" I called back, waving. New attenders did a couple of double takes before they caught on to the prank.

We served a sit-down dinner at the hospitality house after chapel each Sunday. With the blessing of the chaplains, we watched for new singles in the services, inviting them to come. Through the years we found that if we made contact soon after a single man or woman arrived in the area we were more likely to get them involved in the house activities.

I prepared dinner for thirty to forty each Sunday. Twenty could sit at our massive table. We set up other tables for the rest. The food was ready in the oven when we returned from chapel.

Early in our ministry we determined that meals were not to be an end in themselves. They required large outlays of energy and money and we wanted them to count for eternity. So we worked hard to direct the conversation around important subjects. But there was also lots of laughter.

Chapter 41

PEOPLE FOR ETERNITY

At the fall of Vietnam to the Communists in 1975, the U.S. government made a concerted effort to evacuate the orphans from that war-torn country. The project was called Operation Baby-Lift. C-5 jumbo jets from Travis were dispatched for that mission. Mike Pageant, one of our regular men and a keen Christian, was aboard one of those planes when it crashed in Saigon. The whole world wept over that tragedy as it was broadcast over TV. Mike's death was a blow to all of us at the house. One of our other faithful men, Jeff Krohn, had the privilege of escorting Mike's body back to its final resting place.

The day following the crash, Terry Cole, a staff sergeant, knocked on our front door. We knew it was someone new since everyone came through the back door without knocking. "I brought you some fried chicken," he said shyly.

"Uh, thanks," Tom responded with some hesitation. "Would you like to come in?"

"If the chicken stays, I stay!" was Terry's reply as he cautiously entered the room. He was visibly shaken. Soon we learned that he had been scheduled for that flight to Vietnam but Mike had volunteered to go instead. Terry realized that Christian had died in his place.

As Tom shared with Terry about Jesus Christ and how he voluntarily died in our place for our sin, he listened carefully. He knew he wasn't ready to die, but had never been to church and knew nothing about the Bible. We invited him back for Wednesday Bible study. Again he listened intently and within a few days invited the Lord Jesus to come into his life. How he changed! His life had been so empty and now he couldn't learn enough.

Terry served on a medical evacuation team so was frequently gone. But when he returned he always came out the house. One of his first times back happened to be a work day. He and Tom were outside working in the yard when Terry asked, "How do you finance this place? Everything is free to us guys, but I know the money has to come from somewhere."

Tom responded, "My family and I are supported by churches and individuals who love you guys in the military. The expenses of the house are provided voluntarily by those who come."

"I'd like to contribute," Terry said. They went into the house where Tom wrote Terry a receipt for the fifty dollars he gave, explaining how the money would be used.

Two weeks later Terry again returned from a trip on a work day. "Uh, Tom," he asked, "are you still taking donations?"

"Sure," Tom replied with a smile.

"Well, I have some more to give," he said. Again they went inside where Tom wrote a receipt, thanking him for his gift. The next time he came the same scenario was replayed.

The next summer we were on a deputation trip, scheduled to speak at the Wednesday night service at First Baptist Church in Lake Orion, Michigan. We had never been there before so watched the map carefully as we drove. But we got lost—very lost. When we arrived ten minutes after the service had begun, the pastor was patiently leading the singing. We quickly unloaded David's bass guitar and amplifier and moved toward the piano and platform as the relieved pastor introduced us. We sang a few songs and then began our slide presentation.

We showed a slide of Terry Cole working in the yard at the hospitality house. Tom shared the story of his consecutive giving on work days. Instantly the pastor jumped up wanting attention. Tom, thinking perhaps he had said something offensive, quickly stepped aside. "I declare this Saturday a work day!" the pastor shouted and sat down. The congregation exploded in laughter. Ironically, that body of believers has faithfully supported our ministry since that day.

Cindy (McGeehan) Zulli recalls her experience at Travis:

> I grew up in a devout Catholic family in Salt Lake City, Utah. My parents not only gave the three of us children love and affection, but a healthy respect for God. They saw that we attended church regularly. They worked hard and sacrificed much to send us to private Catholic schools. I had everything relating to religion that a person could want.
>
> However, in my senior year of high school my heart grew restless and my mind confused about what I believed. Waitressing part-time, I came in touch with people of all different cults and religions. They were all so sincere, convinced theirs was the right way, yet they were all so different. My insecurities increased as graduation approached. One night on the way home from work, I sat in my car and cried, *God, how do you want me to worship you? What is the true way?*

Cindy McGeehan

After graduation from high school I joined the United States Air Force. I attended tech school at Chanute AFB in Illinois and then received orders to Travis AFB in Fairfield, California. There I was trained as an aircraft mechanic for the Air Force's largest cargo planes, the C-5s and C-141s.

For the next two years I was the first (and only) girl in the shop of about sixty men. I saw it all—the gestures, the harshness, and the shop talk that accompanies a man's world. To the older men I was a daughter to be protected; to the younger men I was a sex symbol to be exploited. Pioneering this new career field left me with challenges I was unprepared to handle. I wasn't sure I would make it. But one man in my shop was different—Staff Sergeant Louis Alier. He came to me, was friendly, and asked where I went to church. "I'm a Catholic," I responded.

"Oh, so am I! I'm a Catholic Christian!" he replied excitedly. *What is a Catholic Christian? Aren't all Catholics Christians?* I thought to myself.

Louie then invited me to the Travis Hospitality House. "It's a home away from home for military men and women, with home-cooked meals, friendship and fellowship around the Bible." His invitation appealed to me because he was genuinely interested in my spiritual life. I agreed to go.

On Friday night, Louie and his wife Gina picked me up at the barracks. When we arrived at the hospitality house, I was impressed with the atmosphere. The thirty-five or forty other military people were friendly and happy, warm and loving. We sat at tables for the delicious meal, then the tables were put away and chairs set up for the fellowship hour.

I met Tom and Dotty Hash and their three children. I felt so loved by them. They seemed to be just like my own family—genuinely concerned for me. Dotty began the program with the liveliest, most uplifting piano music I had ever heard. Then we all joined in with singing—a celebration like none other. John Hanson, a nearby pastor, was the guest speaker. He presented the Gospel and the claims of Christ, explaining that we could know for sure, without a doubt, that if we were to die tonight we would go to heaven. He said an individual must have a personal *relationship* with Jesus, not just a *religion* to join.

On February 21, 1975, at twenty years old, I stood to my feet, bowed my head in prayer and asked Jesus to forgive my sin and be my Savior. Immediately my heart, my mind, and my soul were at peace. My soul-searching questions and doubts were settled in this new personal relationship with the Lord. My question, *How do you want me to worship you, God?* was answered when Louie showed me John 14:6: "Jesus said to him, I am the way, and the truth, and the life; no one comes to the Father, but through Me." (NASB) That verse became bedrock to my Christian life.

With all the opportunities to sin available to me, my life as a young single military girl could have been a disaster. But the Lord graciously rescued me, saving me by his undeserved and unmerited grace! From the moment of my salvation experience, I had one great passion—to grow and be used by God.

The hospitality house became my new home. I was so eager to learn what the Bible was all about and how to build my new life on *all* the promises God had for me. Every time the doors opened I was there. I attended the regular Bible studies and special meetings, the local field trips and annual Horn Creek conferences in Colorado, the evangelism outreaches in the air terminal on the base, and the prayer meetings and work days at the house. Barry Will, who also made a commitment to Christ that same night I did, became my dear brother in the Lord. He was a support to me, even loaning me his car whenever I needed it. Mike True taught me how to get serious with God in prayer. We would walk down the road in front of the house, talking to God openly, genuinely, and with childlike faith. Tom baptized me, along with Barry and several other new believers, in Lake Barryessa on Easter Sunday. Brrrrrrr....it was cold!

Tom and Dotty became role models for me, not only as my spiritual mentors, but also as a pattern for a Christian marriage. I wanted everything they had: a solid, growing relationship with Jesus; a strong marriage; a godly family; and a vital ministry touching the lives of people for eternity. Tom's life verse, Philippians 1:6, became my life verse: "For I am confident of this very thing, that he who began a good work in you will perfect it until the day of Christ Jesus." (NASB)

With my enlistment almost completed, I realized I needed formal Bible training. Tom and Dotty told me about Western Bible College in Denver, Colorado. So as soon as I received my discharge, I began my studies there with missions as my major and a theology minor.

My freshman year was another challenge, but Tom and Dotty, who were now serving at the OCSC home office in Denver, continued to encourage me. In fact, Dotty even helped me make the curtains for my dorm room.

At the end of my freshman year, I returned to the Travis Hospitality House as a short-term missionary to help Harold and Edna Matolka, the new directors. There I met Dan Zulli, a security policeman on base, who had recently come to the Lord and was attending the house. I had no idea that the Lord would lead us together someday.

I returned to college and received my degree three years later. I graduated on May 7th and married Dan on May 8, 1982. Dan finished his enlistment uncertain whether to re-enlist or get out. As a new Christian, he loved the military but wasn't really fulfilled in his job—he wanted to serve the Lord full time. During one service at the chapel, he gave his career to the Lord and surrendered to serve him.

Not long after that, Dan talked with Tom Hash. "Since you love the military and want to be in ministry, why don't you pursue the military chaplaincy?" Tom advised him. That was like manna from heaven! Dan got out of the Air Force and entered Dallas Theological Seminary in Dallas, Texas. He became a reserve chaplain and then pastored a Bible church in Dill City, Oklahoma. All that time we were praying and yearning to return to active duty in the chaplaincy.

In 1993 the Lord answered our prayers—Dan was called back on active duty as a full-time Air Force chaplain. The foundation laid in my life at the hospitality house served not only to ground me in the Word of God and my walk with him, but also provided the background for our ministry with military men and women.

One Thursday morning a new lady came to my women's Bible study. She introduced herself as Kathie Timko. I noticed that she listened intently to every word as I taught. After the study she lingered and asked if we could talk. She poured out her story:

"I am a believer in Christ. I really love the Lord and want very much to please him. My husband, Barry, has just gotten out of the Air Force. Our marriage has been rocky and we are presently separated. About two weeks ago Barry became a Christian. But I am so confused. I have recently met a man who is involved in a ministry in this area and we have become very, very close. There has not been any immorality—he is simply helping me grow in the Lord and we have fallen in love. What shall I do?"

We turned to the Word of God and read several passages and Kathie soon admitted that she knew the Bible did not support her actions toward this extramarital relationship. "But how can something be so wonderful and yet be wrong?" she wept. We talked for a long time and I became convinced that Kathie really did love the Lord but she also loved this other man.

"Kathie, you will have to make a choice," I challenged her. You must choose between obedience to the Lord or disobedience. What will it be?"

She sat in silence for a long time. Then we prayed together. She was sobbing softly as she prayed, "Lord, I love you and I also love this man. But I love you more. I will obey you."

We both looked up through our tears and hugged. Then Kathie said, "I'm going home. I'll call Barry and ask him to come home. Even though my heart doesn't support this action, I know it's right and I want to please God."

Kathie walked out the door with firm steps of resolve. She kept her promise. Barry returned home to Kathy and their little daughter, Robyn.

We learned that Barry had been led to the Lord by Mel Anderson and he was being discipled at Pastor Hanson's church. Barry and Kathy became active at the church and at the hospitality house. Healing came to their marriage.

Before long they responded to God's call to prepare to serve the Lord and moved to Chicago to attend Moody Bible Institute. While there, God blessed them with a second daughter, Blair. But soon they discovered that Kathie had breast cancer. She underwent extensive treatment and seemed to recover well.

Sensing God's call to serve as a missionary pilot, they moved to Elizabethton, Tennessee where Barry began his flight and aviation mechanic training at Moody Aviation. But Kathie's cancer returned and after a long illness she was called home to be with the Lord. Barry remained on at Moody Aviation as a flight instructor.

Barry and Kathie had been friends with Deborah Goube and her family for several years. Deborah had been widowed five years earlier and had two children, Jeremiah and Ammi. Eventually the Lord led Barry and Deborah together and they married. God is good and his plan is perfect. But how different this story would have played out had Kathie chosen to disobey God. "Therefore, to one that knows the right thing to do, and does not do it, to him it is sin." (James 4:17, NASB) God honors obedience!

Russ Baird was a quiet young man who came regularly to the hospitality house. He loved God's word and grew in his walk with the Lord. One time, in response to an urgent financial need at the house, he sold his newer car, bought an older one, and gave the profit to meet that need. We were deeply humbled by this selfless gesture. Toward the end of his enlistment, Russ sensed the Lord's leading to attend a Bible college to prepare for Christian service. He sought Tom's counsel and they decided on Montana School of the Bible (later Big Sky Bible College which subsequently was closed).

During his first year there, he met a lovely girl and they were married that summer. During the next Christmas vacation, they traveled to Kentucky to visit Russ's parents. On the return trip they became engulfed in a blizzard on the plains near Denver, Colorado. Russ pulled the car off the road, left the engine running, and hoped someone would come to rescue them. They were found the next day. Russ and his wife both died of carbon-monoxide poisoning when snow covered the exhaust pipe on the car. We were deeply grieved when we learned of this tragic accident, and deeply moved to learn he had designated one-third of his military insurance policy to OCSC.

Chapter 42

EAGLE WINGS

By fall of 1976, Tom and I were feeling the effects of a demanding ministry. We paid a visit to our longtime friends, Dr. Roland Icke and his wife, Muriel, who lived in central California. After complete physical examinations, Dr. Icke said that even though he detected no serious problems, he sensed that we were near a state of burnout.

"My recommendation is that you step aside from the ministry for about six months to recharge your batteries," he said gently.

We had high regard for his advice, for the Ickes had cared for a multitude of missionaries through the years, often taking them into their own home to speed their recovery from illnesses.

We returned to the hospitality house and shared the diagnosis with the folks there. Everyone was deeply concerned but none of us knew just what to do. We eventually developed a plan for us to take a two-week vacation with the regular folks carrying on our responsibilities.

It took a week to accomplish that transfer, but soon Tom and I were on the road with our little trailer in tow.

Driving north along the coast of California, we reached a dense forest of redwood trees. There we pulled into a campsite deep in the woods and stayed there for two weeks. We slept, read the Bible and other books, hiked, and just plain rested. It remains one of the most refreshing times of our lives. Even though it wasn't the six months Dr. Icke had prescribed, it was like an oasis in the desert to our weary bodies and souls.

When we returned to the hospitality house everything was going at full force. We quickly plunged back into the ministry but knew a permanent change needed to be made.

Before long plans were in place for us to spend the summer of 1977 away from the ministry. The Lord provided a young couple who were considering joining OCSC to take our place during that time.

After their arrival we worked frantically to prepare for the turnover. After all, three months was a long time to be away. The folks at the house prepared an elaborate celebration for our last night there—a welcome for the interim couple and a farewell for us. By the time the crowd arrived, Tom and I were exhausted, but we had a great time anyway. As most of them were leaving, I was standing at the sink washing the punch bowl. My head was pounding, my back ached, my feet burned with pain and I still had hours of work to be ready to leave by 7 a.m.

I glanced up to the wall beside the sink and read again the verse I had taped there: "But they that wait upon the Lord will renew their strength; they shall mount up with wings like eagles; they shall run, and not be weary; and they shall walk, and not faint." (Isaiah 40:31.) *Oh, Father,* I pleaded, *I desperately need those eagle wings tonight!*

Just then the door opened and one of our regular girls stepped inside. "Come on in. It's okay," she said gently to someone outside. I walked to the door to see what was happening. There stood a teen-age girl dressed in scanty shorts and a halter top. "I found her on the parkway trying to hitch a ride," the young airman said. "I found out she was a runaway so I brought her here. I knew you would know what to do to help her."

"Come on in," I said, inwardly crying out for the eagle wings. That definitely was not my area of expertise, but I took the girl aside and we began to talk. At first she was reluctant to say anything, but eventually her guard subsided and she told me that she was fourteen years old (she looked at least seventeen) and couldn't get along with her mother. Her father was an officer in the Air Force and frequently away from the family. She had run away several times before.

We talked about her disillusionment with life and I shared the love of Christ with her—how he had come to give his life so she could have forgiveness of sin and a new life. After several hours of talking and praying—it was now about 2 a.m.—she agreed to let me call her mother. Earlier I had promised not to do that unless she agreed. Now she was ready and told me her name and phone number.

Of course, her mother was tremendously relieved when I told here where her daughter was and that she was okay. In a few minutes she drove into the driveway. I referred them to a godly chaplain who could give them counsel, prayed with them, and they drove off.

Thanks for the wings, Father, I prayed and dropped wearily into bed.

We were able to rent the home of a Christian family in Denver who were away for the summer. We had a restful three months. The children all had summer jobs and Tom and I simply rested. When we returned to Travis in September we were ready to jump heartily back into the ministry.

Chapter 40

"...THE ACCOMPLISHMENTS OF OTHERS"

Under the ten years of Dick Patty's leadership as Executive Director of OCSC, the mission had grown significantly. But in 1976 he became seriously ill and was eventually diagnosed with cancer. As a result, the doctors performed what they called "mutilative surgery" on his lower intestinal track. They were confident the cancer was removed, but Dick's recovery was long and slow. Yet he faithfully carried on the leadership of the mission with the able help of Sid Hendry and others in the office.

Eventually the Board of Directors of OCSC determined that Dick needed relief. After a long search, they asked Chaplain Dave Meschke, who had served on the board for many years, to become General Director. After much prayer Dave responded, "I will accept that position but it must be under the condition that I have some help. I would like to ask

Dick Patty to become Director of Europe Ministries and Tom Hash to become Director of Asia Ministries." The board agreed, as did the Pattys and Hashes. So after twenty-one years of active duty in the U.S. Navy, Dave resigned his commission and took retirement. The turnover was planned for the summer of 1978.

As the plan developed, it was determined that Dick and Margaret Patty would move to Europe and establish a field office there, but Tom and I would live in Denver. The dynamics of our living in Asia were complicated by the vast distances between our servicemen's centers there—we could be at any of our places as quickly from Denver as we could travel between countries. Also, Dave Meschke was eager for Tom to be available to help with his adjustment to his new role as General Director.

Six months before our scheduled departure from Travis, Harold and Edna Matolka, OCSC missionaries, came to stay with us. They were awaiting visas to go to Okinawa to serve in our center there. They entered into the ministry wholeheartedly and were loved by all of the group. Several months later, when their visas were denied, we were all sure God had brought them there to be our replacements.

We were very excited about our future role, for the Lord had been preparing our hearts for years to assist new missionaries in getting started in ministry. We had trained four couples at Subic for extensive periods of time. At Travis we had invited numerous new couples who were in the process of raising their support to come and spend at least two weeks with us. During the first week we took them through our activities, spending hours sharing our philosophy of ministry as well as our methods. Then the following week they ran the work while we observed and critiqued. We loved doing it and each couple expressed gratefulness for the hands-on exposure to the work.

In June of 1978 the Hash family packed up all of their worldly goods to move to Denver. We must have been quite a sight as we pulled out of the driveway with David at the wheel of the rented truck, Tom and I in our car towing the little camper trailer, and Danny and Lori following behind in Danny's Chevy station wagon.

The curtain was falling on a significant five-year chapter in our lives. Tears welled up as we recalled the farewell party the night before when nearly everyone we knew came to share crazy stories and bid us a tearful goodbye. We carried with us painful farewells but also deep thankfulness to the Lord for what we had seen him accomplish in the lives of so many, including our own children, as he had faithfully "filled our rooms."

We knew our future role would take us out of the direct ministry into a leadership position of overseeing our missionaries in Asia. But our life verse, Philippians 1:6, played

The family when we left Travis in 1978
From left: Tom, Dotty, Danny, Lori and David

over and over in our hearts and minds: "Being confident of this very thing, that he who hath begun a good work in you will perform it until the day of Jesus Christ." And Dick Patty's wise words kept ringing in our ears: "After many years of fruitful ministry, we must now find our fulfillment in the accomplishments of others."

POSTSCRIPT

Numerous times we have been asked which place we enjoyed the most. We are still unable to say. Each place of ministry was unique, each place God did a mighty work in our hearts, each place God used us in the lives of the people who filled our rooms, and each place we grew to love a group of people unlike any other we had known. We can honestly say that we were thoroughly happy at each place of ministry even though there were many trials. That joy continued during our role as Director of Asia Ministries, then Director of Americas Ministries, and now as Cadence Historians.

Another question frequently asked concerns rearing children effectively in a servicemen's home or hospitality house setting. That subject was and still is elusive, frightening, and to the thinking of some, impossible. Even after more than forty years of history, it is still the urgent subject of discussion and apprehension between the missionaries. The measure of success or failure is also elusive. The best measure, obviously, is how the children turn out. To those of us who were in the midst of having babies, training toddlers, and seeing to their education while running a busy in-home ministry, the underlying uneasiness came from wondering how this kind of life would affect them. Those of us who were blazing the trail through virgin territory had to simply rely on the Lord to lead us in each decision, trusting him with our childrens' outcome.

The philosophy Tom and I came to embrace (we actually "fell" into it rather than choosing it), was that our ministry and family were an integrated union. Therefore, we did not try to protect the children from the ministry, nor the ministry from the children. We did, however, develop clearly defined parameters for both. As tots, the children were watched closely. We didn't allow them to antagonize the servicemen, nor to manipulate them. (Of course, through the years they did lots of both, but we always sought to be alert to their activities.) When the children were small, I faithfully followed my own axiom: *Small children owe it to their parents to go to bed early.* Until they were in their pre-teens, all three of our children were normally in bed by 7 p.m. That gave them adequate sleep and us the freedom to carry on the ministry in the evenings. On weekends, they accompanied us on the trips and excursions, giving them exciting exposure to the host country where we served as well as to cross-cultural missions. And we spent that entire time as a family.

Even though our ministries were very large and demanding, we made conscious efforts by word and action to assure the children they were more important to us than the "guys." When they were small, demanding much of our time, we found ourselves making choices hundreds of times each day. My 20/20 hindsight estimates we did well about fifty percent of the time. One of my most frequent and urgent prayers was, "Lord, please don't let my sin leave an indelible mark on my children." Even though I failed so often with the children, God knew my heart, and protected them.

In our forty years as missionaries, we have seen God take practically every young first-term missionary through the refining process. Those who respond well and allow the Lord to take them through the fires of adversity usually continue to serve the Lord the rest of their lives; those who resist become missionary casualties.

Many years after the stories that are written in this book, our own children, their mates, and our grandchildren flew away to foreign lands as missionaries. We knew they would not be exempt from the refining fires. But we joyfully sent them off, knowing that our loving Heavenly Father would be very careful to see that the trials only refined, not destroyed them.

Give of thy sons to bear the message glorious;
Give of thy wealth to speed them on their way;
Pour out thy soul for them in prayer victorious,
And all thou spendest Jesus will repay.

—from *O Zion Haste*
Mary A. Thomas and Jame Welch

When we became missionaries, it was a lifetime commitment. We knew God would provide for our daily needs as we served him. So early in our missionary career we asked God specifically for two times we assumed we could not make preparation: the education of our children and old age.

Well, our children are educated and now we are old. He remains faithful, still filling our rooms until the day he calls us home to fill his rooms for all of eternity.

Cadence Press
Tom & Dotty Hash
13803 W. Amherst Way
Lakewood, CO, 80228

(303)989-5659

FILL *these* ROOMS

A STORY OF GOD'S FAITHFULNESS

ORDER FORM

(Satisfaction Guaranteed)

POSTAL ORDER:

Cadence Press
Tom & Dotty Hash
13803 W. Amherst Way
Lakewood, CO, 80228

(303)989-5659

NAME:

ADDRESS:

CITY: STATE:

ZIP: PHONE: ( )

Book: ***Copies @ $13.^{00} ea.*** ***$***

Audio Cassettes: ***Sets @ $20.^{00} ea.*** ***$***

CO residents add 4.3% sales tax ***$***

Shipping: $3.^{00} for the first item and $1.^{00} ea. additional item $

TOTAL: ***$***

CP
cadence press

MAKE CHECK PAYABLE TO CADENCE PRESS

FILL *these* ROOMS

A STORY OF GOD'S FAITHFULNESS

ORDER FORM

(Satisfaction Guaranteed)

POSTAL ORDER: ***Cadence Press***
Tom & Dotty Hash
13803 W. Amherst Way
Lakewood, CO, 80228

(303)989-5659

NAME:

ADDRESS:

CITY: STATE:

ZIP: PHONE: (   )

Book:	***Copies @ $13.00 ea.***	***$***	
Audio Cassettes:	***Sets @ $20.00 ea.***	***$***	
CO residents add 4.3% sales tax		***$***	
Shipping: $3.00 for the first item and $1.00 ea. additional item		***$***	
TOTAL:		***$***	

CP cadence press

MAKE CHECK PAYABLE TO CADENCE PRESS